TALK OF THE TOONY

GREGOR TOWNSEND

Talk of the Toony

HarperSport
An Imprint of HarperCollins*Publishers*

HarperCollinsPublishers
77–85 Fulham Palace Road,
Hammersmith, London W6 8JB

www.harpercollins.co.uk

First published in 2007 by HarperSport
an imprint of HarperCollins London
1

A CIP catalogue record for this book
is available from the British Library

ISBN 13 978-0-00-725113-1
ISBN 10 0-00-725113-0

Printed and bound in Great Britain by
Clays Ltd, St Ives plc

All photographs supplied courtesy of Gregor Townsend
with the exception of the following: Fotosport 16 (middle);
Getty Images 11 (bottom), 13 (top), 16 (top and bottom).

Mixed Sources
Product group from well-managed
forests and other controlled sources
www.fsc.org Cert no. SW-COC-1806
© 1996 Forest Stewardship Council
FSC

Contents

Dedicated to rugby in the Borders,
and the hope that it can rise again.

Have you ever stopped and wondered why
Border rugby is so strong
I'll tell you how it started, just listen to my song
How the Reivers wrought disorder
And the rule of law was lame
And the Bonnie Scottish Borders became
The Kingdom of the Game

Frae Gala, Hawick and Melrose
The Gospel quickly spread
The magic of its spell rose
Frae Selkirk don tae Jed
Frae Kelsae doon on Tweedside
Tae the muckle toon they came
And they fought tae find the best toon
In the Kingdom of the Game

Their features carved in granite
Their hearts as stout as stone
They won the ball and ran it
They made the game their own
Now many Border Callants
Bring honour and great fame
Tae the heartbeat of the Nation
Tae the Kingdom of the Game

'The Kingdom of the game' (Henry Douglas)

Preface

Happiness isn't something you experience;
it's something you remember.

Oscar Levant

15 September 2006

I suppose we are never angrier than when we feel ourselves to be at fault. In only the third game of this season – my final season – I played as badly as I've ever done in my career. I was playing for the Border Reivers down in Wales, and we succumbed to another defeat – this time against the Ospreys. However, my own disappointment was much greater than that of my team-mates. This wasn't entirely to do with my error-strewn performance. The match also forced me to admit an undeniable truth – my rugby career was all but over.

Throughout my career, I would set myself goals of getting into club, Scotland or Lions teams, but my real focus was on trying to improve every time I got my hands on a rugby ball, trying to play the perfect game. A few months previously I had announced publicly – and set as a goal – that I was going to retire at the end of the season. It wasn't the most positive of targets and for the first time in my career, I began to feel demotivated. Now, showing signs of being unable to reach the standards I had set for myself, I feared that I'd lose the respect of others, never mind my own self-respect.

Professional sportsmen never know when the best time is to retire. The preferred option is to 'go out at the top', when you are still at the height of your powers. I couldn't see the logic in that – surely you would want to achieve as much as was possible? Another option is to wait until injuries force you out of the game. My body had been crying 'enough' for some time – a broken ankle, torn shoulder ligaments and a cortisone injection in my neck were some of the things I'd faced in the previous two years – but I couldn't resist working myself back to some sort of match fitness and playing once more. In the weeks following the Ospreys game, I realized just when the right time to take your leave was – when you start to feel that rugby has become a job. When the exciting becomes mundane and challenges mere chores, then it is time to call it a day.

My last two years back in Scotland have had precious few highlights, as the overriding memories are of recovering from a stream of injuries and of striving to just make it through the day, whether it was a weights session, rugby training, video analysis or rehab work. At times I was getting by on the bare minimum, and I knew it. It's not a sentiment I want to associate with the sport I love, especially as I've felt blessed at the opportunities that rugby has given me.

For the past seventeen years I have been playing, thinking and living rugby. It has taken me from the Scottish Borders to the great playing fields of the world: Twickenham, Stade de France, Lansdowne Road, Stadium Australia and Eden Park. I have crammed in eighty-two Tests for Scotland and two more for the British Lions and I have been in a privileged position to witness the incredible changes that have taken place in the game over the last two decades, as rugby has transformed into a fully professional sport. I have also been in the unique situation of playing club rugby in five different countries, and my experiences in France, South Africa, England, Australia and Scotland have not just helped my rugby but enriched my life.

Rugby has given me so much and has had a hold over me for over half of my life. I've found the game compelling and, if given a choice, I wouldn't have wanted to play any other sport. I believe that, at its best, there isn't another sport that comes close in terms of excitement, commitment and spectacle. Rugby demands bravery from its players and can contain unforgettable moments of individual brilliance and equally momentous passages of immense team effort. What is it that gives rugby its special qualities? For me it's no single thing, but the sum of its wonderfully diverse parts – its history, its personalities and its camaraderie.

One of the best quotes I've heard about rugby was from a TV interview with Philippe Sella I saw when I was playing in France. He said that to be a true rugby player you have 'to take the game, but not yourself seriously'. Most of the people I have met during my rugby career would fit this description, although it seems to be less of a prerequisite now that the sport has been chiselled down from a fun-loving amateur game to a hard-nosed, image-conscious professional sport.

Throughout the book you will see that I am an avid collector of quotes. I can only apologize for borrowing from others so much, but as Michel de Montaigne once said, 'I quote others only the better to express myself.'

My rugby career has been a series of experiences and lessons and it has been the main source of my misery and joy. I've had highs and lows, triumphs and disappointments and through playing for Scotland and the Lions I have experienced the whole range of sporting emotions. The spine-tingling combination of fear and excitement before an international match is something you don't experience in other walks of life. There is a sense of adrenaline and anticipation that is the equivalent of arriving at church on your wedding day; the moments before you turn over an exam paper; and attending a job interview – all rolled into one. It is something I will yearn for each year come the Six Nations.

There have been times when I've been able to step out of the moment and see that rugby has taken me to the pinnacle of sporting intensity and achievement. These are memories that stay with you forever, private recollections that make you realize how lucky you are. Standing facing an All Black 'Haka' with hundreds of camera flashes going off around the stadium made me aware how far-reaching the game had become. And I'll never forget standing arm-in-arm with my Lions colleagues at Newlands Stadium in Cape Town as we approached kick-off time in the First Test. It was a balmy evening and there was a gentle breeze in the air. I was incredibly focused, but I felt myself become an onlooker as the crowd began to sing the new South African anthem 'Nkosi Sikelel' iAfrika'. It is a beautiful, mesmerizing song and I couldn't help but hum along with the thousands of proud supporters as I realized that this was going to be one of the most significant nights of my life.

In addition to the memories, it is the people you meet over your career that make it all the more special. There are too many to mention but rugby seems to have so many 'good guys' – people like Derek Stark, Neil Jenkins, Tabai Matson, Jason Leonard, Anthony Hill, Carl Hogg, Tony Stanger, Francois Duboisset, Lisandro Arbizu, Semo Sititi and A. J. Venter. This book is a tribute to these and the many others that have helped me over the years. In putting this book together, I've been reminded of just how many people have been involved in my journey, and I would like to thank those, especially my family, who have shared in and contributed to the many wonderful times I've experienced.

There will no doubt be many occasions in the future that I will be wishing I was still part of a squad on tour or preparing for a Test match somewhere, but the thing I'll miss most is the vision of a scrum-half fizzing a pass through the air into my outstretched arms, and the thrill of running on to that ball with a world of possibilities stretched out in front of me.

CHAPTER 1

Borders Crossing

Inspiration starts with aspiration.

Mary Lyon

Craig, my brother, was inconsolable. He was trying hard to hold back the tears. I asked him what had happened.

'Someone's called off – I'm going to have to tell the others we can't play.'

For the previous month he'd been organizing a team to enter the Ward Sevens – the highlight of the rugby calendar for any Gala youth. He had managed to recruit six of his mates from the 'ward' we lived in – a ward being a designated area of the town – but he had just found out on the morning of his big day that one of the team was down with the flu. He couldn't enter a side with six players and so his hopes of winning the 1980 Under-10 trophy seemed lost.

I saw an opportunity and I wasn't going to let it pass me by.

'Dad, if I play then there would still be a team.'

'No chance – you've never played a game of rugby before.'

'But I've run about with Craig's friends lots of times.'

'No.'

Since the age of five I had been going to mini-rugby sessions on a Sunday morning and had joined in with the older boys who played touch rugby in the dead-ball area of Netherdale after Gala matches had ended. I knew I would be fine in my brother's team. For the next ten minutes I pleaded with my parents to allow me to take part. I had just turned seven years old and they were obviously very reluctant to let me play. However, faced with two screaming kids, it wasn't long before we persuaded them to change their minds. Craig was given instructions that I was to be picked as a winger and only involved in play as a last resort.

As I ran out on the Netherdale pitch on a sun-drenched afternoon, the day's events flashed by. My mum said it was comical – it looked like everyone else was a foot taller than me. I only received two passes throughout the day, but she said I got a huge cheer both times I touched the ball. We went on to win the tournament and I remember spending the evening taking the trophy round the houses in our ward. And so, in the same weekend that Mount St Helens erupted in North America, my love affair with the game began.

I was brought up in the town of Galashiels (or 'Gala' as it is better known locally), which is situated right at the very heart of the Scottish Borders. It is a busy town on the A7 road from Edinburgh to Carlisle and lies in the bottom of the steep-sided valley of the Gala Water, a mile upstream from its confluence with the River Tweed. Other Borderers from rival towns sometimes disparagingly call Gala people 'pail mercs'. This refers to us being – allegedly – the last town in the Borders to get indoor plumbing, thus leaving 'pail mercs' (local dialect for 'bucket marks') on the backsides of those using the outside toilets. I have myself been abused as a 'pail merc' – (amongst other things) at Mansfield Park in Hawick.

Gala folk much prefer to be known as 'Braw Lads or Lasses'. The Braw Lads Gathering in late June is one of several summer festivals in the Borders and is the focal point of the local calendar, with hundreds of horse riders marking boundaries around the town. The day also commemorates the town's history, notably an incident in 1337 when a party of English soldiers, resting nearby after picking and eating wild plums that had made them ill, were surprised and defeated by a band of locals. I'm amazed Mel Gibson hasn't made the story into a film yet!

Borders history has long been closely tied to the fluctuating fortunes of the textile trade, which used to be far larger than it is today. There has been a steady decline since the Second World War and the many woollen mills that once proliferated in towns like Gala and Hawick have now all but disappeared. The local communities thrived during the nineteenth century, the height of textile boom. In Gala alone there was a population increase from 1,600 in 1825 to 18,000 by 1891 – nearly 4,000 more people than live in the town today.

Efforts at establishing a more balanced economy by introducing electronics factories in the town in the 1960s have also seen a reversal in fortunes over the last ten years, with most employers relocating to Asia. However, the area's future now seems to be on more of an upward curve. The Waverley Line – the train link from Edinburgh that was lost in 1969 – will be reinstalled in 2011 and the trend for young people to leave the Borders to seek work and opportunities elsewhere in the UK is much less pronounced nowadays. This might be to do with house prices being much lower than in Edinburgh, but it has created a positive vibe about the Borders once again.

I suppose most people would describe their upbringing as 'normal'. Looking back, there was nothing out of the ordinary with my childhood. Life was constructed around the pillars of family, school, church, work and sport. My personal beliefs come from my family. I believe that I formulated all my values from them. My parents stressed the importance of being humble, modest and never taking things for granted.

My dad has always been my rugby conscience. He will notice a missed tackle or a poor bit of play that others would not have seen and is quick to remind me that I can always make improvements to my game. Only hearing positive things about yourself might seem more pleasant, but avoiding the truth won't make you a better player. I remember early on in my career that he hadn't spoken to me about an upcoming international, which I thought was strange. But on match day, when I got my boots out of my bag, I found little notes just saying 'concentration'.

From my mum I have inherited other qualities: a desire to please and not to let anyone down. She is an eternal optimist and has been incredibly supportive to my brother and me in everything we have done. Whilst I've realized that you can't please everyone, I would still like to aim to reach her standards of being good natured and helpful with everyone she meets. Craig was a talented centre who played a few seasons for Gala and Exeter, although golf has always been his preferred sport. One of my proudest moments came when I caddied for him in the Scottish Amateur Championship, even though he went out in the quarter-finals. He's also responsible for our family recently having to make the unusual adjustment of supporting the 'Auld Enemy' – after spending some time working for the RFU as an Academy Manager, Craig is now the manager of the England Sevens team.

My dad was a print setter for a local paper – *The Southern Reporter* – before becoming an estimator for a printing firm in Gala. My mum still works today as a library assistant at the Borders campus of Heriot-Watt University, less than 100 yards from Netherdale, home of Gala rugby club and the Border Reivers. Our house was on the west side of the town near the summit of Gala hill, which I've recently found out has a tenuous link to the film *Braveheart*. In 1296 William Wallace pursued the Earl of Dunbar – who had betrayed him to the English – to the top of the hill, where the Earl had taken refuge.

I am descended from rugby stock – my dad played in the centre for Gala and twice for the South. His father, John, was also a centre, but was forced to move from Gala to Melrose in the Thirties due to the presence at the time of Scotland international Doddie Wood in the side. My mum might not have such a direct rugby lineage, but it is impressive all the same. Her second cousin was the late Jock Turner, a classy midfielder for Gala and Scotland in the Sixties, and one of five players from the club to have played for the Lions.

My folks have a strong work ethic – a common trait in Borders people. I suppose I must have inherited some of this, as my paper round was the toughest in Gala, reaching 102 papers a day at one point. On one occasion I was even waiting to pick up my papers before the shop owner had arrived.

As I sat outside the paper shop I saw my dad approach, looking slightly bedraggled.

'What do you think you're doing here?'

'I was going to ask you the same question – I'm waiting for the shop to open.'

'Have you seen what time it is?'

In my zombie-like state of semi-consciousness, I hadn't checked my watch that morning. I looked up at the town clock, which loomed large over us. It was 3 a.m. I was four hours early. Fortunately my dad had been awoken by the noise of the door shutting as I'd set out on my very early shift. I made a mental note to check that I set my alarm properly before I went to bed.

I have two images of my young self. The first, prior to enrolling at Galashiels Academy, is of a manic, sports-mad, stubborn, attention-seeking lad prone to a tantrum or three – basically a parent's nightmare. The second image is of a shy, solitary and curious boy uneasy with handling praise. Later I became more geared to using humour rather than bravado to get people's attention. I still like to get the last word but this second description is much more in line with my present character.

My parents were a huge influence in helping me get involved in as many sports as I could squeeze into my days. At twelve years old, newly enrolled at Galashiels Academy, I played rugby on Saturday for the school first year team. Then, every Sunday, Mum and Dad ferried me up and down the A7 to play football for Hutchison Vale, a renowned boys club in Edinburgh. John Collins, another Gala lad, also turned out for Hutchie at the same time as me, but for their Under-18 side. He was a much more talented footballer and went on to captain Scotland – in the same month that I captained the Scotland rugby team – during an illustrious playing career. In the summer I shared my time between playing golf and cricket and competing for Melrose Athletics Club. At other times of the year Craig and I would turn to other sports – these ranged from marking out a chalk tennis court on the road outside our house to creating a jumping course (usually when *The Horse of the Year Show* was on TV) in the woods nearby.

Sometimes I didn't need anyone else to keep my sporting obsession going. There would be many a night I'd kick a football against a wall beside our garage, or take my misshapen orange Mitre rugby ball and practise drop-kicks and up-and-unders. I must have been happy in my own company as this usually evolved into a match, passing to myself and side-stepping past some imaginary defenders. I became stand-off for Scotland against a world XV, honing my Bill McLaren-from-the-commentary-box impersonation as I scored yet another try. I did the same at golf, often playing the top nine holes at the local Ladhope course with four balls and commentating on each shot as I pitted myself against the likes of Nick Faldo, Seve Ballesteros and Sandy Lyle. Perhaps speaking to yourself on a regular basis isn't that great an idea, but I'd choose it over today's 'PlayStation generation' who spend an inordinate amount of time indoors watching television or playing video games.

I also have to thank my parents for making me attend the Boys Brigade. This created a foundation that was very worthwhile because of the discipline the BB instilled – like going for badges, keeping the uniform clean for weekly inspection and working as a team. During my teenage years when there were many other distractions, I hardly ever missed a Friday night parade or a Sunday Bible class and I went on to gain the Queen's badge, the Brigade's highest honour. I came under the influence of some excellent role models like Al Christie and Riddell Graham – people who had given up their time to help others. It wasn't all hard work and for me, it was an excellent outlet for my competitive nature. We competed against other battalions in the Borders at things like drill, table tennis and cross-country. But my personal highlight was a game called 'Murder Ball', which we played each week. It was really just a raw form of rugby played indoors, but because of the confined space and hard floors it was sometimes more physical than the real thing.

I was, as you may have guessed, a fairly competitive youngster, although winning itself wasn't the sole motivation for me. I just wanted a chance to be out there doing some sort of sport and I was forever organizing games of football during break time at school. Looking back I must have taken this just a little too seriously. As there was only one rugby tournament – the Ward Sevens – for primary school children at the time, I concentrated my efforts on getting teams together for the handful of football five-a-side competitions that were held during the year. I remember arranging trials and selection meetings and even doing a poll with everyone in the school – St Peter's Primary – to decide what would be the best name for the side. I had obviously come up with the two or three names that were on the ballot sheet. For the record, 'Liverpool Lads', 'Rangers Reserves' and 'Tottenham Toddlers' were the options. Not the most inspiring of choices I must admit.

Probably because I played more football at primary school and then went on to play on a weekly basis in Edinburgh, I was much more committed to football than to any other sport. I loved playing for Hutchison Vale and went with them on a tour to Holland, although I never really felt part of the football scene as all my team-mates were from Edinburgh and I couldn't make the midweek training sessions. Moving to Gala Academy meant that there were now weekly games of rugby to get stuck into and although I still harboured dreams of being a dual international for Scotland, I knew something would have to give. The following season saw the end of my football career as the games changed from Sundays to Saturdays and I had to decide which sport I would have to sacrifice. It wasn't a difficult decision to make and probably the correct one – I had started at Hutchie Vale as a striker but ended up as a defensive midfielder, running all day but not possessing enough skilful touches to make it as a professional.

By that stage I was also a huge fan of the Scotland rugby team. I had first been to a Murrayfield international in 1982 – there had been a record crowd that day and my dad had to hold me above his head to avoid the crush outside the stadium. Being a Rangers supporter as well, I'd been to Tynecastle to watch them play Hearts and also to Hampden to see them play Aberdeen in the Scottish Cup Final. Whilst it was great to see my heroes like Ally McCoist and Davie Cooper close up, there was an unpleasant edge to watching football games at the time. The atmosphere was very threatening and was probably one reason why my dad had bought us tickets for the Aberdeen end at Hampden. However, the Aberdeen supporters were just as abusive as the raucous Rangers fans packed into the other end of the ground, and what made matters worse was that I was too scared to celebrate any of Rangers' goals when they went on to win the match on penalties.

Having spent my youth watching Scotland win two Grand Slams in the space of six years, it is something of a disappointment to have been a member of the Scotland team for eleven years and not to add to this total. I suppose playing in the side that were crowned the last-ever Five Nations champions in 1999 is a pretty good recompense, but that year's narrow defeat at Twickenham grates a little more with each passing year. However, I remain convinced that I helped Scotland topple the French in 1984.

With France leading 6–3 at half-time and their key players like captain Jean-Pierre Rives, stand-off Jean-Patrick Lescar-boura and full-back Serge Blanco growing in influence, a Scottish Grand Slam was looking less and less likely. Sitting in the schoolboys enclosure, I repeated a prayer throughout the second half. I urged God to grant my wish of a Scotland victory, and I wrote 'Scotland win' and 'Scotland Grand Slam' over and over again with my finger on the wooden bench upon which I was perched. My prayers were answered as Jim Calder scored the decisive try, diving over at a lineout after the French failed to control the ball. The media later described the score as a brilliant piece of instinctive play by Calder. I still think there was an element of divine intervention involved.

The year 1984 was an inspirational one for Scottish rugby supporters and I had been hooked all that season as the team worked its way to the Grand Slam. The 32–9 hammering of the Irish was their best game of the championship, with my favourite player, Roy Laidlaw, scoring two tries. As two Gala players were at the heart of that season's successes, it resonated even more. Captain Jim Aitken scored the match-winning try in Cardiff and full-back Peter Dods kicked seven-teen points in the win over the French. A couple of days after the decider against France, just after I had started that morn-ing's paper round, I remember seeing Peter Dods in the dark, an electrician by trade, also beginning his working day. This was a fairly normal occurrence – such was the nature of the amateur game and also the number of internationalists living and working in the Borders.

The abundance of rugby knowledge in the area was plain to see and I was lucky that I had been able to come under the influence of some very astute teachers. After being invited to attend a summer sports school, I had sessions from Jim Telfer and Jim Renwick, one of the best ever Scottish players. He showed us how to use a hand-off and how to accelerate into the tackle – advice that I still draw on to this day. I also tried to watch and imitate those who played in my position, which is the best and fastest way to learn a sport. Although I had started as a scrum-half, I was now certain that stand-off was the best position to play. Watching the 1984 Grand Slam video, I noticed that when he was kicking to touch, John Rutherford placed his right hand underneath the ball, not on top as I had been previously taught. This adjustment, and later copying how Craig Chalmers struck his drop kicks, helped my kicking game immeasurably. I remember getting up in the middle of the night with my dad and my brother to watch Scotland play France in the opening game of the 1987 World Cup. As well as desperately hoping for a Scottish win, I was also starting to imagine myself running out in the future as a Scotland player.

I played sufficiently well to be selected for Scotland Under-15 against Wales Under-15 in 1988. I know it might sound clichéd, but the first time I wore the Scottish jersey was a hugely uplifting experience: something about the blue jersey made me swell up with pride. My performance in the game itself wasn't anything special, and we lost 23–6 in front of a large Borders crowd. I hadn't exactly frozen on this elevated stage, but I hadn't done anything that suggested I'd attain any higher honours in the game.

It wasn't until a year later that I convinced myself I could make it to the highest level. And on top of that, this epiphany came during a match in which I was on the wrong end of a fifty-point hammering. I managed to get picked for the South Schools team at the end of that season and even though Midlands Schools beat us heavily, I knew then that playing against better players only improved my own game. My build may have been more akin to the gable end of a crisp, but I played really well and scored two tries, one of them a long-range effort.

That season had seen a major improvement to my game, mainly because I was playing two, sometimes three, matches every weekend. Most people will probably agree with the maxim that being grown up isn't half as much fun as growing up. This is certainly true in terms of my rugby career. The pressures, frustrations and emotional swings involved in professional rugby were not evident back when I was fifteen years old. Although my limbs were usually aching by the time I clambered into a bath on a Sunday night, I couldn't wait to play the following weekend. On a Saturday morning I was now turning out for the senior side at the Academy and the following day I played for the Gala Red Triangle, which ran an Under-16 team. After a couple of months of the season, Craig asked me if I would be interested in also playing for the Under-18 side, the Gala Wanderers, who played on Saturday afternoons. The last time I had played with my brother was eight years previously and my parents had feared for my well-being. This time around they let me decide if I was ready. I soon became a regular and playing alongside my brother was a thrill, especially when we won most of the sevens tournaments at the end of the season.

These early games for Gala Wanderers were an essential part of my rugby education. Physically inferior to the other players, I had to use pace and evasion to get past opponents. There was also a much rougher edge to youth rugby than I'd been experiencing at school – my first game against Selkirk Youth Club ended up in a mass brawl that even involved some of our replacements on the touchline. It showed me that you could never afford to take a backward step in rugby. I also received some excellent guidance from our coaches, Johnny Gray and Arthur 'Hovis' Brown.

Enthusiasm is a crucial characteristic for any successful coach. This is even more the case when coaching youngsters. Johnny and Hovis had this in spades, and it was such a joy to train and play for them. They are real characters, full of

banter and proud Gala men. Being coached by them made
you feel you were part of something much bigger. I used to
love hearing their stories. They also knew the game inside out
– Johnny having coached the South to victory over Australia
in 1984, and Hovis being full-back for Scotland in the Seventies before Andy Irvine came on the scene.

We were never dictated to or told to play in a certain way
and I'm sure this freedom was a major help in enabling us to
win the Scottish youth title at Murrayfield the following
season. We had some really promising players like Mark
Ballantyne, Greig Crosbie, Alan Bell and Alan Johnstone, but
our antics must have driven the coaches mad at times. One
night after a heavy snowfall they still wanted us to train –
instead we went outside and built a snowman and then
pelted them with snowballs. I'm sure Johnny was wishing he
was still preparing to play the likes of Mark Ella and David
Campese.

Like anyone else in Scotland, on 17 March 1990 I was celebrating the fact that we had beaten England to win the Grand
Slam. Everything about that day at Murrayfield was a credit
to the values of Scottish rugby at the time: humility, passion,
graft and togetherness. Four days later I felt very privileged to
run out on the same ground to play in the Schools Cup Final
against St Aloysius. In fact during the next month I played on
five occasions at Murrayfield. I had made it into the Scotland
Schools side and we played three matches at the ground,
together with a match against Ireland at Lansdowne Road.
Unfortunately, all four games were lost.

The Schools Cup Final had also ended up in a defeat and
left me with an embarrassing reminder each time I returned
to the home of Scottish rugby. Before the match we were in
the home dressing room, a vast area underneath the old West
Stand. As was the tradition at the time, we had a pre-match
'psych up', which involved slapping our legs and faces then
grabbing someone and wrestling with them. With memories

of David Sole leading out his troops the previous Saturday, we were all pumped up. On the way out, in a rush of adrenalin, I kicked the door to the changing room. Unfortunately, my boot went right through the plywood, leaving a sizable hole. Each time I returned over the next few weeks, I was racked with guilt. Just as well the West Stand has now been replaced or I think the SRU would probably come looking for some compensation!

Following the success of Gala Wanderers in winning the national title at Murrayfield, I came under the radar of the Gala selectors. This I know, because my dad was still one of the selectors at the time. He had told me they wanted to give me a run at the end of that season, when I was still sixteen years old, but both he and my school coach, Rob Moffat, were not keen on the idea so it never happened. I had enjoyed an outing for Gala in the Kelso Sevens a few months later, but I presumed my final year at the Academy would be spent once again playing for the school in the morning and the Wanderers in the afternoon. That was how things were panning out until we broke up for the October holidays.

For a Borders youngster with a talent for sport, rugby was seen as the only true way to express your natural abilities. I grew up in the golden age of Borders rugby. We had some great ambassadors for the area – people like Gary Armstrong, Roy Laidlaw, John Jeffrey and John Rutherford – all of whom successfully blended courage, modesty and skill. The Scottish League officially started in 1973, the year I was born. Between then and 1990, the year I made my debut for Gala, there was only one occasion when a non-Borders team won the championship. So, when I was asked if I would be available to play for Gala in their league match away to Stirling County, I jumped at the chance.

A club's tradition and history are what make it special. If the club is also your home town, it makes it something to aspire to be a part of. Even though it had been a few years since Gala's run of three championship titles in the early Eighties, at the start of the Nineties the side still had a reputation of being a tough team to play against. They invariably finished in the top half of the table. One key difference that separated Gala from the likes of Hawick or Melrose was that they lacked a ruthless streak and a sizeable forward pack. However, Gala possessed many talented individuals. Players like Ian Corcoran, John Amos, Mark Moncrieff and Mike Dods were some of the most skilful in the country and were on the fringes of the Scottish squad. However, it was the more experienced players like Hamish Hunter, Peter Dods and Dave Bryson that I turned to as I prepared for my first match at that level.

Brideghaugh, Stirling's home ground, was almost completely waterlogged after some torrential rain, but the game went ahead. We went on to lose 12–10, but I'd put in a decent enough performance. I relished the step up in intensity and the fact that everyone was taking things seriously. There had been times when I felt that there weren't many of my team-mates at school or youth level who cared that much about rugby. This time, however, I could see the guys were visibly upset at not coming away with a win. The Gala players had been great with me and were already talking about next week's fixture as if I'd be playing.

Although Gala's traditional rivals had always been Hawick, it was Melrose – just four miles away – who had emerged as the team we most desperately wanted to beat. Melrose set the benchmark in Scottish club rugby, and would go on to repeat the feats of Hawick who had dominated the championship in the Seventies and early Eighties. Well marshalled by their inspirational coach Jim Telfer, they were aggressive and relentless up front and had halfbacks who knew how to control a game. One of those half-backs was Scotland stand-off Craig Chalmers, who had played for the Lions and won a Grand Slam in the previous eighteen months. I was due to face him on his home turf in only my second game for Gala.

Against the odds, we defeated the reigning champions 19–15 in a game that was much more open than it had been at Stirling. I had a pretty mixed game, making some good breaks but also missing tackles and struggling with my restarts. I once read in a coaching manual that the biggest room in the house was the room for improvement and that definitely applied to my game – I knew I had many things to work on. That was why I had already decided I would return to play for the school team the following weekend. I thought it would be a better way to work on my basic skills, as well as offering a chance to finally win the Scottish Cup after two Final defeats in a row.

Later, some said that my return to schoolboy rugby had been bad for my game. They said that as I had continued to dominate games bad habits had developed. For years I would have argued with this sentiment. I worked very hard on my kicking and passing under the expert eye of Rob Moffat, often spending lunch hours during the week out on the pitch. I also achieved my goal of captaining the Scottish Schools team and leading Gala Academy – finally – to a Scottish Cup success. However, my form a year later, when I became established in the Gala side, was not as good as I expected. Part of the reason was a frustration borne from being unable to find holes as easily as I had done at Under-18 level. Throughout my career I have always felt my game has improved every time I've had to make a step-up to a better standard of rugby, but it wasn't immediately obvious that I had made real progress in my first season of senior rugby. Although my last season at school was very enjoyable, maybe I should have decided to stay with Gala after the win at Melrose.

Near the end of the season, I managed to play the odd game for the club and made it into the side for the 100th Gala Sevens, which attracted international teams such as Canada and Fiji. Despite incessant rain, thousands turned out at Netherdale and they were treated to a wonderful exhibition of sevens rugby from the South Sea Islanders. The annual sevens season in the Borders is the region's rugby heartbeat, and the five spring tournaments are still an established part of Borders life. The abbreviated form of the game was the brain-child of Ned Haig, a butcher from Melrose, where the first ever sevens tournament took place in 1883. Melrose Sevens today draws crowds of up to 15,000 and it was a pity and a mistake that the SRU did not give the town the right to host the Scotland leg of the IRB Sevens circuit.

The 1991/92 season – my first full season with Gala – was delayed because of the Rugby World Cup. This coincided with my first weeks at Edinburgh University where I'd enrolled to study history and politics. The season started well as we got our revenge on Stirling, winning 31–9. I made a break that led to a try and featured Kenny Logan falling for an outrageous dummy that was shown on the BBC's *Rugby Special* as part of their intro for the next few years, much to Kenny's irritation. Gala were undefeated going into Decem-ber as we prepared for the biggest game of the season, at home to Melrose. This was one of two matches in a month that got me a reputation for being brilliant one minute, lousy the next.

It was a bitterly cold day and the pitch was barely playable from an overnight frost. This hadn't deterred 5,000 support-ers turning up at Netherdale. Melrose made a dream start to the contest, galloping away to a 28–3 lead after only twenty minutes. Apart from a try from their hooker Steve Scott, the other three Melrose scores all came from mistakes by yours truly. I learned some harsh lessons as a bout of nervousness led to two fumbles and a loose pass. A paralysing feeling had enveloped me but I came back to score a cracking try late in the first half. We lost 28–16 and, although I was devastated by the start I had made, I knew that once I had recovered my composure I had played really well. James Joyce once remarked that mistakes are the portals of discovery – I discovered that day that temperament is a key factor in achieving sporting success.

I thought that the Melrose game might have dampened down the expectations that had been building up around my play, but less than two weeks later and after only three months of senior rugby, I was selected to play for Scotland 'B' against Ireland. At eighteen years old, I was set to become the youngest ever B cap. I spent a week giving press interviews and being photographed for the Scottish papers. I remember one dodgy photo I had to have taken with my dad, which for some strange reason involved us both cleaning my golf clubs.

An article appeared in the *Daily Telegraph* that had the headline 'Scot set to rival Barry John'. It quoted John Jeffrey as saying I was Scotland's 'outstanding hope for the future'. The *Telegraph* had even managed to get in touch with Barry John himself: 'I have only seen him on video and heard rumours. Although I wouldn't want to burden the boy with unnecessary expectations, there is clearly no limit to what he might achieve.' While flattering, I found it daft and I believed that it was both a reflection of the state of the game (which at the time was dominated by kicking) as well as a lack of rugby stories since the end of the World Cup.

It was nice to hear illustrious people say such things, but all I wanted to do was play and improve – expectations weren't in my control. There's a quote from Henry Ford that you can't build a reputation on what you are going to do. I wanted to be judged on how I was performing in the present, not on whatever potential I had. All I could do was remind people that I hadn't done anything to justify this talk, remind them of my mistakes; and together with the media I helped build up my image of being 'prone to errors'. The irony is that I spent the last few years of my career trying to tell them I wasn't prone to errors after all.

For the B international we stayed in Edinburgh's opulent Balmoral Hotel, which was in a different world to the room I

had been given that year in the university halls of residence
in the same city. My room was G1 – something I wouldn't
forget in a hurry. G1 meant the first room on the ground
floor, situated next to the main entrance of the halls. This
frequently meant I'd get a restless sleep as drunken students
arrived back at various times through the night talking loudly
or singing. This wasn't as bad, though, as the times I would
hear a knock on my window, followed by the request, 'Could
you open the main door? Sorry, I've forgotten my key.' It
drove me mad. I lapped up the luxury of the Balmoral and
felt that this was a much better way to prepare for a game.

A few of the Scotland team were congregating in the hotel
lobby as I wandered about after dinner.

'Toony, you want to come for a walk along Princes Street
with us? It's a tradition the night before a big match, and it'll
help you sleep later.'

One of the others suppressed a laugh at this, but I couldn't
see what the joke was. I agreed to join them for a leisurely
walk. We were a group of around half-a-dozen, all from the
Borders, which was comforting to me – not just the fact that I
knew the other players, but in that I presumed that Borders
rugby guys would know how to best prepare for a match.

After making it to the end of Princes Street we skirted by
the Castle on our way to the Grassmarket. Up ahead, my Gala
team-mate Gary Isaac shouted back to me, 'We're stopping at
the next pub for a drink, before we turn back to the hotel. It's
just a lemonade – you coming with us?'

'Of course', I replied.

I didn't want to walk back on my own and everyone else
seemed keen to get into the pub, in fact they seemed to start
walking more quickly than before.

We had walked up a hill at the end of the Grassmarket into
darker territory. We stopped and were now facing three pubs,
all of which did not look the most salubrious of establish-
ments. What I later realized was that we had been drawn into

Edinburgh's ersatz red-light district – affectionately known by locals as the 'pubic triangle'. This had not happened by coincidence. Within seconds of entering the bar, most of my team-mates were seated next to the stage where a stripper was well into her routine.

Like any hormonal teenager finding himself surrounded by half-naked women, I was initially in a state of shock. I tried my best to relax, and after ten minutes it's fair to say my mind was no longer on the fact that I was making my debut for Scotland B the following day. Just then the door to the bar swung open and in walked the three members of the Scotland management team. We had been busted and thoughts were running through my head that we'd be sent back to our clubs for a lack of professionalism. However, it turned out that the Scotland management had arrived not on a search and rescue mission, but clearly with more personal agendas. We quickly made our excuses and left, although we couldn't shout to one of our team-mates at the other end of the bar. We left him stranded, beer in one hand, stripper in the other. Curiously, neither players nor management ever mentioned the incident again.

The next day I played a game that was almost the reverse of my performance for Gala against Melrose. On this occasion, I played some of my best rugby to date for the first sixty minutes. I don't think I had ever kicked as long and as accurately, and my half-back partnership with Andy Nicol was going very well. However, just after the hour mark I committed an absolute howler, which saw the Irish take the lead for the first time.

From a scrum near the halfway line I called a pretty standard backline move called 'Dummy rangi, rangi'. This may sound like something that is shouted at a toddler's birthday party, but all it involved was that I ran across the field with my inside-centre dummying the outside centre before I finally gave the ball to the full-back on a scissors pass.

However, for whatever reason, full-back Mark Appleson stayed out wide as I took off on my lateral run. In attempting to show him that he was supposed to be running towards me, I stuck out the ball in one hand. Irish centre Martin Ridge didn't need a second invitation and stole the ball from my fingertips to run in unopposed from fifty yards. In hindsight, this was not my wisest career move to date. Just to rub salt in the wound, I dropped a ball close to my goal-line near the end of the game – another mistake which resulted in an Irish try. We lost the match 29–19.

Press cuttings now began to appear with words like 'mercurial' and 'enigmatic' used to describe my game. These were to stay with me for the rest of my career. After the disappointments of the Irish match I had the chance to bounce back immediately as I was selected at stand-off in the National Trial for the Reds (possibles) against the Blues (probables). We blitzed the shadow Scotland team, winning 27–18, and my performance exorcized a few of my Murrayfield demons. While I was probably still too raw to have any chance of being included in the Five Nations, it was now obvious that rugby had become an integral part of my life. And more than that, it was about to take me all over the world.

CHAPTER 2

Odyssey

Life is far too important to take seriously.

Oscar Wilde

'Benzo – Where are you?'

There was no response.

Grudgingly, I picked up the sledgehammer once again and looked at the wall in front of me. I could have done with some help, and I cursed my workmate, Benzo (Stuart Bennett), under my breath. Covered in a thick coat of sweat that only a humid Australian afternoon can generate, I tried to knock right through the wall. I failed miserably. After a few more whacks, I'd only made a small hole. We had been told that we'd be able to rip at the plasterboard once a gap appeared, so I dropped the sledgehammer and went at it with my hands. Eventually, I saw some daylight. I relaxed in the knowledge that it would be much easier work from now on.

Almost immediately, Benzo's head appeared through the hole I'd made. I recoiled in shock and he burst out laughing. But it wasn't him that had given me the fright. Instead, my acute alarm was down to the swarm of huge cockroaches pouring out of the new opening. Benzo was not smiling for long. This was the glamour of my first season playing abroad.

In the two years after leaving school, I discovered very quickly how richly rewarding a successful rugby career could be. These were the amateur days so there was no financial return, but opportunities abounded. Within this period rugby had taken me to Australia, Hong Kong, Fiji, Tonga, Samoa, France, Italy, Spain and Dubai. This was a time when enjoyment was almost as important as winning – an ethos that underpinned the amateur game. It was also when I made the most improvements to my play as I absorbed the lessons and benefits from what felt like an endless succession of amazing adventures – a rugby odyssey.

After the high of beating a Blues side led by Gavin Hastings at Murrayfield, I was selected once more for Scotland B, this time in Albi against the French. Despite losing 27–18, we competed well and my own game was solid and mercifully error-free. It had been the last chance for players outside the Five Nations squad to impress the selectors in an attempt to win a place on the summer tour to Australia. Although I was never really in the running to play for the senior team that spring, being a part of the Scottish Students squad for their Five Nations Championship was just as challenging – and much more fun!

John Rutherford coached the side – a bonus for me as 'Rud' was rightly regarded as the best number 10 Scotland had ever produced. He gave me little tips like how to kick into the wind, but the best thing for me was the fact I had a coach who was a former stand-off. I felt that we viewed the game from the same perspective, which helped me no end. It was also obvious that Rud's temperament must have been a major reason he had performed so well at the highest level. I was starting to discover that being relaxed in pressure situations was a better way to succeed than getting so pumped that you tighten up. Rud was always very laid-back and an ideal coach for a team like the Students, who could be a wild bunch at times.

After losing to a strong England Students team, we went to Dublin for our second game of the tournament. As we had only met a few hours before the game the week before, we didn't know how rigorous our match preparations would be before the Irish game. After our arrival, the captain, Graham McKee, announced to the squad that we would meet in the hotel bar to talk things through for the following day's match. It seemed like we were taking a much more detailed approach to our preparations this time around.

Once the squad had assembled, McKee stressed to us the importance of beating the Irish: 'Guys, we may have a talented squad but it's no use if we can't get a win tomorrow. I think I know how we might be able to do that.'

He had our attention.

Just then he turned round and nodded to the barman: 'Two compulsory pints of Guinness for everyone!! No one is allowed to leave until they have finished them both.'

Such was the hedonistic atmosphere surrounding the Students Five Nations – bonding together was as important as training together. We didn't take ourselves seriously at all, but we went out onto the pitch prepared to die for one another. Unfortunately, this sometimes wasn't enough.

Going into the last five minutes of the match against Ireland, McKee asked the referee, Irishman John Cole, what the score was. He replied that we were trailing 21–19. The next time we got hold of the ball we broke through the Irish defence and scored. As a try was still only worth four points, we believed we were now leading 21–23. However, something didn't seem right – both teams began kicking the ball into touch at any opportunity. Mr Cole had in fact got his sums wrong, as we had actually been 21–16 in arrears prior to our late score. Much to the puzzlement of the Irish, our front-row celebrated the score with 'victory' leaps that, in retrospect, must have looked distinctly out of place.

The following afternoon I stood on the terracing at Lansdowne Road with the thousands of other travelling Scots, thankful for the many hip-flasks of whisky that were being passed around to keep us warm. It was great to play a form of international rugby and then experience the real thing the next day from a supporters' point of view. There weren't many better sporting occasions in the world than a Five Nations weekend in Dublin.

Our match against the Welsh had been yet another narrow loss, this time played in driving rain at Llanelli's Stradey Park. We soon forgot about the result. At the after-match dinner, just as things were starting to get out of control, one of the Welsh players announced it was a tradition at Llanelli to get hit over the head with a metal beer tray. Phil May, the ex-Llanelli and Wales second row shouted in agreement and picked up a tray and whacked one of the Welsh players. He then turned to us and said someone had to do the same to him. For whatever reason, I was unanimously voted as being that someone.

Tentatively I took the beer tray and gently tapped Phil May's bald head. My feeble effort was met by howls of derision and I was urged to do it again – this time with feeling. I didn't hold back, hitting Phil May so hard that the metal tray was bent in two. I was worried for a moment that I might get a punch from the big man; instead he slapped my back saying, 'Well done – you're next!'

The resulting sore head was alleviated an hour later by one of the funniest things I've ever seen throughout my rugby career. We had headed back to Swansea, where we were staying, and got dressed up in our kilts before going out on the town. As we arrived in the town centre, there were a number of people shouting at us to lift up our kilts. One car had stopped at the traffic lights, and a group of girls had rolled down the window, urging us to show them if we really were 'true Scotsmen'. Our prop, Stuart Paul, did the honours, lifting up his kilt and 'mooning' to them. This wasn't enough for one of the girls who asked for a closer look. Stuart obliged and tried to place himself on the front windscreen. We all watched in disbelief as his bodyweight suddenly proved to be too much for the car – the windscreen caved in. Managing not to fall into the car himself he joined the rest of us who were by then already running as fast as we could to seek shelter in a pub. We didn't stop laughing all night. I can only imagine what the girls felt like to see a kilted Scotsman's hairy arse coming towards them at close range!

Following the Five Nations, I received the good news that I'd been selected to tour with Scotland to Australia. I also had a rather more unexpected phone call from the Irish Wolfhounds asking if I'd be available to play for them in the Hong Kong Sevens. I was eighteen years old and was being asked to play a lot of rugby, probably too much. I had just played for the Students and Scotland Under-21s and was all set to play sevens for Gala. However, I enjoyed playing so much that I found it hard to say no. An opportunity to play in Hong Kong was too good to turn down.

I had been drafted into the Wolfhounds side as a replacement for Stephen Bachop, who had played stand-off for Western Samoa in the World Cup the year before. I had apparently impressed the manager during the students international in Dublin. What I didn't realize when I met up with the squad was that our time in Hong Kong would be just like an extension of a weekend's partying with the Scottish Students. There were some great characters like Dave Beggy, Paddy Johns and Jonny Garth on that trip and it was certainly an eye-opener for myself and another draftee, young Irish winger Niall Woods. During our week together, the only time we didn't go out to bars like 'Joe Bananas' and the 'Bull and Bear' was the night before the opening day of the tournament. Not surprisingly, we failed to qualify for the quarter-finals of the main competition, losing the pool decider against France.

We didn't fare that much better in the Plate, going out in the semi-finals to Tonga. This was more disappointing than our defeat to the French, as winning the Plate had been a realistic goal. However, by that stage a tropical storm had made it a much more level – and extremely muddy – playing field. When the storm hit, it hit hard. Torrents of water sluiced through the stands, turning the grounds into a swamp. I looked on in amazement and admiration as Fiji sailed through the tournament, seemingly unaffected by the mud and rain. They went through their full repertoire of skills in the most horrendous conditions, just like they had done at the Gala Sevens the previous year. Even New Zealand, whom they met in the final, were left chasing shadows as Waisale Serevi and player of the tournament Mesake Rasari dominated proceedings.

I knew the Scotland tour to Australia would be much more professional – anything led by David Sole had to be. Sole had been Scotland's Grand Slam winning captain two years before, famously leading the side out against England at Murrayfield. I got to witness both the intense and inspirational sides to his character, in what proved to be the final time he wore the dark blue jersey.

Early on in the tour I was Sole's room-mate. Being amongst members of the 1990 Grand Slam team was a daunting experience at the best of times – a bit like being a pupil asked to spend some time in the staff room with a group of teachers. They gave the impression of possessing amounts of self-confidence I could only dream about. Sole also appeared to have something about him that gave him automatic authority; an almost eerie, potentially crazed nature. He could have been well cast ahead of Jack Nicholson in *The Shining*. I had seen him snap at one of the players for turning up late on one occasion, so I decided to keep out of his way and try to be early to meetings for a change.

Sole's performance as a substitute in our third game of the tour against Emerging Wallabies in Hobart left everyone in awe. It also inspired the team to come back from 4–24 to draw the match 24–24. He was magnificent – it was one of those moments when you feel privileged to be on the same pitch as a true rugby legend. What made it all the more special was that Sole, normally a loose head prop, came off the bench to play at openside flanker. He took the game to the opposition at every opportunity, continually cajoling us to do better, and on one occasion lifting the huge second-row, Garrick Morgan, clean off his feet in a tackle that saved a certain try. The second half also coincided with an upturn in my form.

We had lost our opening match in Darwin by a point to a Northern Territory Invitation XV. Although the weather was stiflingly hot and the opposition had brought in some quality guest players, my disappointing kicking performance had much to do with our subsequent defeat. Things continued in the same vein for me in Hobart until we began our comeback. However, my final two games on tour were much better and I ended up winning the man-of-the-match award in my last outing against Queensland Country. While it was pleasing to improve each time I played, I knew there would be many people who thought I would never be able to control an international match from stand-off. Otherwise, my first Scotland tour had been a blast.

I struck up great friendships with Derek Stark, Ian Smith, Sean Lineen and Tony Stanger and I discovered that touring with Scotland wasn't all hard work. The squad seemed to be very conspiratorial and keen to have fun together. We had a couple of 'kangaroo court sessions' during our month in Australia – this was basically a variety of ways to get drunk as quickly as possible. After two weeks we realized that having to drink large amounts of Bundaberg Rum was a sure-fire, one-way-ticket to oblivion. It was used as a punishment for those misbehaving while the court was in session. No one escaped from having to consume a shed-load of alcohol. First-time tourists, points scorers, those that had done something stupid that week, those that hadn't – everyone was called upon to empty their glasses.

Saturday matches were usually followed by a 'happy hour' back at the hotel. This was a chance for us to play drinking games. It sorted out the weak – guys like me – from those experienced at this type of thing. It also got us prepared for our night out – a compulsory activity for those who had played that day. 'Work hard, play hard' seemed to be an unwritten rule on tour.

Another rule was that of 'Dirt Tracking'. This happened the night before a match and involved those players who weren't in the squad for the following day's game. The theory was that they were to find out which bars and clubs were the best for everyone to visit the next night. What everyone really wanted was for the players to get wasted so there would be a few stories to tell at the 'happy hour' the next evening. Incredibly, the management at the time sanctioned this. In fact, the team manager paid for a meal with the 'Dirt Trackers' to get them started on their way. What with going out with the midweek team after our matches, I think I was drunk at least three times a week in Australia. At times amateur rugby wasn't good for your liver!

I think I was a bit of an enigma to the older guys – I combined some daft things like attempting to wash my clothes in a tumble dryer, and trying to keep up with my studies by reading books such as Plato's *Last Days of Socrates*. I was the nonchalant, disorganized student and I soon had a reputation for always being the last person to turn up at meetings. While most people called me 'Toony', I was renamed 'Hint-End' by Tony Stanger on tour. 'Hint-End' is Scottish for 'tail-end', which was usually where I was – wandering around with my head in the clouds. I didn't really mind my tag as it gave me an identity. I played up to the stereotype even though it insinuated that I was immature and unreliable. Being known as something was better than being ignored, even if it was a negative. I realized that others laughing at your expense seemed a sure-fire way to be popular within a rugby squad. I helped this no end by my efforts at horse riding.

We spent a day at a ranch out in the bush, enjoying an Aussie 'barbie' and getting to ride around on quad bikes. There were a few guys riding horses and I was asked if I wanted to join in. I had never ridden a horse before, but this only seemed to encourage my team-mates who wanted to see me at least have a go.

I didn't have a clue what to do and I naively thought the horse would just trot around at a leisurely pace. However, within seconds my horse had started to pick up some speed. My feet had come out of the stirrups and I lost hold of the reins. I was clinging on to the saddle and feeling very uncomfortable. For some insane reason I thought giving the horse a kick would act as a brake. As you can imagine, the opposite happened. The horse was in complete control and heading fast for a boundary fence. I decided to jump off.

It was a long way to the ground and I crashed down onto the dirt. I was very sore but hadn't broken any bones. Through the dust, I could see my team-mates were hysterical with laughter. Well at least it had been funny for someone. If I had any thoughts about getting back on the horse they were quickly dispelled as my eyes and face started to swell up. The tour doctor then informed me I had an allergy to horses. At that moment I hoped I had got all the bad luck out of my system, as the following day we were due to go bungee jumping.

Next stop on my world tour was Italy. Number 8 Carl Hogg and myself had agreed to be available for the Students World Cup, even though we had both just toured with Scotland in Australia. It had already been a long season and we only had three days' rest at home before leaving for Italy, but we felt it would be worth it. The coaches, David Bell and John Rutherford, had reassured us that we would be used sparingly in matches and could lounge by the pool instead of training. As it turned out, we trained every day and we were two of only three players to play every minute of every game.

I would describe us as a rabble with good intentions. Although our squad was similar to a Scotland 3rd XV in terms of quality, the SRU only provided £10,000 of the total £30,000 costs. This meant that players had to pay £250 each for representing their country. France, on the other hand, ranked their Students behind only the senior national team in their priorities. Our shoestring budget provided us with the scariest plane journey I've experienced and some very basic accommodation once we got to our Italian base in Arenzano, a seaside town an hour from Genoa.

Despite a ramshackle and chaotic beginning, we bonded as a group and went on to play some great rugby. We qualified for the last eight as runners-up, having lost to a strong French side that included the likes of Fabien Pelous, Thierry Lacroix and Olivier Brouzet. Although we had been leading them after the break, their experience told and it was no surprise to see them go on and win the tournament. I think we had won their respect, though, and we had a good time with them afterwards in the bar. Our players couldn't believe their luck the next day when the French turned up at our hotel and handed us some of their stylish Eden Park kit in exchange for some of our gear. They must have felt sorry for us – our T-shirts wouldn't have looked out of place at a primary school gym class.

The subsequent draw for the quarter-finals gave our management a few headaches. The matches were to be played over two days the following weekend, although we only had enough money to stay in our hotel until the Sunday morning. We put in a request to have our game against Argentina brought forward to the Saturday but the opposition refused, citing the need for an extra day's rest. It was an embarrassing situation but didn't ultimately affect our preparations. Mind you, I remember the look of disgust the hotel manager gave us as we stayed an extra night on credit.

We put in a valiant effort against the Argentines, who had a huge pack and looked like they had a lot of postgraduates in their team. The French squad had turned up to support us and sang 'Flower of Scotland' as best they could from the stands. We were very much in the game and the final result – a 29–18 defeat – was down to their superior scrummaging and a costly mistake by me. I was close to running on empty by the second half as too many matches that season – my first season of senior rugby – had finally caught up with me. A charged-down kick gifted Argentina six points at a crucial stage of the match and left me distraught – not for the first time that year. I was glad the summer break was on the horizon.

I spent my time working as a plasterer's labourer in Gala and trying to get on top of my studies. I had been forced to put back my exams until September having been in Australia when I was originally due to take them. Being a model student at Edinburgh University didn't really fit with my efforts at furthering my rugby career. There were many times I would have to miss lectures and tutorials, but I had deliberately chosen a subject – history and politics – that wasn't too intensive in the hope that I would have free time to catch up and also fit in some extra fitness and weight training.

University had a similar raison d'être as amateur rugby – enjoyment. I've heard university described as a holiday of indulgence, which is hard to deny. I suddenly found myself free to drift, happily suspended from the real world. It was no wonder I became known for having my head in the clouds. Spending an hour discussing the American mid-term elections or listening to a lecture on seventeenth-century Scottish history was a delight and if rugby had turned professional five years earlier, I would have missed it terribly.

As well as a sense of freedom, I enjoyed the anonymity of university life. Strolling through the Edinburgh's Meadows on the way to a lecture with hundreds of fellow students was a pleasant departure from the expectations and pressures of trying to break into the Scotland team. I remember lining up for the national anthems at Lansdowne Road two years later and being distracted by someone trying to wave at me. I looked around and saw a guy who was in my political theory tutorial. His face was a picture of utter disbelief – he hadn't a clue that I was a Scotland rugby player.

I became less anonymous when I was presented with a sponsored car from a garage in the Borders. My name was emblazoned on both sides and I used to dread parking it in case anyone noticed me. Years later, Duncan Hodge, a top bloke who also played stand-off for Scotland, admitted to me that his student mates used to try and find my car after a night out and then urinate over each of the door handles. I suppose I had been asking for it.

The following season I was quickly back in the groove with Gala, enjoying an excellent run of games. However, we blew our chances of winning the championship on the penultimate week of the season. We were only a point behind Melrose with two games to go, the first of which was away to already-relegated Dundee. Our final fixture was a home match against Melrose and all the talk in the Borders was about what a fantastic climax to the season it would be – almost like a play-off for the title. There was predicted to be a record crowd at Netherdale and I think we got carried away with it all when our focus really should have been on first beating Dundee. I remember talking with the Gala players on the bus to Dundee about moves that might work well against the Melrose backline. We were far too complacent against a fired-up home team and lost the match by a point. It always brings a smile to Andy Nicol's face – the Dundee captain that day – when I remind him that it was the biggest disappointment of my time playing for Gala.

That season also saw me move position for the first time in my career, as I was picked at outside-centre for the South in the Inter-District championship and also for Scotland 'A' in a one-off match against Spain in Madrid. I continued to run at stand-off for Gala, but there was now a lot of speculation that I might get a start in the number 13 jersey for that season's Five Nations. As Sean Lineen had recently retired, pundits predicted that the Scottish midfield would include either Graham Shiel or myself at centre to play alongside established backs Craig Chalmers and Scott Hastings.

The selectors showed their intentions with the team they picked to play Italy in December. It was Gavin Hastings' first game as Scotland captain, although caps were not awarded for the fixture. I was chosen as outside-centre, partnering Scott Hastings in the midfield. Duncan Paterson, the team manager, said that the five debutants were very unlucky not to be winning their first caps. Scotland, like other countries at the time, still deemed Italy not to be of a standard worthy of awarding Test-match status.

Although we just sneaked a 22–17 win over the fast-improving Italians, I'd felt reasonably comfortable and was getting increasingly used to playing at 13. There were only two more games before Scotland's opening Five Nations match against Ireland and I was given two further opportunities to play at centre. First up was an A international against Ireland and then the National trial. This time I was picked to play for the Blues (probables). Unfortunately the timing of my first real rugby injury couldn't have been any worse as I tore my medial knee ligament after only twenty minutes. It was only a minor tear, but it was enough to keep me out of action for three weeks, consequently missing the Irish match. Even the help of a machine used to heal horses' joints couldn't reduce the recovery time. After Scotland won their opening game, Graham Shiel held onto his place in the centre and I had to be content with sitting on the bench for the remaining three matches.

By the time of our final match, away to England, I was resigned to the fact that I wouldn't be winning my first cap that season. At the time, replacements could only come onto the field for an injured player. As no one in their right mind would want to quit a Test match unless it was a serious injury, we didn't even bother leaving our seats during play. All the subs were aware that if any player suffered a bad injury our team doctor, James Robson, would throw a towel onto the ground – these were the days before the medics had a radio link with the coaching staff. After twenty minutes of the game, Craig Chalmers was being treated for an injury and I got told to do the obligatory warm-up just in case. I thought this was unlikely as Craig usually got up with a shake of the head and carried on playing.

I was on my way down to the touchline when I saw the doctor's towel being lobbed onto the field. The blood started to drain from my body and I became as nervous as a long-tailed cat in a room full of rocking chairs. What made me even less comfortable was what coach Ian McGeechan then told me. He said that I was to go on at inside-centre, a position I had never played before, with Graham Shiel, who had been at inside-centre all season, moving to stand-off. I didn't have time to feel disappointed about this bizarre and unexpected decision but the little confidence I had in reserve now evaporated. I did the necessary stretches as I waited for Craig Chalmers to be carried from the field. I couldn't help looking up at the huge stands opposite, which didn't do much to console me. I also started thinking of friends and family watching the game on television. My focus certainly wasn't on playing inside-centre against quality opponents like Will Carling and Jeremy Guscott.

The first ten minutes were a blur – I ran about in a daze unable to control my movements, and certainly not any movements associated with tackling. This was no doubt due to trying to work out what to do at inside-centre and also due to an element of being self-conscious in front of 70,000 people. It was as if I was running around with my eyes closed.

Unfortunately, the opposition ran towards me on a couple of occasions with the ball. It really seemed like I couldn't remember how to tackle and I was as effective at stopping them as a speed bump is at stopping a car.

Martin Bayfield was one of two players who ran through me and when I later joined him to play at Northampton he thanked me for my efforts in getting him selected for the Lions Tour in 1993. In fact there is a photo from the match in the clubrooms at Northampton of me poised to tackle him. Luckily the photo wasn't half a second later as 'Bayfs' strode on to make what was undoubtedly his longest break of his international career.

If Geech had been thinking of the players that might become Scotland regulars, I'm sure he must have already put a line through my name. However, I got my act together after twenty minutes and by the second half I was desperate for the ball, enjoying the atmosphere instead of being intimidated by it. England had hit a purple patch where they ran us a bit ragged, but we were much more competitive after this. Considering our midfield after Scott Hastings went off injured was Graham Shiel at stand-off, myself at inside-centre and Tony Stanger at outside – all three of us playing out of position – we had done well to keep the score down to 26–12.

We drowned our sorrows at the after-match dinner – an event that seeks to destroy those that have just won their first cap. A tradition at the time was that new caps had to finish whatever was in their glass each time someone came over to them with a drink. Predictably, this happened quite frequently. To make matters worse, I was forced to drink port because the red wine on the table wasn't deemed strong enough. I soon became very drunk, and was back in my hotel room with my head in the toilet before midnight. Mind you, I fared better than when lock Ian Fullarton won his first cap in New Zealand in 2000. He didn't even make it to the toilet and has the memory to tell his grandchildren that he was sick all over the shoes of Jonah Lomu, who had been sitting beside him.

In the midst of trying to win my first cap, I had been involved in the build-up to the inaugural World Cup Sevens. In November, I was part of the Scotland team that went to Dubai and shocked everyone by winning the tournament. There were maybe only a handful of international sides present, but we had beaten France, Queensland, Natal and England along the way. The setting was as far removed as it was possible to be from anything we could have experienced back home in Scotland – we played in extreme heat and the pitch consisted of tightly packed sand. I had imagined that playing rugby on sand would be much the same as running on a beach, but this was very different and very painful. It was as if a thin layer of sand had been put on top of concrete and even though we wore knee and elbow pads, we still ended up having our skin lacerated every time we hit the ground.

Two days after my first cap at Twickenham the next leg of our sevens preparations took me to Australia, Fiji and Hong Kong. Known at the time as the 'debacle', the best we achieved in the three tournaments was a quarter-final appearance in Hong Kong against Western Samoa, the eventual winners. Our win in Dubai, where we had mixed a kick-and-chase game with traditional Borders sevens rugby, had led us down a cul-de-sac. Sevens rugby was evolving very fast and the best exponents were those that had a physical edge to their play. We had opted for stamina over explosiveness and weren't in the same league as the leading nations. Samoa's performance in Hong Kong and later England's triumph at Murrayfield demonstrated that the abbreviated game was now all about power. Despite our poor results and some punishing bouts of endurance training, the sevens tour was very enjoyable – we only had a squad of ten players and we became quite a close-knit group. Also, our time in Fiji was terrific, as none of us had experienced anything like it before.

As soon as we had boarded the bus at Nadi airport and on the three-hour trip south to the Fijian capital Suva, we saw people playing rugby wherever we went. Usually in bare feet, in fields sometimes having to dodge past trees, Fijians were out throwing a ball around. There can't be another country in the world where rugby is so popular. On the morning of the tournament, all the teams were driven in open-top buses through the streets of Suva. The parade brought out thousands of exited locals, many of whom mobbed our bus, but their interest wasn't in any of the players. Our assistant coach, John Jeffrey ('JJ'), got the locals very animated and we could hear them saying excitedly 'White Shark' over and over to each other.

The Fiji tournament was another disappointment as we failed to qualify from our group – just like the previous week in Australia. However, the skill on show from the local village sides was amazing. Six out of the eight quarter-finalists were Fijian – having consigned Australia, the All Blacks and us to the Plate competition. That the Fijian national team turned out to be the eventual winners was solely due to the presence in their team of one man – Waisale Serevi.

I had always wanted to call my first born after my favourite rugby player. David Campese was my rugby idol for years but by 1993 the two potential options were Zinzan or Waisale. I don't think I would have persuaded my future wife with either of these choices. Waisale Serevi, known as 'the wizard' by his team-mates when he later played for Leicester, was the instigator of the Fijian wonder try of the 1990 Hong Kong Sevens which is one of my all-time favourite sporting moments. Under pressure from a strong All Black defence, Serevi took a low pass and instinctively passed it between his legs to Noa Nadruku who, as he was being tackled, flicked it on to the captain Tomasi Cama. Cama then sprinted fifty

yards – hitch-kicking all the way – to score the tournament-
clinching try. Serevi was a magician and I had seen him close-
up in the 1991 Gala Sevens and the 1992 Hong Kong Sevens
where he danced through the mud to win yet another sevens
trophy for Fiji.

While in Fiji, I think I had bored my team-mates senseless
eulogizing about Serevi. I felt it was justified when he
proceeded to produce a master class of sevens rugby on the
final day of the competition. Unknown to me, JJ had spoken
to Serevi and told him that I was his biggest fan. So, between
them they decided to have some fun at my expense. As I was
watching one of the ties I got a tap on my shoulder from none
other than Waisale T. Serevi.

'Hello Gregor. Can I have your autograph?'

'Well, y-y-yes. Erm, of course.'

Although somewhat surprised, I thought I couldn't turn
him down and it wasn't until I started to sign my name that I
noticed JJ laughing with the rest of the team. I'd been
stitched up.

In Fiji, the rugby-mad public treated Serevi like royalty. He
was married the weekend before we arrived in the country,
and the national paper devoted almost all of its pages to cover
the event. I remember a local rugby supporter raving about
Serevi and a try he had scored at a recent sevens tournament.
It involved him flicking up the ball with his feet as two
defenders were chasing him. I wish I had seen it.

It was probably with this in mind that I tried to do something similarly outrageous in the World Cup Sevens that were
held at Murrayfield in March. As I went back to cover a kick
that had been put in behind our defence I could sense that
there was an Argentine player very close to me so, instead of
diving on the ball, where I would inevitably be tackled as I
tried to get back on my feet, I chose the element of surprise
and back-heeled the ball past the oncoming defender. With
Serevi as my inspiration I had tried the most unlikely of

options and it had worked. Unfortunately as I was in the process of picking up the ball, I got smashed by another Argentine player.

The back-heel was to be my only good memory from the World Cup as I suffered the ignominy of being dropped. I watched the action from the bench for the next two days and it was obvious that our three-week tour had drained our energy levels and belief. Although I wouldn't have said so at the time, being a replacement was probably no bad thing as Scotland ended up in a dismal eighteenth place.

A number of players who had taken part in our many squad sessions and the three-week tour had since been dropped or were out injured. The attrition rate had been horrendous, and for those left standing, there was little left in the tank. Just to rub salt into the wound, England were crowned world champions after having decided not to enter any other sevens event. Their lack of any meaningful preparation had left them fresh to play a high-octane brand of power sevens. We had reached the end of the road a long time before.

I remember chatting to Tony Stanger prior to the tournament about injuries – he had hamstring problems and missed the World Cup while I was struggling with a groin strain. But I couldn't resist carrying on playing and I made myself available for the Scotland tour to the South Seas at the end of the season. Although we were due to play the Test sides of Fiji, Tonga and Samoa, the SRU deemed that no caps would be awarded. The reasoning was understandable – with the Lions touring New Zealand and a spate of injuries, just three players in our tour party had played during the Five Nations.

Travelling in the South Pacific was a peculiar experience. The 180th meridian of longitude, which indicates where the western hemisphere comes to an end, passes through the Fijian island of Taveuni. Situated some 400 miles to the east is Tonga. However, the King of Tonga – more of whom later –

decreed that, geography notwithstanding, the 180th meridian would be stretched eastwards to embrace his kingdom and thus enable Tongan time to be thirteen hours ahead of GMT instead of eleven hours behind it. This meant that the Tongan people would be the first in the world to greet the new day, but caused us no little confusion as we toured the South Sea Islands. On one occasion, we boarded a one-hour flight from Tonga on a Tuesday night and arrived in Samoa – our destination – on the Monday night. Robin Charters, our jovial president quipped, 'I haven't had a drink since tomorrow!'

As with the West Indies and cricket, so with the Pacific Islands and rugby. Rugby – union and league – suits Polynesians, who enjoy the physical challenge. They thrive on making big tackles and running with the ball in hand. In addition, they tend to have oodles of flair and daring. Fiji have dominated sevens rugby for the last two decades and we've seen at a number of World Cups how good Samoan rugby is. This is achieved with little help for creating a professional structure in any of the three countries. Samoa once played in the Super 10 competition – a forerunner of the Super 14 – but have been largely ignored ever since the game went professional. It is a disgrace that the All Blacks have never played a Test match in Tonga or Samoa, but are quite happy to fly around the world for revenue-generating games at Twickenham. If rugby really has ambitions of being a global game then it must stop snubbing the Pacific Islands – and Argentina for that matter – and include them in international tournaments such as the Tri-Nations or the Super 14.

Being dropped seemed to be becoming a habit, as I didn't make the starting line-up for our First Test match against Fiji. My performance in the opening game of the tour was patchy and my kicking was all over the place, despite us winning 51–3 against Fiji juniors. I thought the coaches might have taken into account the fact that I hadn't started a fifteen-a-side match for over three months and was understandably rusty. My battered confidence needed games, and I hoped I could play myself back to form. Certainly, I knew I had lost an edge to my game – a spot of soul-searching was inevitable.

I felt I was being forced to grow up too quickly and began having second thoughts about what direction my life was taking. With questions being raised about my future as a stand-off, I felt a long way from home. Coach Richie Dixon tried his best to put me at ease with the comment: 'Gregor, we have belief in you and I know you'll soon be back playing well. You've got to concentrate on playing your natural game – that's when you're at your best.' This was a great help – although waiting a week on tour for a chance to prove yourself is a long time, especially in a barren place like Tonga where we were staying in the island's only hotel. I knew my next game against a Tongan President's XV, bolstered by many of their Test side, wasn't going to be criticized for a lack of desire or concentration. I was determined to bounce back.

The match still ranks as one of the hardest games in my career, both in terms of the pressure to perform and in having to face such hard-tackling opposition. We were all wearing elbow and knee pads as in Dubai – this time because the grass pitch felt as hard as an airport runway. The Tongans were incredibly physical in the tackle, sometimes even if you had already passed the ball seconds before. We were fiercely competitive ourselves and battled to a 21–5 victory. I scored sixteen points (which included a try) and my confidence was restored. I remember calling my parents later from the hotel – I think we all felt relief and joy that I'd come through my toughest examination to date as a fledgling international.

I had always felt that I just needed another chance to show what I could do, and that I was capable of getting rid of the errors in my game from the previous week. But I knew deep down that this was a turning point in my career. I was determined to kick on from here. I had decided that I wasn't going to pay heed to those who advised me to rest in the summer.

Coaches, the medical staff and even some players had been questioning the wisdom of my intention to go and play club rugby in Australia after the tour, especially given my continuing groin pain, but the last month convinced me to leave Scotland and learn rugby away from perceived opinions. It was also a place where I knew I could play attacking rugby. Having won back my confidence, I couldn't wait to play more rugby. I finished the tour in good form.

I was recalled to the Test side and we went on to beat Tonga 23–5. It was a much less intense match than that in midweek, and I think the experience of meeting royalty before the game may have slightly altered our focus. The seventy-five-year-old King Taufa'ahau Tupou IV (an absolute monarch who had been in power since 1965) was seated on a makeshift throne up in the main stand of the national stadium in Nuku'alofa, Tonga's capital. The King wasn't only famous for his longevity, but also his waist size. He had previously made international headlines when he entered the *Guinness Book of Records* as the world's heaviest monarch, tipping the scales at a staggering thirty-three stone. We were made to walk up the steps to the King to shake his hand before the game could begin. For some strange reason he was wearing a motorcycle helmet – it was as if we had slipped into some surreal parallel world.

Tonga consists of 170 islands, but its population – at 100,000 – is less than that of the Borders. The locals seemed much more aloof than the ever-smiling Fijians, and there were times when they looked like real warriors surveying the enemy as they watched us walking about. This might have had something to do with the garish tour outfit we had been issued with: knee-length royal blue socks complemented grey shorts, white shirt and a royal blue blazer – it's no wonder that the Tongans looked like they wanted to kill us!

Before we left for our final destination – Western Samoa – a few of the squad were asked to lead a training session at the former school of Australian backrower Willie Ofahengaue. They wanted to know what sequences to run from lineouts, so we showed them how to get quick off-the-top ball out to the stand-off. We explained that this was the easiest way to get a strike runner over the advantage line. Then I gave a flat ball to inside-centre Ian Jardine who was running at half-pace, trying to show the Tongan lads the best angle to attack the opposition line. Out of nowhere a fourteen-year-old schoolboy poleaxed him with a chest-high tackle. Jardie, struggling to get back to his feet, congratulated the lad on his defence and added that it wasn't necessary to put in tackles against us. It was a reminder to never to let down your guard while in Tongan rugby circles.

Samoa – a tropical paradise – was my favourite destination. The people seemed to be somewhere in between those we'd met in Fiji and Tonga – friendly and welcoming but taking no prisoners on the rugby field. We lost the Test 28–11 but this was by no means a disgrace. After all, this was the same group of players that had made the World Cup quarter-final two years before and included future All Blacks Alama Ieremia and Junior Tonu'u in their line-up. In temperatures reaching 36°C – so hot in fact that before the game we had to move from the touchline into a shaded area to sing 'Flower of Scotland' – Samoa were too strong for our development side. A month later they pushed the All Blacks all the way, eventually losing 35–13 in Auckland.

Having just turned twenty, I had experienced a lot in two years of senior rugby, but it was being suggested in some quarters that my rugby career was faltering and that my game was characterized by errors. Learning over the summer could only help me improve – and doing it outside Scotland was likely to make it more pleasurable. A year previously I had wanted to stay out in Australia after the Scotland tour to play club rugby, but was forced to return to compete in the Students World Cup. Tony Stanger had turned out for

Warringah and it was through him that I had established contacts to join up with the Sydney-based team for a three-month stint.

Going to Warringah wasn't just an opportunity to improve my rugby experience – it was also a chance for me to grow up on my own terms. Only 25 km away from the city, on Sydney's northern coast, Warringah Rugby Club is close to many magnificent beaches and headlands. The club captain, Rob Blyth, and his wife Leanne provided me with a room in their house alongside the Kelso flanker Stuart Bennett. From Borders farming stock, Benzo kept his side of the room as tidy as a neglected pigsty, and our living space inevitably began to attract cockroaches and spiders as big as your hand. Benzo played really well for the club and gained respect for his combative approach. He was different to Aussie backrowers at the time in that he played the game much closer to the ground. He was always first to a loose ball and was much better than them at clearing rucks. Up against more physical players, managing to break into the Warringah first-grade team was a superb achievement.

Warringah organized jobs for its itinerant players – like Benzo and myself. First we were demolition men, but once the plagues of cockroaches grew too much for us, we were given the positions of groundskeepers at the rugby club. Our first task was to clear away the large rocks that were scattered around the outside of the pitch and car park. Feeling a little like Paul Newman on the chain gang in *Cool Hand Luke*, we set to work. Our Calvinist spirit drove us to clearing most of the rocks by midday, much to the horror of the head groundsman – this one job was supposed to take us three months. We soon slowed to the rate of a rock a day, playing games of cricket with our spades and the numerous golf balls that had been hit over the fence from the nearby driving range.

Warringah were known as the 'Green Rats', after the 9th Australian Division that defended Tobruk during the Second

World War. Although they had never won a Premiership title, the team had a reputation for uncompromising rugby. They were coached by Steve Lidbury, a former backrower who been capped twice by the Wallabies in the Eighties before switching to rugby league. On a Thursday night after training we always went out as a squad to a pizza restaurant and Benzo and I used to make sure we sat near our coach. With his muscular frame and quick wit he always dominated conversation, and he was soon recalling anecdotes from his time playing for Warringah, the Wallabies and Canberra Raiders as well as stories from his other employment as a security guard. Despite having to retire after breaking his neck, he continued to play touch footy with us and was an astute coach. He must have been some player in his day.

I think Libbo liked me as a player, and he moved me into stand-off (or five-eighth as it was called over there) after two appearances for the club at outside-centre. For the first time in my career I had a coach that really appreciated my kicking game. Although I'd made a lot of improvements, this was probably more due to the fact that there was hardly any kicking in Australian rugby, which was in stark contrast to the situation at the time in the northern hemisphere. Watching paint dry was occasionally a better option than attending a British rugby union match in the early Nineties, as the ball very rarely got past two phases without someone kicking it in the air.

In contrast, it seemed that most coaches in Australia insisted on the ball being kept in play, as up-and-unders left too much to chance. My centres always wanted me to use them to set up another phase and the only kicks we tended to utilize were diagonals, which forced the opposition to kick to touch and give us the throw at the lineout.

Australia had won the World Cup two years before through some terrific attacking play, which was a credit to the standards and attacking philosophy of their club competition.

In successive weeks, I encountered two of the driving forces of that World Cup victory – captain Nick Farr-Jones and record try scorer David Campese. My first match in the number 10 jersey was against Farr-Jones' Sydney University side, which went well as I was voted man of the match in our home win. I could tell that Farr-Jones was a natural leader and organized his team from scrum-half. He impressed me not just with his ferocious commitment but also his goal-kicking ability that had kept his side in touch for long periods of the match.

Next up was an away fixture against Randwick – the most famous club in Australia. They were known for playing a quick-passing game, and their pancake-flat alignment was pioneering. The Ella brothers had once strutted their stuff for the 'Galloping Greens', as they were called, and they continued to deploy a similar attacking style. I remember seeing my opposite number, Lloyd Walker, arrive at the ground with his family at the same time as me. Walker had played several times for the Wallabies, but I fancied my chances against him that day. He looked old, overweight and I expected him to be slow off the mark. I was later shown a masterclass in how to play in heavy traffic, and how to make a defence open up for you.

Walker was so flat from scrum and phase ball that I could almost touch him. At first, I left him alone for my open-side flanker to deal with, as Randwick had some devastating runners out wide who posed much more of a threat. Walker's lack of pace didn't prove to be a drawback for him – he started so close to the advantage line he was soon getting in behind us, causing panic in our defence. When I later changed track and marked him directly, he began to deliver some deadly accurate wrist-passes to runners on either side of him. We never once managed to line someone up in the Randwick backline and knock them back in the tackle.

Out wide, Campese was a continual threat. I also noticed a tenacious edge to his game, which proved to me that you don't get to the top unless you are mentally tough. Libbo had instructed me to test out Campese with some high balls, but to make sure they landed shorter than usual so that the pack got the chance to ruck the living daylights out of him. This we did on a couple of occasions. It all seemed to no avail, as Campo got back on his feet without complaint and played superbly thereafter. I realized he must have had to endure that sort of treatment right throughout his career.

During the previous season I had seen seasoned internationalists being laid-back, but it finally hit home in Australia that I needed to relax much more around game time. At Warringah, in the lead up to kick-off, the backs nonchalantly threw a ball around in the car park, chatting to each other as if they were about to go out to train, not play an important match. I loved this mindset – it implied that this was no different from training and there was no added pressure to worry about. Once on the field they were passionate and totally committed to the cause, effectively embodying the spirit of the club – never to give in, just like the Rats of Tobruk.

I used to live by a quote I'd read somewhere: 'If you've never made a mistake, you've never made a decision.' Now I was getting much better at recognizing the two benefits of failure: first, if you do fail, you learn what doesn't work; and second, the failure gives you the opportunity to try a new approach. As the game was fought out on the gain line it was really high-pressure stuff, which brought out the best in me. Players were bigger, more physical and the pitches were hard and fast. I loved every minute of it.

We climbed up the table and I was playing consistently well – by far the best rugby of my career. Unfortunately I had to return to Scotland for my exams, which I had missed because of the Scotland tour to the South Seas in June. Warringah tried hard to get me to stay. They arranged to have the exam paper faxed out to a university in Sydney, and said I could fly home to Scotland and pick up anything I needed to help with my studies before coming back a couple of days later. In the local paper, the *Manly Daily*, Libbo had said, 'I am going to block his way to the airport, handcuff him, anything to get him to stay.'

I was worried that Libbo might prove to be all too persuasive in terms of stopping me from returning, as I was reluctant to muck around Edinburgh University any more than I needed to. I'd cut a few corners already in the first two years of my course and I knew I would have been further distracted if I was to sit my exams in Australia. I left Warringah with two games still to play. Unfortunately, the club went on to lose the Grand Final. Looking back, I wish I could have stayed. However, at the time there was another reason I wanted to return home. The new club season in Scotland was just about to begin. First up for Gala was an away trip to arch-rivals Melrose – a game I didn't want to miss.

We won 14–13 and I carried on my Warringah form, once more in direct opposition to Scotland stand-off Craig Chalmers. I was buzzing with confidence and played well the following week against Boroughmuir. We again won away from home, which meant that we had now beaten the champions from the previous two seasons in our opening two matches. I remember former Scotland centre Sean Lineen daring me to take a quick drop-out against him during the game. I dummied the normal kick to the forwards to my left before knocking the ball along the ground to the right, past his despairing dive. After having shown caution and self-doubt at times during the previous season, Sean might have been right in thinking that I wouldn't have had the audacity to try something like that, but my experiences in the summer had made me much stronger mentally.

Having shown my resolve in Tonga and then become much more relaxed and rounded in Sydney, I felt I was ready-made for international rugby. A year earlier I had been too caught up in other people's opinions and expectations of my talent and there would have been times when I'd actually have been thinking 'I shouldn't be doing this', even when I was making a break. Pace and willingness to have a go had always been my two biggest assets, but I now had a greater awareness of other aspects of play and was confident in my decision-making. Things couldn't have been going any better – which is often the exact moment that adversity chooses to seek you out.

CHAPTER 3

Don't Cry for Me, Argentina

We judge ourselves by what we feel capable of doing,
while others judge us by what we have already done.

Henry Wadsworth Longfellow

On a clear day the Buenos Aires Sheraton has stunning views over the Rio de la Plata and beyond the river valley to the Uruguayan capital of Montevideo. Sadly, clear day or not, my room was positioned on the other side of the hotel. As I got out of bed I opened the curtains to gaze across the rooftops of the largest city in Argentina. Below me I noticed that the streets were crammed to bursting with emotional, flag-waving Argentines – just like a scene from *Evita*. I resisted the temptation to climb out onto the hotel balcony and deliver a song. Instead, I rushed downstairs to see what the celebrations were for.

In the hotel lobby, members of the Real Madrid team, who were also on tour in Argentina, were gathering. I met up with Bryan Redpath and Stuart Reid – two team-mates who were, like me, keen to join in with the carnival atmosphere on the streets of Buenos Aires. However, several Argentine policemen were blocking the hotel's exit.

'I'm sorry, you can't go outside today. Or tomorrow. There is a demonstration being held in Buenos Aires.'

'Surely we'll be okay to go to the shops on the other side of the road?'

'No – it is for your own safety.'

'What about the Real Madrid players? Look – they're joining in with the locals.'

'Yes, but it is okay for them – they are not British. Don't you know it is Malvinas Day?'

The penny finally dropped – the Malvinas, of course, are better known in English as the Falkland Islands. The policeman explained to us that Malvinas Day is officially titled 'The Day of the War Veterans and the Fallen' in the Falklands Islands. What the people were also demanding was the recovery of these islands.

I looked back at the crowds outside – the passion I had earlier seen in their eyes now looked a lot more like anger than celebration. Even though the Falklands War had ended over ten years before, it was clearly still an emotive subject for the Argentine people. And our hotel was situated right next to the focal point of their fury – a memorial for those killed in the conflict. We were more than happy to agree to police demands to stay in our hotel for the full forty-eight hours. Unfortunately Claudia Schiffer, who we had spotted a few times earlier that week, had just checked out, so as time passed we grew more and more frustrated and bored. Although I suppose it was preferable to being out on the streets.

Argentina was a tour I wish I could forget. My torment in trying to become an established Test player continued thousands of miles from home and I had to endure another character-building episode, just like in Tonga. Loss of confidence, loss of form, injuries and public criticism are the sporting equivalent of the Four Horsemen of the Apocalypse. I met all four on my own personal tour of hell.

Before the tour, I had squeezed so much playing and travelling into my first three years of senior rugby that at times I wondered whether I would ever have the chance to stop and reflect – not least on how lucky I had been. Luck, of course,

will always run out at some point, and before I knew it, I had
more than ample time to take stock as my career was halted
by injury problems.

My time in Australia had taken my game to a new level
and I was playing with confidence and verve on my return to
Scotland. However, following my second match back for Gala,
my wrist was in severe pain and I couldn't really take a grip of
anything without wincing. An x-ray showed that I had
broken my scaphoid, which meant I was facing ten to twelve
weeks on the sidelines. There is never a good time to get
injured, but being struck down when you are in the form of
your life is hard to take. I knew that getting back to that level
wasn't going to be easy.

During my time out, I did a lot of speed work with Charlie
Russell, a local sprint coach. As I had a lightweight plaster on
my arm I was able to run at close to 100 per cent. Pace has
been, and always will be, the most vital component when it
comes to beating a defensive line, no matter how organized
and compact that line is. I was sceptical whenever I was told
that I was quick, but I surprised myself when during the Scotland tour to Australia in 1992 I took on winger Iwan Tukalo
over 100m and won. I'd always felt that my overall speed
wasn't that great, just my change of pace or acceleration. This
is what I worked on with Charlie. As a favour in return, I
agreed to run for him in the New Year Sprint at Meadow-
bank. A handicap race held over 110 metres, the Sprint has
been staged in Scotland on or around New Year's Day annu-
ally since 1870.

As it was my debut on the pro-circuit, I was given an arbi-
trary handicap of six metres. This meant that I was left with
104 metres in front of me. There was another runner with a
handicap of 6 m, but the rest of the field started the race in
front of us, the furthest being given a handicap of 25 m. Trying
hard to go on the 'B of Bang', I managed to get pulled back for
a false start. In professional athletics, you get docked a metre

for jumping the gun, so I was now facing the daunting prospect of being the back-marker in my first ever professional sprint event. The other competitors suddenly seemed to be quite far up the track. I finished in sixth place, which I was told later was a reasonable first-time effort. Mind you, there had only been six people in the race! I was desperately hoping my return to rugby wasn't going to be such an anticlimax.

I was lucky to have missed playing against the All Blacks, as they had rampaged their way through Scottish rugby – winning 84–5 against the South and 51–15 at Murrayfield against Scotland. I had a month to play my way into the selectors' thoughts before Scotland's first match of the 1994 championship, away to Wales. My form was nowhere like it had been before my wrist injury. However, after the desperate performance against the All Blacks, the Scotland selectors seemed eager to make changes.

While it was obvious that I had lost momentum following my lay-off, I was selected at stand-off for the A side against Ireland, only a few weeks before the Five Nations. We won the game comfortably and my own performance was composed, but lacking the attacking edge I'd developed in Australia. Despite this, the media began to raise the bar of expectations once again after I was picked in the number 10 jersey for the Blues team in the national trial. Craig Chalmers had been demoted to the Reds. At the time the SRU Director of Rugby, Jim Telfer, commented on the recurring theme of the media building me up, by saying: 'You begin to wonder if we expect him to bring on the oranges at half-time on top of everything else.'

The trial game as usual was a torrid affair, but a small personal triumph for me – I notched up a try in our 24–14 win. The score involved a one-on-one with Craig Chalmers, which made it even more enjoyable. With only two weeks to go before the Welsh match, I was quietly confident that my first start for Scotland would be in my preferred position of stand-off. After all, if I had been selected there in the trial, which had gone well, surely the selectors would follow this through for the next match?

Regrettably, this wasn't to be the case, although I did make the Scotland starting line-up for the first time – at outside-centre. As Scott Hastings was injured, the selectors opted for the experience of Craig Chalmers at stand-off and I was partnered in the centres with the hugely underrated Ian Jardine. The game was to be a disaster for Scotland – we were soundly beaten on the scoreboard as well as in the all-in brawl that had erupted early in the match. Given the terrible weather, our limited style of play and our poor performance, my first start in the Five Nations almost felt like a non-event.

I was by and large a spectator in the first half, and I didn't touch the ball until the thirty-third minute, and even then it wasn't from a pass. This wasn't too much of a surprise in those days because Scotland tended to adopt a kick-and-chase approach to the game. Although I was itching to be involved, I didn't let myself get frustrated and I tried to be positive when the ball eventually did come my way.

My involvement in the play increased tenfold when I was moved to stand-off after Craig Chalmers left the field injured in the second half. By that stage the match was beyond us, but at least we did try to chase the game as much as we could. I enjoyed my first taste of international rugby as a number 10 even though I now had the dubious distinction of having played three positions – stand-off, inside- and outside-centre – in what was only my second cap. Little did I know then that this was to be a recurring feature of my Scotland career.

I did my best to take the game to the Welsh and nearly got on the end of a chip-and-chase to score a try. I knocked over a drop-goal, although the referee, Patrick Robin, inexplicably ruled that it had fallen under the crossbar. Admittedly, it was a wobbly effort but the players on both sides knew that it had been good. Television pictures later showed that my drop-goal was a valid one and that I should have registered my first points for Scotland. Soaked to the skin, I tried my best to persuade Monsieur Robin that the ball had gone over the bar. My lack of French meant that I was reduced to playing a game of charades with the referee to explain my frustrations. Unfortunately, it was all to no avail, which really upset our hooker Kenny Milne, who was claiming a share in the drop-goal that never was.

Kenny had come to my aid before the match as I was facing an extremely embarrassing situation just before going out to win my first full cap. Trying to relax in the changing rooms at the Arms Park, I noticed that other players in the side were changing their studs for longer ones – the pitch had become a mud bath due to some torrential rain. My studs weren't too bad but, being a student, it was ingrained in me not to turn down anything that was free. 'I'll take a handful of those, please' I said to one of the forwards, who handed me a dozen shiny new studs.

I waited patiently for a pair of pliers, and then set about changing my studs. Obviously my technique wasn't the best as I broke the insert on a couple of studs, thus making my boots quite unusable. This was potentially disastrous as the game was less than an hour away. The only player who had a spare pair of boots in their kitbag was Kenny Milne, so I was saved the mortification of running around in lopsided boots. The downside to wearing Kenny's boots, though, was that they were a size 9, which was one size smaller than I normally took. It was a painful lesson that reminded me to be more organized in my match preparations.

The 29–6 defeat to Wales, which had followed on the heels of the hammering by the All Blacks, dealt a further blow to the confidence of Scottish rugby. The result in Cardiff, however, wasn't the most important issue – rather the fact that we had been bullied up front and were unimaginative and leaden-footed in the backs. Next up was the Calcutta Cup game and there was much soul-searching and hand-wringing throughout the land as to how we could get back to winning ways against the Auld Enemy. And at a time of crisis, who better to turn to than a real live talisman – Gary Armstrong.

Gary had actually retired from the international game some nine months previously and had been playing at full-back and centre for his club, Jedforest, before being persuaded to make himself available once more for Scotland. He is a heroic figure to supporters and players alike and, having been named at stand-off for the first time, it was an honour to be selected as his half-back partner.

I remember in my first year at Edinburgh University going into a pub that was a local for the motorbike community and a small number of students who were attracted by the cheap beer, where the walls were covered with photos and newspaper cuttings of Gary who was obviously loved by the clientele. I don't know if he was aware about this unlikely shrine to him, but it illustrates the high regard in which he was held by Scots from all walks of life.

The match was to be the most emotional fixture at Murray-field since the Grand Slam game against the same opponents in 1990. Gary started the match as if he had never been away from the Test arena and was desperately unlucky to have a try ruled out early on for a double-movement. Fortunately, Rob Wainwright scored soon after this and our forwards began to get the upper hand in their battle with the hulking English pack. This was a remarkable transformation from the Welsh game and maybe had something to do with the rucking session that Jim Telfer had taken with the forwards at our hotel on the morning of the match. Officially, Jim wasn't allowed to coach the team as he was now in the salaried position of SRU Director of Rugby. His appearance on the Saturday morning certainly focused the minds of our forward pack – he didn't hold back during the intense session, which was all about keeping a low body position and flying hard into rucks.

However, I was disappointed with my own contribution as I was kicking most of the ball I received from Gary. This was, in fact, our game plan and at times it brought success – our try had come from an up-and-under – but I didn't utilize the quick ball that came my way to run at the opposition. My role in the game could have been a lot more influential. The absence of conviction was due to a lack of confidence, which was probably the first time in my career I had felt this way. The events of the closing minutes very nearly erased from my memory my lack of attacking ambition, as we looked to have won the match in injury time.

England had clawed their way back into the game and led 12–11 going into the last minute of the match. According to a newspaper headline the following day, I was 'A hero for sixty seconds'. From slow ruck ball wide on the left I managed at last to drop a goal for Scotland, following two earlier misses in the match and my disallowed effort against Wales. This time I was very grateful to the referee as I'd struck my kick very high and I wasn't totally sure myself whether it had gone inside or outside the left upright.

As the game moved deeper into injury time, I was anxious that we might be denied our hard-earned victory. I had a vision of Rob Andrew dropping a goal just like he had done to win the World Cup semi-final 9–6 against Scotland in 1991. It was with this in mind that I sprinted out of defence to try and charge down my opposite number, as Andrew had positioned himself in the pocket to go for the winning kick. I lunged forward at the right moment and his drop-goal attempt crashed against my arms. When I saw Ian Jardine secure the loose ball I was now sure that we were going to win the match. Unfortunately, the referee had other ideas.

As we surged forward, the New Zealand referee, Lyndsay McLachlan, blew his whistle to award a penalty for handling in the ruck … to England! This was a stupefying decision, as we had recovered the ball – why would we have wanted to handle in the ruck for ball that we had just won? More importantly the ball came out on the English side, which meant that whoever had handled the ball on the ground had wanted to turnover Scottish possession.

A few days later, television pictures confirmed that an English hand had scooped the ball back from the ruck. The guilty party was Scotland's nemesis, Rob Andrew. The only thing that could excuse the referee from his appalling decision was that England had navy cuffs on their white jerseys. But surely McLachlan was aware of this anomaly before his game-changing aberration? It was suggested that England would now be stitching green cuffs to their sleeves for their next match against Ireland.

Anyway, Jon Callard held his nerve and his successful penalty-kick gave England a 15–14 win. The referee blew the final whistle immediately after the ball sailed through the uprights. We were absolutely gutted and a nation was seething with outrage. Our captain Gavin Hastings even broke down in tears during a television interview after the match. This won him many more admirers and he told the squad the following week that he had received hundreds of letters of support – which even included one from my mum!

Despite the agonizing result, in what is always our most important fixture of the year, we had won back respect and confidence by the way we had played. However, the one-for-all unity of the amateur era wasn't in much evidence when I read an article by Craig Chalmers in the *Sunday Post* the day after the game. He wrote that Scotland would have played much better if he had been selected at stand-off instead of me. It wasn't the last time that he resorted to the tactic of criticizing his rivals in the media, and I kept his article to give me motivation in our fight for the number 10 jersey. I was determined to do my talking on the pitch, although I was disappointed by the selfish actions of a supposed team-mate.

I kept my place at stand-off for our next match away to Ireland but I knew there were a number of areas in my game that needed to improve; notably kicking, passing off my left hand and tackling. Above all, though, I was disappointed that the Scottish public had yet to see me attacking the opposition with ball in hand, the best part of my game. Now, in my third year of senior rugby, I had learned to stop breaking for the sake of breaking and was responding to situations more as they arose rather than forcing play. However, this had made me somewhat conservative in the match against England, which was probably the first game of my career that I hadn't managed to break the advantage line at least once.

It is often said that the fear of failure is more stimulating than the reward of success and I've heard many coaches and players shout before a game: 'We've got to be scared of losing today!' I agree that losing sometimes hurts much more than the equivalent feeling when you win, but I don't think it's a good way to motivate players. A culture of fear leads to worry and anxiety, which is not a winning attitude. Being positive and concentrating on the *process* – not the end result – is a much surer route to success. I resolved to be free from worry and tried to express myself much more in Dublin.

We drew with Ireland 6–6 after having dominated the first half, in which we played into the teeth of a howling gale. Gary was monumental at scrum-half, despite playing for most of the game with a broken hand. The match was also my best performance yet for Scotland, as I made a couple of breaks and tackled well. It was our first time for almost a year that we hadn't suffered a defeat, but we knew that it was the second game in a row that we should have won.

With Gary now injured, I lined up with Bryan Redpath at half-back for our final Five Nations match at home to the French. Although we only had five caps between us, I thought we would work well together. As it turned out, we didn't have the immediate understanding I had hoped for and my own game was again as frustrating as it had been against England. To cap it all off, I threw an interception pass that gifted France seven points at a stage in the game when we still might have come back to win.

After the match Gavin tried to console me, saying that if my pass had hit its intended target we would have scored a try. The move was a simple miss-one loop, which had achieved its aim of committing the French midfield. With Gavin and Kenny Logan outside me, a clear overlap had presented itself. As we had predicted in our pre-match analysis, Philippe Saint-Andre rushed in from his wing to try and block my pass. Because of my poor execution, plucking the ball from the air was his reward for this 'blitz' style of defending, and he ran unopposed all the way to the try-line.

A lack of experience can only go so far in explaining my poor decision at throwing the interception pass. Just as in the England game, I had attempted a pass that I would never have tried in a club match. But when you are not confident in your actions, hope replaces certainty.

Normally, I would have relished the fact that Saint-Andre had come off his wing to pressure my pass. This is an ideal situation in which to hold onto the ball for as long as possible so that the defender has to make a decision as to what to do next. Because I was moving forward, Saint-Andre would have had to come in and tackle me or go out to tackle Gavin. Either way, at least one of our players would have been in space. However, instead of waiting for his actions to make the decision for me, I presented him with an opportunity by trying to pass the ball to Gavin as soon as possible. It was a 50–50 pass, which more often than not is punished at international level. We lost the match 20–12.

I suppose everyone in sport has to navigate a learning curve, but my problems had nothing really to do with either the opposition I was facing or the step up to Test level. The reason I hadn't played to my potential was entirely to do with my state of mind. Although this was exasperating, I realized that it was probably much easier to remedy than a physical weakness or any problems coping with the speed and intensity of international rugby.

Two years later, Scotland coach Richie Dixon made the wise decision to introduce a sports psychologist, Dr Richard Cox, to work with the team. Dr Cox showed us an example of how the dangers of having doubts about your ability can have a direct affect on your performance. He produced a document that included quotes that were familiar to me. The text was in fact an interview that I had given to the *Sunday Times* a few weeks after the French game and the gifted Saint-Andre try. Dr Cox described it as an ideal example of the importance of self-belief in sport.

> *During our internationals at Murrayfield in 1994 I sometimes went for a pass when there would be no way I'd do that in a club game. I went in thinking that I must not make mistakes, but that meant not trying things. I was thinking I would be dropped if I made a mistake. Now, I realize I was thinking wrongly.*

Getting over injury problems and trying desperately to balance the expectations of others had made me incredibly frustrated. Worryingly, this had also left me short of confidence. I viewed rugby as a game that I took enjoyment from and I had always tried to play without constraints. I knew I hadn't been true to myself over the past few months in this regard, and was no longer doing things that had always come naturally to me.

After the Five Nations were over I managed to start taking pleasure in the game once again as I played sevens rugby for Gala. We had a superb group of sevens players – guys like Grant Farquharson, Jim Maitland and Ian Corcoran – and we won the Melrose and Jed Sevens, as well as our own tournament. We very nearly made it four wins out of the five spring tournaments, losing in the final at Langholm. Away from the glare of expectation at Murrayfield, I was smiling on a rugby field once again. I also went to the Hong Kong Sevens for the third time and did my best to enjoy my twenty-first birthday party, which was held in a student pub in Edinburgh.

However, it was whilst playing in the sevens circuit that my injury problems began to get close to unbearable levels. My wrist had been sore during the Five Nations but it was my knee that was more of a worry – it had given me constant pain since the beginning of the year. Nevertheless, I didn't want to take a break from rugby and I was again trying to fit in as much as possible.

To try and alleviate my knee pain, I adopted an unconventional recovery technique at the suggestion of the sprint coach I'd worked with the previous year, Charlie Russell. He said to me that the best thing I could do was to sit downstream in a river for ten to fifteen minutes after every training session. He said this had worked for a few players, citing as an example Kelso's Eric Paxton, who had sat in a river after a hamstring tear and had been able to play the following weekend. Ice baths may be common rehabilitation practice nowadays, but this cold-water treatment was almost unheard of back in 1994. Although it wasn't a pleasant experience, it certainly kept the swelling down a little, and provided some interesting viewing for one surprised Borderer.

For my outdoor ice bath I had been using the Caddon River on the edge of Clovenfords, which was a ten-minute drive from Gala. Late one night after a training session, I drove up there on my own to try to ease the pain in my knee. With my three jerseys and a waterproof jacket I was almost ready to sit in the water for fifteen long minutes. The finishing touch was to place a hot-water bottle under my jerseys to keep my heart warm as I sat down on the riverbed. It was a dark night, and I switched on my Walkman to try and think about something other than my freezing legs. I closed my eyes and hummed along with Kylie Minogue.

After ten minutes of sitting downstream, I thought I heard the noise of a dog barking which I found odd as I'd never heard it before in the song I was listening to. Something made me look around, and I nearly jumped out of the water when I saw a man standing above me on the riverbank. He was pulling back on his dog's lead, which was excitedly barking at this strange person lying in the river below. There was no doubt that I'd had a shock at the sight of someone suddenly appearing out of the darkness, but I can only imagine how surprised the Clovenfords local was feeling stumbling across someone shivering and mumbling a song at ten o'clock at night while partly submerged in the burn below!

As I was trying my best to recover from my dual injuries, the summer tour to Argentina was looming on the horizon. Touring, I hoped, would give me an opportunity to become more consistent at international level. During the championship I had performed much better away from home than at Murrayfield. If I could overcome my knee and wrist problems, I aimed to excel in Argentina and enjoy the thrill of touring once again. To the wives and families of international players it may be a four-letter word but, in the amateur days, a tour was the absolute highlight of the season. Nothing else really came close.

Despite rugby being a minority sport in Argentina, it was a notoriously tough place to play, and there had only been a few teams in history that had managed to win a Test series there. In our first few days in Buenos Aires, we were soon aware of the dominance of football in the culture and daily lives of the populace. Locals were far more interested in Boca Juniors and River Plate than a touring rugby team from Scotland, and there were posters of Diego Maradona everywhere. Argentina's major concern seemed to be if Maradona would be fit for the forthcoming football World Cup, not whether their rugby side could extend a proud home winning record.

We undertook the challenge with a severely weakened touring party, as most of our senior internationalists – Gavin Hastings, Scott Hastings, Gary Armstrong, Kenny Milne, Doddie Weir and Tony Stanger – had decided that their best preparation for the following season's World Cup was a rest from the summer tour. At the time, there seemed quite a bit of logic in this, but looking back from an era where the game is much more physically demanding, it seems as if maybe a few of the players just didn't really fancy a month of rugby in Argentina. In the weeks prior to our departure, injuries robbed us of more key personnel – Andy Nicol, Craig Chalmers and Derek Stark from the backs and Iain Morrison and Rob Wainwright from the forwards. The words 'on a hiding to nothing' hung over those of us who left for Argentina.

The spate of call-offs led to the appointment of the unlikeliest of captains – Andy Reed, our second-row from Cornwall. Andy had the rather harsh nickname of 'Boring Bob from Bodmin', but he didn't seem to mind that players teased him about his rambling stories. In 1993 he had burst onto the international scene playing well and looking very much like a modern day second-row forward – physical but also able to get around the field. Although he had been a member of the much-criticized Scottish front five on that season's Lions Tour to New Zealand, he had still kept up his good form for Scotland in the lead-up to Argentina.

The management obviously selected him because he was one of the few players that had made themselves available to tour and who had played well in the recent Five Nations. However, there are many more factors than just form involved in choosing a captain. Whether it was because of his Cornish accent or a lack of leadership experience, Andy found it a tough act to follow the likes of Finlay Calder, David Sole and Gavin Hastings as Scotland captain. Although he struggled at times with the role, he tried his best and was one of Scotland's better players on tour.

Just as with the previous year's tour to the South Pacific, prior to leaving I hadn't played any fifteen-a-side rugby for a couple of months. I was determined to start the tour totally focused, as my rusty performance in the first match a year before in Fiji had cost me my place in the Test side. Despite increasing pain in my wrist and knee, I viewed the tour as the final opportunity of the season to boost my confidence before taking some time away from the game and resting my injuries. Unfortunately, this was to be wishful thinking – by the end of the tour I would have been happy never to touch a rugby ball again.

Things seemed to be very promising early on and I got off to a much better start in Argentina than I had done in Fiji. On a hot afternoon we played some good attacking rugby in our opening match against Buenos Aires. Only some decidedly dodgy refereeing decisions denied us a deserved victory as we were held to a 24–24 draw.

It was another ten days until the First Test against the Pumas, but most of the players involved in the Buenos Aires game were rested for the next two matches. We were constantly reminded that Argentina was one of the hardest places in world rugby to tour, but our first three outings against their best provincial sides hadn't been that menacing. Our major problem had been the interpretation of the laws by the local referees in charge of our matches outside the Test Series.

The Argentine game plan was based on a strong scrummage, aggressive defence and a considerable amount of mauling by both backs and forwards. It wasn't attractive to watch but has proved to be effective. The First Test was played in a hostile atmosphere at the FC Oeste stadium in Buenos Aires. The excitable spectators all seemed to have these long red horns, which annoyed my flatmates no end when I brought one back to Scotland. The horns created a noisy backdrop to the game, more like a football match. However, the game itself was nothing to shout about.

We weren't able to control the play as we would have liked and we seldom strung more than two phases together. This was mainly because the Argentine midfield rushed up very quickly in defence and their forwards continually spoiled our lineout ball. Although it was an error-strewn match, it was clear that we had been the better side. That we lost the game 16–15 was largely due to our inability to finish good build-up work. Also, our goal kicker, Gala's Mike Dods, obviously hadn't borrowed his older brother Peter's boots, having missed five attempts at goal.

I was frustrated with my own performance in that I hadn't been able to rise above the general malaise and dominate proceedings. While I hadn't done myself justice, I was more disappointed that as a team we didn't perform and weren't able to get an historic win in Argentina. This would have been even more memorable given the fact we were missing a number of established internationalists.

It was a gloomy scene in the changing room, but at least we knew we had the means to win the Second Test the following Saturday. I had just finished icing my aching knee and showering, when head coach Dougie Morgan came over to give me news that left me reeling: 'Gregor, I've just spoken to the press and I told them that you had a shocker.' How do you respond to that? For several moments he looked at me as if he wanted me to agree with him.

'Cheers' was all that I could say to fill the silence that hung between us. It was the end of our conversation. As soon as he walked away, I was angry with myself for not fighting my corner – to point out to him that I hadn't been the only one.

'Blamestorming' is a term used in business for those sitting around in a group, discussing why a project failed, and who was responsible. I remember after international defeats at Murrayfield, the coaches and selectors used to stand in the middle of the changing rooms discussing quietly amongst themselves what went wrong. The players knew what was being talked about as we returned from the showers to get changed. If any of the selectors mentioned your name or turned to look in your direction it wasn't a good sign. Still, it was preferable to the very public naming-and-shaming I received in Argentina.

I felt a shiver run right through me even though it was a warm evening in Buenos Aires. I was concerned with my coach's view of the game, which was one I didn't share. It would have been hard for me to argue that I'd played well, but there had been no glaring errors. Stand-off is at times an exposed position, especially when you have to lead the attack from slow-ball, as was the case in the First Test. I was finding out just what John F. Kennedy meant when he once said that 'victory has a thousand fathers, but defeat is an orphan'.

Criticism should be done in private with the aim of trying not to repeat mistakes and improve the player in question. Having just turned twenty-one, there were many areas I needed to work on and my performance in the First Test flagged up two or three that I needed to sort out very quickly. I have always been a harsh critic of my own game and, although I felt I had played badly, that had also been the case for the majority of the team. Only two or three players had played well. Naively, I thought that during the press conference Dougie had maybe gone on to say that more than half the team had been shocking too. I also hoped that he had been joking when he said that I'd had a shocker or that the press hadn't taken him seriously.

I had previously got on well with Dougie despite the fact that he had dropped me from the Scotland Sevens team during the World Cup the year before. We would later have a very good relationship during his time as Scotland manager leading up to the World Cup in 2003. He was terrific in this role and the only member of the management that contacted me after my retirement from Test rugby, and I greatly appreciated his kind letter. However, back in 1994, when what he

had said after the First Test began to sink in, I couldn't envisage us ever being friends again.

Dougie's comments about my performance became *the*
story of the First Test. ITV, who had filmed the match, broad-
casted Dougie's comments, which were backed up by the tour
manager, Fred McLeod. For the next couple of days I wasn't
really aware of the story that had blown up back in the UK,
but I was miserable and started to feel a long way from home.
I had been publicly criticized by our management and to
make matters worse, there didn't seem to be any attempts
being made to remedy the situation. It didn't take a genius to
work out that I wasn't going to be selected for the Second Test
against Argentina.

My fears were confirmed when the midweek team to play
Rosario was announced and I was named at centre – one of
only two players to be selected who had played in the First Test.
At training it looked obvious that Graham Shiel was being lined
up to move from number 12 to stand-off, as he had already
been given the goal-kicking duties ahead of Mike Dods.

With my knee and wrist injuries deteriorating, the last
thing my body needed was to play another game just four
days after a Test match. But on the other hand, lining up
against Rosario, I was glad to be back out on a rugby field so
quickly after my so-called 'shocker' and I was determined to
show that the weekend's events hadn't affected my self-
belief. I wanted to play as if I didn't have a care in the world.
It was frustrating that the coaches had selected me at centre,
not allowing me the opportunity to prove what I was capable
of in the number 10 jersey. Even though I didn't get much
ball, I managed to put on a decent pretence of being confident
and found a couple of gaps. However, we lost 27–16 to
Rosario, an Argentine side who had unexpectedly moved the
ball wide.

The following day back in Buenos Aires, I bought a *Times*
newspaper, which was now a few days old. Interestingly for

me it included a match report from our game against Argentina. The headline said it all: 'Townsend shocking in narrow Scots defeat'. The majority of the article was concerned with Dougie's outspoken comments. I realized that it would have been an even bigger story in the Scottish press. Speaking to my mum and dad on the phone I tried to sound as upbeat as possible. They told me there had been debate in the media about Dougie's criticism of me and that most commentators seemed to think it had been unmerited. There had even been letters of support for me printed in *The Scotsman* newspaper.

I am sure Dougie had made a heat-of-the-moment remark and later regretted what he said. This was maybe why he came to speak to me so soon after the press conference, but even though the manager Freddie McLeod sent me a courteous letter after the tour, Dougie never backtracked on his comments about my performance. I'm certain, however, that he hadn't intended to create a story that was to dominate our build-up to the crucial Second Test. Dougie had been through a tough season already – no wins in seven games – and this had been another narrow defeat to go alongside the agonizing loss to England in the Five Nations. Perhaps my interception pass in our last championship match against the French was in his thoughts and he had finally lost patience with me. Nevertheless, there should be no scenario that justifies publicly hanging a player out to dry in what I believe is the ultimate team game. Coaches who do this deflect the criticism away from themselves and the team, whether or not that is their intention. There's a great quote by American football coach Bear Bryant, who said: 'If anything goes bad – I did it. If anything goes good – we did it. If anything goes really, really good – congratulations guys, you did it.'

Back in Buenos Aires I got a surprise by being named at stand-off for the Second Test – a strange change of fortune but I wasn't complaining. It was the beginning of a volte-face in the management's dealings with me. I am positive that this had much to do with the influence of the SRU Director of Rugby, Jim Telfer, who had flown out to Argentina to take in our final match. He talked me up to the press and was being very positive about my long-term international future. He even stayed behind after our final team run when I did some extra kicking, offering me encouragement and helping return the balls to me. Jim had never coached me up to this point and this treatment was a surprise, as he had a reputation for being a hard taskmaster, more used to shouting at his players. He was genuinely trying to help and I had always felt he rated me as a player. I was touched that he was going out of his way to get me in a better frame of mind for the following day's match.

I played better, making some yards with the ball-in-hand and knocking over a drop goal, but in many ways it hadn't been that different to my performance in the First Test. The team improved slightly, although we still couldn't shake off the Argentine spoiling tactics and we suffered yet another narrow defeat. Our goal-kicking again let us down as it had done throughout the tour – our overall strike rate was a mere eighteen goals from forty-nine kicks. On this occasion, Graham Shiel and Mike Dods missed five attempts between them. In contrast, Argentina's Santiago Méson had a 100 per cent return and we succumbed to a 19–17 loss.

We almost salvaged a win in the last minute, but a couple of bizarre incidents – or maybe fate – kept us from scoring. First, late in the second half Argentina tried to make a substitution but didn't actually take anyone off and, for a few minutes, had sixteen players on the field. The illegal 'replacement', Leandro Bouza, was fast becoming my nemesis – he had charged down a clearance kick of mine to score a try two years earlier in the Students World Cup quarter-final. As luck would have it, he again got his hands to another kick, this time charging down my attempted drop-goal. Finally the referee noticed there was one too many Argentine players on the field and we were back to fifteen against fifteen going into injury-time.

As we progressed into the Argentine 22-m I called for the ball, seeing that we had an overlap to the right. However, calling for the ball on the left-hand side of the ruck was our ebullient hooker, Kevin McKenzie. He was probably the loudest member of our squad, and it was no doubt for this reason that Bryan Redpath passed the ball to him instead of his half-back partner on the right. Wee Kev then lined himself up for a drop-goal that would have made him an instant hero. However, infamy beckoned as he scuffed the ball tamely along the ground. He will be forever remembered not for having the guts to go for the winning kick, but as that Scottish hooker who nearly had a fresh air trying to drop a goal. It was an ignominious – yet fitting – end to what would remain the only tour that very nearly managed to do what I once would have thought impossible: destroy my enthusiasm for rugby.

CHAPTER 4

Breakthrough

*Courage is the ability to get up when things are getting you down,
to get up and fight back. Never to know defeat, let alone accept it;
to have principles, be they of fitness or morality, and stick by
them; to do what you feel you must do, not because it is the
popular thing to do but because it is the right thing to do.
Courage is skill, plus dedication, plus fitness, plus
honesty, plus fearlessness.*

Bill Shankly

At the end of the tour to Argentina my left knee was injected
with cortisone to try to put an end to the pain I'd suffered
throughout the season. It had been a difficult twelve months
and I was desperate for a change of scene. Along with my
close friend and fellow Scotland cap Derek Stark, I set off to
Florida for five weeks. As our trip coincided with the football
World Cup in the US, we spent our time watching the round
ball game and avoiding thinking about rugby.

My knee didn't improve, despite the injection. Also, something wasn't right with my wrist – I winced whenever we did
any weight training (or when Derek coerced me into being
his beach volleyball partner). When I returned to Scotland I
had to undergo two operations. The first was on my knee to
clean out my patella tendon. Then, after a precautionary x-
ray on my wrist, it was revealed that my scaphoid had broken
once again, the fracture probably occurring during Scotland's

Five Nations campaign. The next step was to have a pin inserted in my wrist with some bone grafted from my hip to keep it sealed. It was late summer, I hadn't touched a rugby ball since the Argentina tour and had to face being out of action until Christmas.

Even though I endured two bouts of invasive surgery, I wasn't as disappointed as perhaps I should have been. The pain in my knee and wrist had troubled me so much the previous season that I knew that something had to be done if I was going to be able to play anywhere near my capabilities again. Normally injuries are incredibly frustrating but in this instance they allowed me to take some time away from my problems at handling the expectations of others and my lack of assertiveness at international level. Argentina had convinced me that an extended break from rugby could provide me with some much-needed relief.

I was also thankful that I hadn't been involved with Scotland in their solitary Test match in the autumn. They were beaten 39–10 by South Africa at Murrayfield – a ninth match without a win. I returned to full fitness in December, playing first for the South then a few games at stand-off for Gala. My form was good, but more importantly I was hungry, confident and keen to express myself.

The time I spent out of the game made me realize that the thing I missed most was actually playing matches. It was what I was good at and it was a part of my life that filled me with joy. I knew that the window on a rugby career wasn't open for too long and my injuries had sharpened my focus to attempt to play without inhibition and fear of making mistakes. They say that ambition is enthusiasm with a purpose and this was exactly how I felt coming back from injury. Less than a month later I was selected at outside-centre for Scotland in a Five Nations warm-up match against Canada.

It wasn't an enjoyable game for the outside-backs – the ball remained a stranger to us for almost the full eighty minutes.

However, on this occasion I couldn't blame stand-off Craig Chalmers as the weather was atrocious in Edinburgh. By the second half, sleet had turned to heavy snow and the intrepid supporters that had turned up at Murrayfield must have wished they had stayed at home – although at least they could say they had witnessed a Scotland victory. Despite narrow losses to England and Argentina, the best we had managed throughout 1994 was a draw against Ireland. Canada was my first ever win in a Scotland jersey. It wasn't much, but at least it sparked a tiny bit of hope going into the following week's Five Nations Championship.

We followed the victory over Canada by winning our opening match at home to the Irish. This boosted the squad's confidence considerably and saw the criticism of our coach, Dougie Morgan, quieten down. Our much-maligned captain, Gavin Hastings, also experienced an end to what had been months of sniping from the media. He would never again be criticized in what was the final season of his playing career.

Big Gav was an inspirational figure for the squad, especially to the younger players like myself, Kenny Logan and Craig Joiner. Having your full-back as captain usually means that you intend to play fluid, open rugby. Although we weren't there yet with this Scotland team, Gavin always encouraged the backs to move the ball and have a go at the opposition. As he stressed to the squad, this would be the only way we could play if we were to win our next match, which was against France.

Paris in the springtime was full of romance, in rugby terms at least, and provided me with a wonderfully memorable day. Scotland hadn't managed to win in Paris for 26 years and had never recorded a victory at the famous Parc des Princes, a bowl of a stadium that reverberated with constant noise. Back in 1969, a certain Jim Telfer had scored the winning try at the Stade Colombes, which had been Scotland's last away win against the French. We were determined to replace the black-

and-white images of Jim powering over the try-line, which were always shown on the eve of France–Scotland games.

However, I didn't make the most auspicious start to what ended up being the breakthrough game I'd been searching for. As we boarded the bus for our final team run the day before the match, the manager, Duncan Paterson, called me over. I could tell that he wasn't happy and he showed his disgust by pointing to my shoes: 'Gregor, where do you think you're going with those on?'

'Erm, on the bus with the others?'

'Not with those trainers on you're not. Get them changed or you can't do the team run.'

'But I've only got my kilt shoes I brought for the dinner tomorrow night.'

'Well, that's what you'll have to wear for not bringing your Nike trainers then, won't you?'

For a split second, I thought it was some big joke and I started to smile – hoping this would result in us both having a laugh and boarding the bus as best friends. Unfortunately, he just scowled, putting his body between the doorway to the bus and myself. As other players were waiting to get on board – and realizing that it wasn't worth pushing my luck any further – I trooped off back to my hotel room exasperated and angry. Just why Paterson was upset with me was a combination of my forgetfulness and an over-zealous interpretation of what was still an amateur sport.

Many of the squad were given money or merchandise to wear a certain type of rugby boot, which was perfectly within our rights as amateur players. Earlier that season, I had been contacted by Reebok to become one of their sponsored players, and I have been associated with them ever since. However, we were also supplied with Nike boots and training shoes from the SRU. I think Nike supplied the SRU with kit for their age-group sides and part of the deal was that anyone playing for Scotland had to wear Nike boots. If you look at photos of our win in Paris you'll see a few of the side playing in blacked-out boots. Those of us who chose not to wear Nike had to make sure that no branding was showing. That was after having to convince the management that we had a medical reason for not wearing the Nike boots we had been given. My excuse – which was actually true – was that I'd got blisters from training with the Nike boots. Reebok didn't give me any money for wearing their boots in an international – the £2,000 yearly payment was a flat fee irrespective of how many games and what boots I wore for Scotland.

Reebok would send me a number of items of footwear and other gear, which was mainly stored at my folk's house in Gala together with the kit I'd received from the SRU. In packing my bags for the French match, I must have put in a pair of Reebok trainers instead of my Nikes by mistake. I realized this when opening my kit bag in Paris, but thought nothing more of it. Our final team run wasn't going to be filmed and the odd newspaper photographer who turned up wouldn't be interested in what trainers I was wearing. And I'm sure a global company such as Nike wouldn't have been bothered even if I had had Reebok tattooed to my forehead during our run-through. But it was insignificant details like this that the SRU liked to catch people out on, even at the detriment of Scotland's preparations for such an important match. Sometimes the custodians of the game were more demanding in the amateur days than they are now in the professional era.

A couple of minutes later I was back – the last to board the bus – now wearing black brogues, which didn't really go with my shorts and tracksuit top. If it had been the manager's desire to make me feel very small, he had achieved his goal. I was deeply embarrassed and could tell the rest of the squad had worked out what had just happened. My embarrassment continued at the training ground close to our hotel as I was forced to wear my black shoes to do a few laps of an athletics track and a stretching routine with the rest of the boys. Luckily, when we ran through some team plays, one of the subs let me borrow their trainers until we had finished the session.

I tried not to dwell on the morning's team run and thought back to two years before when I'd sat on the bench for the French game. I had thoroughly enjoyed the peculiar build-up to a match in Paris. We were again using the Hotel Trianon as our base, which was by far the best hotel I had ever stayed in. Even more impressive was the fact that the hotel was only a five-minute walk from Versailles Palace, a stunning building of sublime grandeur surrounded by lavish fountains, a huge lake and magnificent gardens. There are few places in the world that can match the grounds of Versailles for a final get-together as a squad on the morning of a game. It turned out to be the beginning of an unforgettable day.

For a Test match, both teams are usually given a police escort to the stadium. This means that the bus isn't delayed, as other vehicles are obliged to give way. In France, watching the antics of the gendarmes who flank the team bus is something not to be missed. Despite huge traffic jams blocking *la peripherique* of Paris, we never seemed to slow down as our police motorbike outriders banged on car doors, waved us through red lights and forced other traffic onto the pavement. That day, we must have made it to the Parc des Princes in record time.

The pulsating atmosphere in the stadium was the stuff of legend, and we experienced a taste of what was in store during our warm-up. There were traditional French bands all around the ground – drums were banged, trumpets and trombones blared and the deep rumblings of innumerable tubas seemed to vibrate through the pitch itself and up into our boots. It felt as if we were the headline act about to come out on stage at a rock concert. I couldn't wait to get my hands on the ball.

We had agreed that moving the ball wide was our only hope of success, but I wasn't convinced that we would have the courage to start the game playing attacking rugby. However, events in the opening two minutes deprived us of any choice in the matter.

Even though we knew that the French loved to try little kicks ahead for their wingers to chase, we were powerless to stop France's captain, Philippe Saint-Andre pouncing on Thierry Lacroix's neat chip ahead. The game was seconds old and already we were a try down – and at a ground where no Scot had ever tasted success. You could say that, at the very least, this focused our minds! Gavin, who had been caught out of position for the try, rallied his team. And his performance from then on was flawless as he almost metamorphosed into the Scottish rugby equivalent of 'Roy of the Rovers'.

Somehow, the early blow freed us of our inhibitions. We began to play like we had nothing to lose. I took some flat miss passes from Craig Chalmers and surprised myself that I was able to find space against the brilliant Philippe Sella, offloading the ball to Gavin on a couple of occasions. The second of these led our captain surging up-field into the French half. The move was continued through good linking work by our forwards and when we recycled I was standing out wide screaming for the ball. I could see there was a gaping hole in the French defence.

Ian Jardine's pass almost didn't reach me – I had to flick at the ball with my foot and, amazingly, it bounced up into my hands, allowing me to side-step the covering Philippe Benetton to score between the posts. Every aspiring young rugby player has sat at home imagining what it is like to score your first try for your country; very few actually get the chance, but in their dreams the sun is out, the ground is full and it is against one of the best teams in the world. When it happens it is as if time briefly stands still before suddenly going on fast forward. Relief and joy combine in one ecstatic moment. All the hours of toiling on muddy fields on dark evenings, the disappointments of injury – it all seems worthwhile. I tried to run back to my half of the pitch as nonchalantly as possible, pretending that the emotion of the moment hadn't affected me. Inside I was bursting with pride. The stadium and even my own players were temporarily reduced to a blur of colour.

I couldn't think of a better arena in which to score a try and I felt ten feet tall as I ran back to be with the rest of the team – that's nine and a half feet taller than I had felt sliding around with my black brogues at our team run the previous day. With Gavin knocking over a huge penalty kick, by half-time we were in a position to go out and win the game. More importantly, we were all starting to really believe we could win. And, when you start believing you can win games, more often than not, you *do* win them.

I was enjoying the match and I was particularly focused on the various tasks an outside-centre has to perform. With a very dangerous French backline moving the ball at will, I was trying to track the movements of the full-back Jean-Luc Sadourny, and I was able to tackle him man-and-ball a couple of times. We were competing well and making it very hard for the French to get the upper hand in the set piece. However, we seemed to retreat into our shells whenever we nudged ahead on the scoreboard. It made for a decidedly close match.

The last ten minutes had more twists than a liquorice factory and must have been agonizing to watch for our supporters. Revelling amidst the colour, the noise and the sheer whirlwind intensity of the Parc des Princes, I was directly involved in the final two tries of the contest … Unfortunately the first of these tries went to France.

Having been responsible for Saint-Andre scoring an interception try at Murrayfield the previous season, I felt a depressing sense of déjà vu as he again crossed the line to touch down for what looked like being the clinching score.

With the game tied at 16–16 we had won phase possession in our half and, as Craig Chalmers was out of the 22 m, the call was 'miss-one diagonal'. What this entailed was that Craig would send a wide pass to me at outside-centre, missing inside-centre Ian Jardine, and it was then my job to dispatch a clearing kick to the opposite touchline and into the French half of the field. However, for the only time in the game I was indecisive and failed to complete a fairly basic task.

Even though I started in the 22 when Craig moved onto Bryan Redpath's pass from scrum-half, I was unsure whether I was still there or not when I caught his pass and prepared myself to kick. I decided it would no longer be safe to kick to touch as – if I had stepped out of the 22-m zone – France would be given a lineout deep in our half. Instead, I thought the best thing to do was to kick as far as possible into French territory. Frustratingly, I didn't strike the ball as I wanted to. Saint-Andre had also dropped deep and my weak kick gave him the perfect opportunity to counter-attack.

Still, we should have been able to defend better than we ended up doing, as the French were more than fifty metres from our try-line. However, with only Gavin and Craig Joiner outside me when I kicked, the move had the potential to go wrong if I didn't make touch. Saint-Andre and Sadourny easily exploited our lack of defenders. Gavin hadn't come up in a line with Craig Joiner, and I compounded the error of not making touch by not following my clearance. In fact, I had barely moved after seeing the French run the ball back at us, frozen in the hope that Saint-Andre might somehow drop my misdirected punt.

Crucially, Thierry Lacroix missed the conversion, which left a glimmer of hope that we could still win the match. There was probably a feeling of inevitability among our supporters – here was yet another gallant defeat in Paris – and no doubt some of our players began to feel the same way too. However, the urgings and belief of our captain didn't allow us to wallow in any self-pity. Gavin shouted at his troops, looking each of us in the eyes: 'That's it. From now on we run everything.

We're going to get back up the other end of the pitch, score between the posts and win this game. Okay?'

Finally, he looked directly at me. 'Okay, Gregor?' I nodded my assent. I was desperate not to disappoint my skipper and, with five minutes remaining, I knew there was still enough time for us to score a converted try.

We attacked the French with everything we had, but found it increasingly difficult to get out of our own half. I called for the ball wide and took a pass from Craig Chalmers just over the halfway line. With the French defence looking like they were drifting out to the touchline, I stepped back inside to try and find a gap between Thierry Lacroix and Laurent Cabannes. I was tackled by both of them but I managed to wrestle my right arm free in the hope that I could offload once more to Gavin. He had been a constant presence on my outside shoulder every time I had run at the defence, but on this occasion I heard him calling for the ball on my inside.

Gavin had sized up the situation in advance and was aware that a sliding French defence had left a gap. Although I couldn't see him charging up on my inside shoulder, I knew I had to gamble and turn my wrist to send out a reverse pass. Only after letting go of the ball did I see Gavin – who looked more than a bit surprised – surge onto my pass.

In the few seconds that it took Gavin to sprint to the French goal-line he became a Scottish living legend. His angle wrong-footed Sadourny and there was no French player left to stop his run to glory. He still had to knock over the conversion, and showed that his confidence was even greater than normal, as he dummied his run-up to try to catch the French offside. My heart missed a beat when he did this, but he made sure of the two extra points to seal a momentous victory. It would be the only Scotland victory at the fabled Parc des Princes, with France moving to the brand-new Stade de France three years later.

In my old bedroom at my parents' house there is a photograph of the instant the ball left my hand as I flicked the reverse pass that sent Gavin away on his match-winning run to the try-line. The movement became dubbed the 'Toony flip' by the media. Whenever I am back in the room I inspect the picture nostalgically: my focus at trying to get my pass away while being dragged to the ground, and Gavin's look of astonishment as he is about to grasp the ball in both hands.

In the twelve years since that wonderful spring day, the memory of that instant is still strong – the move off my left foot after drifting across the field, the effort to get my elbows high and free from the two tacklers, and finally the almost blind pass as I struggled to look over my shoulder to find where Gavin actually was. One rugby writer commented that it had been the day that I had finally delivered – and I suppose he was right. Paris was my breakthrough match and put an end to feelings of self-doubt that had prevented me from playing to my potential.

It was only once we were back in the changing room that what we had achieved began to sink in – especially for the older players. We had accomplished something special, something that had evaded all the great Scottish players of the Seventies and Eighties. I looked around at the faces of my team-mates and saw unrestrained rejoicing. This elation was illustrated in different ways with groups of players singing 'Flower of Scotland', others hugging each other and even tough competitors like our prop, Peter Wright, crying uncontrollably.

The word quickly spread around the team that most of our supporters were still in the stadium so we went outside to join in the celebrations with them. There were over 7,000 Scots at the ground and we threw our socks and shorts into the crowd as we sang our anthem together one more time. Our team that day – a mix of youth and experience – is worth noting: Gavin Hastings, Craig Joiner, Gregor Townsend, Ian Jardine, Kenny Logan, Craig Chalmers, Bryan Redpath, Eric Peters, Iain Morrison, Rob Wainwright, Damien Cronin (Doddie

Weir), Stewart Campbell, Peter Wright, Kenny Milne and David Hilton.

Inevitably, the dressing-room festivities carried on right through the weekend. The after-match dinners in France usually involved a lot of drinking as we were always placed together at a long table without the distractions of the management or the opposition. We started by smashing all the plates that were placed in front of us. The temptation was too great – they came out piping hot and only needed a tap from a spoon to crack in two. The champagne was flowing and not even a ticking off from our manager could stop us from having fun.

Gavin soon became the focus of our frivolity as we told the French players to approach him every five minutes with a strong drink. As captain, he was duty bound to knock them back. Worse was to follow for big Gav as, naively, he had allowed Damien Cronin (who was playing for Bourges at the time) to write his speech in French. Gavin didn't realize that instead of talking about the match, he was describing to the whole French team and the numerous dignitaries present, the sexual acts he was going to perform later that night with his wife Diane.

Of course, the French found this hilarious and gave him a standing ovation. Gavin looked very pleased with himself. It wasn't until the early hours of the morning that someone eventually told him what he had actually said!

In reply FFR president Bernard Lapasset was magnanimous in defeat. His words were very prescient and I hope his sentiments stand the test of time: 'Rugby is not for the country that is stronger or richer, it is for the country that shows greater courage, discipline and teamwork over eighty minutes.'

After the dinner I went with some of the squad to search for our partners who were supposed to have been at a function with the other WAGS. I had been seeing Claire for almost a year – we had met at university – but this was her first experience of accompanying me on an away trip with the Scotland team. I thought I'd better leave our dinner early, just in case she wasn't enjoying herself. I shouldn't have worried ...

The girls had disappeared. The only people left at the ladies dinner were the wives of the SRU committee. After a quick search, we moved outside – in time to see our partners flying past clinging to the backs of the same motorbike outriders that had taken us to the match earlier in the day. Claire and the girls were buzzing with excitement. In the satisfying glow of the day's magical events, victory in Paris felt like we had won a Grand Slam. And it suddenly began to dawn on us that we were on course to achieve that feat if we continued our good form.

A fortnight later we beat Wales 26–13 at Murrayfield, although I thought our win could have been even more comprehensive if we had moved the ball as we had done in Paris. Nevertheless, we had won our fourth game on the bounce and, more importantly, had a real chance to win the Grand Slam. Our next game, away to England, meant both sides would be going for the Slam – a scenario that had famously occurred back in 1990.

Since their loss five years before at Murrayfield, England had returned to playing a very restrictive game plan. It had brought them success with Grand Slams in 1991 and 1992 as well as being runners-up to Australia in the 1991 World Cup. Yet, they had never fully utilized their awesome attacking potential. For the 1995 Five Nations finale, their backline included the Underwood brothers, Mike Catt at full-back as well as centres Will Carling and Jerry Guscott.

However, stand-off Rob Andrew adopted a kicking strategy, safe in the knowledge that his gargantuan pack of forwards could dominate the game. With a back five of Martin Johnson, Martin Bayfield, Tim Rodber, Ben Clarke and Dean Richards, the English forwards strangled the life out of us and the match as a spectacle. It was ironic that their hooker, Brian Moore, complained afterwards that 'Scotland's spoiling tactics had ruined the whole game.' I suspect that he had been upset by the fact that we hadn't submitted meekly to the English juggernaut.

Although we managed to stop England from scoring a try, I can't say we deserved to win as we hadn't played to our potential. Our work-rate and defence had been exemplary, but we never attacked with the same skill and ambition that we had done in Paris and we missed the direct running of the injured Ian Jardine. However, the 21–12 scoreline flattered England, and we were aware that we hadn't been too far away from winning a Grand Slam. We had built up some great momentum and we were resolved that our belief wasn't going to be affected by the defeat. The squad had real belief that if we developed our attacking edge we could perform well in the upcoming World Cup in South Africa.

From a personal point of view, I felt that I had finally shaken off my previous inhibition when playing for Scotland and, although I would have probably preferred playing in the number 10 jersey, I was now comfortable in the Test match environment. I felt I could beat my opposite number when I got my hands on the ball and I was looking forward to the World Cup on the hard grounds in South Africa. Craig Chalmers had played well that season and I noticed at close quarters that he had an undoubted big-game temperament. There were times against England when I was glad it was him and not myself who was kicking to touch. I was learning more and more with each international and I decided I could wait until next season to make a challenge for what I was convinced was my best position of stand-off.

There was just one more club game to negotiate before the World Cup squad left for a training camp in Spain prior to our departure to South Africa. The rearranged fixture – the last club match of the season – was against Hawick, Gala's traditional rivals. With both teams safely ensconced in mid-table there was nothing but local pride at stake. Little did I know at the time but it was to be my final performance in the maroon jersey. And it was an occasion I was to remember for all the wrong reasons.

After recovering my own chip kick late in the second half, I received a stinging blow to my knee as I attempted to beat the Hawick full-back Greig Oliver. I knew immediately something wasn't right as my leg was very painful and felt unstable when I tried to get back on my feet. The Gala captain, Ian Corcoran, was telling me that I'd be able to run it off, but I knew I would have no chance of finishing the game.

My mind went back to two years previously and the only other time I'd suffered a similar injury during a match. Although I was forced to miss the first game of the Five Nations, my medial knee ligament tear in the 1993 national trial had only kept me out of action for three weeks. With Scotland's opening match in the World Cup almost two months away, I convinced myself that it must be a compara-ble injury and there was no way it would prevent me from going to South Africa.

Looking back now it was obvious that I was in denial. The following day, despite the fact that I struggled to get in and out of the car, Claire and I left for a four-day break in Ireland that we had already planned. In the days before mobile phones I was incommunicado during our tour around the Emerald Isle, and when I got back home there were numer-ous messages waiting for me. In particular, the Scottish team manager and doctor were anxious to assess how serious my injury really was. My knee had improved since the weekend and I was quite relaxed when I met up with the SRU's doctors, Jimmy Graham and Donald Macleod.

An arthroscopic scan revealed that I had completely ruptured my posterior cruciate ligament, which equated to a best-case scenario of three months' rest and rehabilitation. I was dizzy with shock as it meant that I was now ruled out of the World Cup. The whole timing of the news was the thing that fazed me at first. Missing the World Cup felt like a repeat of missing out on my first cap. On top of my wrist and knee problems from the year before, I started to ask myself whether I was jinxed or, even worse, injury prone.

On the way back from the hospital I tried to change my disappointment and anger into goal setting. I decided then that I would return to Australia in three months time when I was due to be available to play again. I also very nearly convinced myself that there were a number of positives to take from my injury. For the first time in four years I would be able to sit my university exams at the same time as everyone else. I was glad to have my student life to fall back on. There followed a lot of sleeping in the university library, getting over late-night studying and regular drowning of sorrows.

Also my daily physiotherapy at the Princess Margaret Rose Hospital in Edinburgh kept my disappointment in perspective. A three-month injury didn't seem so bad when compared to some of my fellow patients. Many had massive operation scars and had recovery periods of over a year. One man even told me that he had already torn his cruciate ligaments on five separate occasions and he didn't play sport of any kind.

Rehab work is a frustrating and seemingly endless repetition of strengthening exercises, but the tedium at least made me determined that I must make the most of the rugby talent I had been blessed with. I had spent the best part of the previous two seasons playing with or recovering from injuries and it was conceivable that the rest of my career could be more of the same.

My rugby mates were great at helping me deal with the trauma and frustrations of missing out on the game's biggest occasion. I met up regularly with Derek Stark, Andy Nicol and Sean Lineen and I remember us all watching Scotland take on France through a drunken haze in the notorious Edinburgh student pub Oddfellows. Our former team-mates put on a tremendous show and were desperately unlucky not to win the match. If they had, they would have met Ireland in the quarter-finals – a match they would have been favourites to win. As it was, Scotland met the All Blacks with Jonah Lomu et al. and they crashed out of the tournament, despite having played well in all of their games.

The 1995 World Cup was a watershed moment in rugby union and all of a sudden it looked as if the game was poised to turn professional. I put it down to wishful thinking and continued to apply to financial institutions in London, hoping I could work there after the summer. It may seem strange, but I was never envious when I looked around at other sports and saw the money involved. Playing international rugby in front of 80,000 crowds was a privilege and I did not feel it was my right to expect money – the sheer experience seemed payment enough.

In Scotland we knew that having a day job was part of the tradition of rugby and there were very strict interpretations of the International Rugby Board (IRB) regulations – the incomparable Scotland and Lions lock Gordon Brown and hooker Colin Deans had both been banned from the sport by the SRU for writing books. But rumours always reached us that other nations were more relaxed. In New Zealand and Australia, players appeared in TV adverts and were permitted to make money from their image. It was also something of an open secret that the French and South Africans paid their players. Benjamin Disraeli once observed that the Conservative Party was a spectacularly well-organized hypocrisy – this could easily have been applied to the IRB and certain national unions in 1995.

For some in Scotland the dilemmas were obvious. Gary Armstrong, our inspirational scrum-half, was a truck driver by day. He was one of the players of the tournament in the 1991 World Cup and from then on had been a target for rugby league – the professional cousin of union that had a history of poaching players. Although very close to signing a league contract, he stayed with the game he loved, going on to play for Newcastle at the start of the professional era. He now owns several trucks himself.

Shortly after the World Cup final in South Africa I was getting my bags packed to return to play for Warringah, who were – thankfully – keen to have me back. However, the day before I was due to leave, I was caught in the shockwave of the seismic changes that were already tearing through rugby union. And I had to face the fact that I might never play for Scotland again.

CHAPTER 5

Rebels with a Cause

Happiness is not having what you want;
it is wanting what you have.

Rabbi Schachtel

Claire passed me the phone, telling me that Gavin Hastings was on the other line. I smiled – Gavin had been great with me over the previous year and I'd missed the banter of the Scottish team since my injury, some three months earlier. It was good to hear from him. I wanted to hear more about the World Cup and what had happened on and off the field. Gavin, however, seemed pressed for time: 'When are you leaving for Australia?'

'Tomorrow afternoon.'

'Oh, right. I need to see you before you leave – it's very important.'

'Can't you tell me over the phone.'

'No, it has to be done face-to-face. Believe me, it is vital for your rugby career to come and see me tomorrow morning.'

'Okay, I'll see you first thing, then.'

The following morning I found myself in an Edinburgh solicitor's office, and Gavin Hastings – recently retired after a brilliant World Cup – is urging me to sign a letter of agreement to play in a rebel tournament. It seemed certain that to sign would prohibit me from ever playing for Scotland again.

Although I had closely followed Scotland's progress in South Africa, I had heard nothing about the proposed breakaway tournament. In fact there had been mounting speculation that the IRB might soon take an historic decision and turn rugby union into a professional sport. It was obvious that rugby was awash with money and the latest World Cup had opened the game to a global television audience. Despite this, the rugby unions of the home nations were determined to keep the amateur status quo. Events in the southern hemisphere finally forced them to take their heads out of the sand.

On 1 April, Rupert Murdoch's News Corporation launched an attempted takeover of rugby league, which was unveiled as 'Super League'. The monies involved meant that rugby league salaries would be doubled or even trebled overnight. Crucially, rugby union players were now being targeted in the quest to make Super League a success. The potential exodus of their prized assets forced the southern hemisphere unions into drastic and revolutionary measures. Ironically, Murdoch's media empire was also to play a key role in this radical change in the union game.

On 23 June, the day before the World Cup Final between South Africa and the All Blacks, the big three southern hemisphere unions (known as SANZAR) announced a ten-year deal with News Corporation worth £360 million. South Africa, New Zealand and Australia would now play each other twice a season in a Tri-Nations Series. Also, the existing Super 10 competition was being enlarged to become the Super 12. It seemed that Rupert Murdoch, who two months before was seen as destabilizing the union game, was now providing the necessary finance that would ensure that rugby union would not lose its best players. That was, of course, if the game turned fully professional. The IRB were scheduled to meet in August to decide what shape or form this new professional game might take.

However, just at the same time as the SANZAR unions were signing up with Rupert Murdoch, his Australian business adversary, Kerry Packer, was behind a scheme to sign up the leading players in the game. The World Rugby Corporation (WRC) was attempting to contract enough players to have a global professional tournament with thirty teams, one of which would be based in Scotland. Every player in the WRC was to be given a signing-on fee, his value determined by his status and no doubt influenced by who was giving out the contracts.

Gavin Hastings was put in charge of getting players signed up for the rebel Scottish team and he had already met with the Scotland team during the World Cup. He told me that they would all be signing their contracts over the next few days. The contract that Gavin placed in front of me was worth around £100,000 a year. This was a substantial increase from the £5,000 I'd earned during the previous season.

The downside was that all players in the WRC competition would almost certainly be banned from playing international rugby. Gavin said that with the number of players worldwide already signed up, the unions would have to work with the WRC or the international game would become a joke. WRC apparently still wanted the unions to run international rugby alongside their proposed thirty-team global tournament. Even if cooperation wasn't possible, there was already a contingency plan in place to play games at football stadiums.

I had never thought that rugby union was there to provide me with financial rewards, so the money on offer from WRC was a non-issue for me. Even though the game was amateur, rugby had taken me all over the world and no amount of money could have matched the honour of representing my country. However, maybe because of the fact that I was leaving later that day for Australia, I was in a dilemma over whether to sign the contract Gavin had placed before me.

As it seemed that the vast majority of international rugby players were in the process of signing up to WRC, I felt that the international game would leave me behind if I didn't sign. While I felt that I had no right to turn my back on the amateur game that I loved, I desperately wanted to be with my fellow Scottish team-mates. So, seeking safety in numbers, I agreed a compromise with Gavin. His solicitors drew up a side letter, which stated that my contract would only be valid if twenty or more of the Scottish squad committed themselves to WRC. This number had to include all the younger players in the squad, like Kenny Logan, Craig Joiner and Bryan Redpath. Although my conscience was slightly clearer, I set off for Australia desperately hoping that the WRC concept would fail.

I had been determined to play rugby as soon as I had recovered from my knee injury. So, less than two weeks after Joel Stransky had dropped the goal in extra-time that enabled South Africa to defeat New Zealand to win the 1995 World Cup, I set off once more to Australia to play for Warringah. Two years previously my three months with the Sydney club had seen me play the best rugby of my career, although I knew that it couldn't possibly be the same on this occasion.

Fortunately, my time there was once again a marvellous experience and, after my knee began to get used to taking contact again, I quickly rediscovered my form. It was much easier to adapt to the club second time around and seeing friends again made me feel Warringah was becoming a home from home. I knew my game was suited to Australian rugby and I was thriving once more in this environment. I felt a sense of freedom on the rugby field and it was a joy to be back playing. I was taking on the opposition, which more often than not was paying dividends – one break from under my posts against Randwick remains a standout memory of my second stint with the Rats.

Also, I felt at the centre of the rugby world as many changes were taking place that would have a profound effect on the union game. The 1995 World Cup had turned out to be of monumental importance not only for the newly democratic South Africa but also for the rugby-playing world as a whole. The pressure was building for the sport to become fully professional. Sydney was to become the epicentre for the machinations and negotiations that were to decide the fate of the game of rugby union.

WRC was based in the city and there were already reports that the players of Australia, South Africa and New Zealand had all signed up with the rebel tournament. The issue dominated the Australian media who seemed to think that WRC was now poised to control the international game. These suspicions were reinforced during the Bledisloe Cup match in July, which Australia lost to the All Blacks. At the end of the match, the Wallaby captain, Phil Kearns, was passed a microphone and spoke directly to the crowd and the television viewers throughout Australia: 'Whatever happens in the future, we hope you and the Union support us.'

His words were a clear confirmation that the WRC had substance, and that it looked like the Wallabies had signed up en masse. The next week a couple of my team-mates at Warringah who were in the New South Wales squad told me that video conferencing between All Black, Springbok and Australian players had taken place. WRC seemed to be holding all the aces.

It was at this time that an open letter was written to the major Australian newspapers by a number of former Wallaby captains, pleading with the current players not to destroy the heritage and achievements of Australian rugby by signing with WRC. To most commentators, however, this appeal seemed to have been too late, and there was now an inevitability that the game would never be the same as before.

Things move quickly in the fluid world of sport and, mercifully, the revolutionary changes to rugby were made not by WRC, but by the game's governing body, the IRB. Consequently, WRC was soon finished as a concept. Francois Pienaar, the Springbok captain, was pressurized into refusing the participation of the South African players. Questions remain unanswered as to why Pienaar eventually changed track, but it was evident that the all-powerful SARFU president, Louis Luyt, had been a significant influence in his decision. Shortly afterwards the All Blacks and the Wallabies sought refuge with their unions and the players were back with the establishment.

Listening intently to the World Service in the early hours of Sunday, 27 August, I received the news I'd been hoping for. Vernon Pugh of the IRB announced that the amateur regulations were to be annulled, rugby was to be open and that there would be no prohibition on paying players. I was both relieved that WRC had not seen the light of day and excited that I could now commit myself full-time to the game I loved. As I looked out of my bedroom window to the shimmering lights of Sydney in the distance, I thought that this wasn't too bad a place to enjoy the final days of the amateur game.

Warringah had made one or two additions to the team I had played with two seasons before, one of whom I had the pleasure of sharing an apartment with in the beachfront suburb of Manly. French backrower Abdel Benazzi, who had just played in the World Cup and had been inches away from scoring a match-winning try against South Africa in the semifinal, had joined Warringah for an Australian rugby experience and an opportunity to learn English. My memories of Abdel were that he was a gentle giant and he became very popular with everyone at the club. He could also eat like no one I had ever seen before. Whole bags of pasta and huge lamb roasts became our standard evening meal together.

On the rugby field Abdel was the same dynamic and aggressive player he had been whenever I had seen him play for the French national team. However, he didn't always find things easy in Australian rugby. Abdel's appearance for Warringah coincided with the French government's decision to explode a nuclear bomb at a test site in the Mururoa Atoll in the South Pacific.

This had become a volatile issue in Australia and there were a number of protesters who turned up at our matches, heckling our respected French international. Some even brought banners that said 'Ban the bomb, Abdel'. Aussies never usually miss a trick to get one over on an opponent and there was a lot of 'sledging' from other teams, but more effective were opposition players shouting to Abdel to pass the ball. Thinking it was his Warringah team-mate calling for the ball he fell into the trap, throwing a couple of interceptions in our match against Western Suburbs.

This game was the only time Abdel didn't play well for Warringah, but he still got a roasting in the Sydney media. He asked me to translate what had been written. I was a bit worried about how he was going to react – he had been described by one journalist as having played with the effectiveness of 'a sparrow with a broken wing'. As I read it out to him, he looked through his English–French dictionary. Steam started to pour out of his ears. I felt sorry for the opposition – in our next match he smashed everybody in sight.

Incidentally, Abdel wrote about his time playing for Warringah in his book *La foi du rugby*. Being teetotal, he was surprised how much alcohol I consumed:

> *Gregor adapted quickly to the Australian lifestyle: at night he drank beer after beer, sometimes to the point that I was worried that he was going to collapse. But the next day, early in the morning, you would find him training very hard, sweating it out … just like the Australians!*

At the time I would have been proud of such an image, but it wasn't true – all my other team-mates at Warringah actually thought I was a bit of a lightweight who went into hiding whenever a Sunday drinking session was planned.

Abdel and I were informed that we had been selected to play for the Australian Barbarians against the full Australian side in Melbourne, which was due to be played the week after Phil Kearns' momentous speech after the Bledisloe Cup match. I was paired at half-back with a rising star of Sydney club rugby, George Gregan. Unfortunately, the Warringah coach, Steve Lidbury, pulled the pin on our involvement, as the club had just qualified for the play-offs. Warringah had given me the chance to start playing again after my knee injury, so I couldn't really argue with his decision.

The Warringah club was generosity personified – again they had organized a job for me. This time they found me employment relevant to my university degree. I worked as a political researcher, first for the Minister for the Commonwealth, Bronwyn Bishop, and then as part of a team in the NSW Parliament. We were assigned to the Opposition leader, Peter Collins, who has since climbed up the political ladder and is now the overwhelming favourite to take over when Prime Minister John Howard eventually retires. Back then his role was much less glamorous, and it was our job to try and catch out the governing party and its leader, Bob Carr. Our chief researcher could have easily given Alistair Campbell a run for his money and my eyes were opened to real politics – not much of which I had studied at university. On one occasion I had the peculiar experience of fixing a public radio phone-in.

At our daily strategy meetings a plan was usually set out as to how our man, Collins, would react to the potential issues of the day, or how he could set the agenda for the various media outlets to pick up on. During one such meeting, we were alerted to the fact that there was soon to be a debate on a popular talk radio show on the subject of road tolls. With a number of new roads and bridges being built in Sydney, the ruling party had recently taken the decision to set up toll-booths on some of these to help with their financing. This judgment had caused a great deal of consternation at a local level. Naturally, our party had come out vehemently opposed

to the imposition of road tolls. It was up to the research team
to make sure we won the radio debate.

So, with little time to work with, we had to find as many
people as possible to phone in their views to the radio show. I
listened in amazement as the majority of the phone-in guests
were our stooges – all with well-argued and distinct reasons
as to why paying a road toll would hurt them personally. Our
chief researcher toted up the scores at the end of the radio
show and we had won the debate by a sizeable margin. I
suppose you could call it politics in action, but it has left me
fairly suspicious whenever I tune into debates on the radio
back in the UK.

Just as in 1993, Warringah finished the season strongly. We
had climbed the table to qualify for the semi-finals, but this
time there would be no Grand Final appearance for the
mighty Green Rats, as we lost out to Canberra, who had only
just joined the Sydney Competition. I must have been doing
something right, though, because at the end of the season,
Rod Macqueen asked if he could meet with me. He had
recently been appointed head coach of the ACT Brumbies, a
newly formed franchise who were to become the third
Australian side in an expanded Super 12 competition.

Macqueen proceeded to offer me a contract to play for the
Brumbies, which was worth £20,000, but it meant that I
would have to be based in Australia from November until
June. Everyone in world rugby was talking about the fantastic potential of the Super 12, which would see the best players
in the southern hemisphere take part as professionals for the
first time. While it was true that the offer came too soon in
my career, I blame Claire for my decision to return to the UK.
I thought it would be impossible for me to spend another few
months thousands of miles away from her.

Rod Macqueen proved himself to be arguably the best
coach of the professional era as he took the scratch Brumbies
side to the final of the Super 12 in only their second season as

well as guiding the Wallabies to Tri-Nations success and then on to becoming World Cup champions in 1999. Macqueen had told me that he thought I would be an ideal inside-centre to play outside Pat Howard, whom he had just signed from Queensland. As events unfolded, Howard changed to inside-centre where he went on to have much success. The chance to work with a coach as good as Macqueen was undoubtedly an opportunity missed and I sometimes wonder how things would have panned out if I had accepted his offer.

However, one negative of the Brumbies deal was that I would have been forced to take temporary leave from the Scotland team. Because the Five Nations had been much more enjoyable that season, plus the fact that I had already agreed to join Northampton (even though there was no contract involved), it was a much easier decision to make at the time than it should have been looking back now. My thoughts turned to England, where I was set to take my first steps in rugby's new professional era.

CHAPTER 6

Last Orders and First Steps

Achievement is largely the product of steadily raising one's levels of aspiration ... and expectation.

Jack Nicklaus

Jonah Lomu had become a global sporting icon almost overnight during the World Cup in South Africa. His devastating performances made him simultaneously the world's best and most recognizable player and his extraordinary impact helped propel rugby into the professional era. After almost single-handedly destroying a very experienced England team in the semi-finals, Will Carling called him a 'freak'. The rest of the rugby world preferred to use the term 'phenomenon'. One year on from the World Cup, Jonah had continued to wreak havoc upon opposition defences. In Dunedin, just over half way through Scotland's First Test match with the All Blacks in 1996, I saw at close-quarters how awesome a talent he was.

Walking back into position to defend an All Black scrum on the halfway line, my inside-centre, Ian Jardine, pointed something out to me: 'Look at that ... Mehrtens has swapped with Lomu.' This was a situation I'd feared for the previous few weeks, ever since I'd seen the All Blacks attempt this particular scrum move. What it entailed was Lomu getting the ball directly from the scrum-half with the intention of running over the top of the opposition stand-off – in this case me. When I'd seen it done on video it had worked very well and I knew they would try it again.

Craig Joiner, our right winger, threw me a lifeline: 'Gregor, we can change positions if you want – so you can mark Mehrtens.' Call it bravery, ego or stupidity, but I turned down Craig's offer.

I tried to work out what Lomu was going to do. It was simple really – he was going to try and run straight over the top of whoever was standing in his way. As the scrum was on our right-hand side of the field, the only person who could help me tackle the colossal figure was my open-side flanker Ian Smith. However, the ease with which Craig Dowd and Olo Brown had been moving our front-row about, it was almost guaranteed that the All Black scrum would get up on the right shoulder and therefore take Smithy out of the game. The only option I had left to help me topple the giant was to cheat.

I looked across at Lomu, about ten feet away, and I noticed a hint of a smile on his face. I think he believed I had no chance of stopping him. As I glanced at his massive thighs and hulking muscles tensing in his neck and shoulders, I almost felt myself nodding in agreement. I tried hard to focus on an area of his body that might be vulnerable, but my attention turned quickly to Justin Marshall who was about to put the ball into the scrum.

Just as hooker Sean Fitzpatrick struck the ball I decided to start my run towards Jonah, miles offside: giving away a penalty was better than having to spend a night in a Dunedin hospital. I was almost level with Marshall as he passed the ball out to Lomu. The referee was no doubt about to blow his whistle to penalize me and put me out of my misery. If only …

Stage one of my plan to tackle the big man had been successfully completed; Lomu had not been able to build up a head of steam and was in fact standing still while I was only a foot away from him. Unfortunately I hadn't thought about adding a stage two, thinking that events would take care of themselves. As I reached Lomu I was still upright and for some insane reason looking to do a smother tackle on the strongest rugby player on the planet. Lomu took the ball in one hand and in the same movement planted his other hand firmly in my chest, which knocked me straight back onto the ground. Rowan Shepherd won't have thanked me for allowing Lomu to then start running full tilt – as full-back he was next in line to be sat down. Eventually, the enormous winger was clawed back by three players, inches short of the try-line. The All Blacks scored from the next phase.

As this was happening I was still lying on the turf close to the halfway line, hoping that I could disappear through a hole in the ground. I redeemed myself somewhat by managing to outpace Frank Bunce for a consolation score, but after the match I returned slower than usual back to the changing rooms, feeling ashamed and embarrassed at my effort at tackling Jonah Lomu. Scotland coach Jim Telfer was already in full flow, angry with us for missing so many tackles. To my surprise he gave me a look that expressed admiration rather than disappointment. He then immediately got stuck into Craig Joiner, castigating him for not changing positions with me to defend against his winger, Lomu. It's hard to interrupt Jim when he gets going, especially if you want to point out that he's wrong. Sorry Craig, I should have told him it had been my decision. At least a mouthful from Jim is preferable to a lifetime of flashbacks of being trampled by a giant.

The New Zealand tour came at the end of the 1995/96 season, which was a pivotal year for the game. It was not only rugby union that was standing at an historic crossroads – my own career path was to take a dramatic turn. While the possibility of playing in a rebel tournament still lingered in the air, I also had to make up my mind as to where I would be playing club rugby the following season. I had just graduated from Edinburgh University and I was eager to gain some business experience. I had previously decided against doing a business degree because of the demands of the course, which would not have been feasible with my rugby commitments. With this in mind I opted to look for employment in London, the ideal location, I presumed, to learn more about commerce.

I enrolled as a graduate trainee in corporate banking with the Royal Bank of Scotland. My place of work was in the heart of the City, less than 100 yards from the Bank of England. I had spoken with two leading English clubs – Sale and West Hartlepool – earlier that year, but my interest in them ended when I accepted a job in the City. The choice now was between Second Division London Scottish and Northampton, who had also just been relegated from the top flight.

I was immediately attracted to Northampton, mainly because Ian McGeechan had been appointed head coach six months previously. His full-time role was a novelty in the amateur game and even though he hadn't managed to lift Northampton from the foot of the table, I knew his coaching intelligence and experience would inspire the players to greater things. His last season as Scotland coach in 1992/93 coincided with my first taste of international rugby, and still vivid in my mind was the amount of preparation and analysis he had managed to do despite holding down a full-time job.

I spent a couple of days in Northampton speaking to Geech (pronounced 'beech' not 'beek') and other leading figures at the club in order to get a feel for the place. It was a big move for me – leaving Gala wasn't easy as I felt real pride in repre-senting my town. I told myself that I would return to my home club a better player, which I presumed would be in a couple of years time. I remember receiving a poem from a supporter – a twelve-year-old girl in fact – pleading with me not to leave. For Borderers it is difficult to see yourself playing for somewhere other than the town you grew up in. I was now going to have to get used to no longer wearing a maroon jersey.

The whole set-up at the Saints was impressive, much more organized than anything in Scottish club rugby, with the guarantee of bigger crowds. I had watched highlights of Northampton's games on *Rugby Special* and the atmosphere at Franklin's Gardens appeared to be excellent. Officials at the club assured me that crowds would still average over 5,000 even though Northampton were no longer playing the leading teams in England. This was way above the numbers attending club matches in Scotland at the time.

My apprehensions of having to play Second Division rugby were largely dispelled by the fact that all the international players at Northampton had committed their immediate futures to the club. The chance to play alongside the likes of Tim Rodber, Martin Bayfield, Ian Hunter as well as rising stars such as Matt Dawson, Nick Beal and Irish centre Jonathan Bell, was more than enough to convince me that I had the potential to learn a great deal from playing with the Saints. The added bonus of having a coach with an outstanding reputation persuaded me to join the East Midlands club. Although at the same time, I had to get my head round the idea of catching a train to London every morning at 7.30 a.m. – my student days were about to come to an abrupt end!

After missing the World Cup, I was now playing rugby non-stop – going straight from Warringah to Northampton. For the second time in my career I came back from a stint in Australian club rugby having played the best rugby of my life. This time though, my season was not cut short by any injury problems. Immediately after my return I played for the Barbarians against Stirling County. I was partnered at half-back with Bryan Redpath and we performed well together – we were good friends and I loved the freedom his wide, accurate passing gave me. I then joined up with my new team-mates at Northampton and found myself selected at outside-centre for a tough derby match at Bedford. I had to quickly get used to a new club – and a new position in the backline.

I was surprised to find that I actually enjoyed playing at outside-centre, which was a stark contrast to my previous experiences of the role. There had only been one occasion – Scotland's win in Paris – when I had received more than just a handful of passes playing in the number 13 jersey. Geech said that rugby can be a simple game – if we did things well – but never an easy one. He had us extremely fit, as our support play would be of paramount importance if we were to be effective at keeping the ball alive at every opportunity. Our game plan was based on attacking at pace from quick ball. Geech tried to get the backline attacking as a unit striking one side of a ruck – the 'whip effect' as he described it. He was also keen to have two points of attack in the backline and for players to group together like an inversed triangle. In theory, the key players in this set-up were the stand-off, outside-centre and the full-back. I relished the chance to play even closer to the advantage line than I had done at stand-off and was used frequently when we attacked the opposition.

In the number 10 jersey, Paul Grayson had the ability and willingness to send out some great wide and flat passes. Grays was a tidy player who had a perceptive rugby brain. He may have lacked a cutting edge and didn't really relish the physical side of the game, but he was consistent and accurate in his passing and kicking, very much like Scotland stand-off Dan Parks.

We quickly realized that playing in the Second Division was going to be a lot more enjoyable than we had all expected. The way we trained and played worked wonders for our confidence and gave us the ideal opportunity to implement a high-paced game plan full of movement and support. I loved what we were doing and relished both our training sessions and the matches. In my first six league games I scored twelve tries and was involved in many others as we blew apart the opposition. Even our two closest rivals, London Scottish and London Irish, who were both promoted during the next two seasons, could not handle our pace and positive approach. We scored over fifty points against each side.

We were playing at a vastly superior level to the other teams in the league, which led to some great rugby, but it was under false pretences. If you're thirty points up on a side – a frequent occurrence for us – you can afford to try things. Individually, it was a marvellous way to improve self-belief and to 'push the envelope', but reproducing that kind of form against top-grade opposition was going to be much more difficult. Nevertheless, it was preferable to the staleness that was prevalent in the English first division at the time, where coaches and players were loath to attack sides with the ball in hand. It was little wonder that players such as Paul, Matt and Tim were soon involved in the England set-up.

The supporters at Northampton appreciated our style of play and the ground was frequently sold out. Franklin's Gardens was considered one of the finest rugby grounds in England. Today, with the construction of new stands, it is one of the best in European rugby. The atmosphere at our matches was superb, and we always seemed to start well as we responded to the welcome from our supporters. Constant renditions of 'Oh, when the Saints go marching in' resounded throughout the ground as well as two or three songs about individual players. I even began to hear the crowd chanting my name.

The song went along the lines of 'Super Greg ... Super Gregor Townsend', and I cringed in embarrassment every time I heard it. In fact, when I recently looked at tapes of that record-breaking season, my body language was not of someone who was enjoying the adulation of scoring tries in front of a home crowd. By the way I was playing I was obviously very confident in what I was doing, but I still wasn't comfortable at accepting praise. Some players were attracted to hearing people talking them up, but I steered away from this, finding it very unfamiliar that some of the supporters were clearly in awe of the team. In the Borders, international players were treated no differently to anyone else and people weren't afraid to tell you when you hadn't performed.

Another difference I found in English rugby was that the organization at the club was based on getting the best out of the players, and there was never a feeling of 'them and us' with the committee. Keith Barwell, a local entrepreneur who had bought the club for £1 million in 1995, spearheaded this approach. Keith had made his fortune by building up a chain of free newspapers and was first and foremost a supporter of the Saints. His main concern was that the club did well and it is a testament to his contributions over the years that Northampton have developed into one of the best run and best supported clubs in Europe.

A beneficiary of the dynamic performances by Northampton was full-back Michael Dods. Like me, Mike had left Gala to work in England and we had found ourselves again at the same club. The national selectors had obviously been keeping tabs on how we had been playing and we were both included in the Scotland team to face Samoa in November. I was chosen at outside-centre where I had been playing the majority of the time at Northampton. However, the Samoan game was vastly different to what I'd been experiencing at club level. We struggled to move the ball wide and were lucky to get away with a 15–15 draw.

Our game against Samoa had been the first time that the team had played poorly in almost a year. During the World Cup, the side had been exceedingly close to beating the French in a crucial pool match and put in a creditable performance against the All Blacks in the quarter-final. With Gavin Hastings and Kenny Milne having retired at the end of the World Cup, our pre-Christmas international against Samoa had been the first without two of our most experienced campaigners of recent years. However, this didn't stop the selectors putting the influential Gary Armstrong and

Craig Chalmers on the bench for our following match away to Italy. It was the first of a number of bold moves that were to pay dividends in the Five Nations.

I received some encouraging news as I was picked at stand-off, even though I'd only played there a couple of times that season. Head coach Richie Dixon and manager Jim Telfer had made a statement of intent, backing me rather than the more experienced Chalmers. Being selected in the number 10 jersey was great, but I was also announced as vice-captain, which was a real fillip. It made me feel secure in the knowledge that the coaches had faith in the way I was playing. It's amazing what a gesture, a comment or genuine praise can do for self-belief. These two decisions gave my burgeoning confidence a huge boost – it was as if I was wearing a suit of armour going into the championship.

Although we lost 29–17 against the Italians, Richie had the courage to send us out with a game plan that was to attack from almost everywhere. He had correctly surmised that the result of the Italian match wasn't that important – what was essential was that we had to get used to moving the ball wide and playing off each other. Most significantly, despite the defeat, the underlying attacking philosophy was left unchanged for our opening championship game away to Ireland. Who knows how much benefit we got from the Italian match as we continued to attack our way right through the Five Nations and within touching distance of a Grand Slam.

Ireland, with a new all-Kiwi coaching staff of Murray Kidd and John Mitchell, were favourites to win the match, which may have been understandable given our results against Italy and Samoa. We were being widely tipped to pick up the wooden spoon. A wet and windy Lansdowne Road didn't affect our attacking intentions and we went at the Irish right from the first minute. I had by far my best game at stand-off in a Scotland jersey, mixing up play well and always looking for an opening in the defensive line. The togetherness and shared ambition that comes from winning away from home was plain to see. It was an essential ingredient in what turned out to be a memorable season.

We had a new-look team with attack-minded players. Combinations, self-belief and understanding between the players were what helped make the individuals we had at our disposal more than the sum of their parts. Guys like Kevin MacKenzie, Michael Dods and Rowan Shepherd had always looked comfortable on the ball at club level and were finally given the chance to show what they could do on the international stage. Our enthusiasm and confidence had yet to be knocked out of us from either the press or the coaching staff. This is often called the honeymoon period in football management – the ever-shortening interval where judgemental comments are held in reserve.

Credit must also go to Rob Wainwright who was an outstanding captain and, despite having a classic public school education – Glenalmond to Cambridge – was universally liked by the squad. He had shown leadership qualities in abundance even when Gavin Hastings had been captain. I remember Rob sending a card to commiserate with me after my knee injury had forced me to pull out of the World Cup. It was touches like this that showed he really cared for his teammates and that being made captain of Scotland had nothing to do with ego or personal gain.

Coach Richie Dixon was enterprising off the field as well, bringing in renowned sports psychologist Dr Richard Cox to work with the side. This was a first for any Scotland rugby squad and there still seemed to be scepticism from some of the management as to whether it would do us any good. For the players, though, it was fresh, original and an excellent tool in our preparations. Dr Cox's one-on-one meetings also gave the players the chance to talk with someone about their ability, without the worries associated with opening up – and showing weakness or overconfidence – to the coaching staff.

Dr Cox's message was simple enough – that the team had to concentrate on positives and visualize actions that would improve our individual and collective performance. Following the Irish game he showed us a video of basic action that led to the team going forward. The clip involved ten passes that Bryan Redpath (Basil) had sent out to me. On every one of these we breached the advantage line as players were hitting the line hard and looking eager to get their hands on the ball.

After our 16–10 win in terrible conditions in Dublin, we went into the match against France full of confidence. The French were desperate to avenge their defeat in Paris the previous season and had been boosted by a home win over England. Their team was at full strength and gunning for a Grand Slam. They had also unearthed a new star in talented centre Thomas Castaignède who had dropped the winning goal against the English. But the French weren't able to handle the pace at which we were now playing. They were very fortunate to have still been in with a chance of winning the game going into the closing stages – we had missed sixteen points with the boot and twice dropped the ball over the line while in the act of scoring.

We produced some scintillating rugby, 'outskilling' the French and at times running them ragged. Nearly everyone in the side had played close to their best – one English journalist even suggested that our starting fifteen should all make the following season's Lions tour to South Africa. The first ten minutes were amazing as we chose to run back the deep French kick-off from our 22. This was the catalyst to us running at any opportunity and making several line breaks, one of which led to a try for Mike Dods. At long last I was taking pleasure in playing at Murrayfield. It is certainly the best running game I have ever had at Test level and I also seemed to have developed a knack for successfully off-loading out of the tackle. After the match we were paid the ultimate compliment from the French coach, Jean-Claude Skrela, when he said, 'Scotland are now playing rugby just as we want to play the game. Now we have to go home and learn from what Scotland have done today.'

However, our 19–14 win drew some criticism from our manager, Jim Telfer. He said that our failure to finish off a lot of good work could have cost us the match. He was right – we should have won by at least fifteen points, not five. Jim, although not officially in a coaching role, had a significant influence over the side. It was the first time he had been the team manager and he approached this in his own inimitable style.

It had always been the tradition that the manager is in charge of presenting the jerseys to the squad – the final act at the team hotel before boarding the bus for the game. Managers would usually add a few words, wishing the boys good luck for the match. Jim took this pre-match preamble to another level. In Dublin, he had arranged the seats for the squad in a circle, with one chair placed in the middle. Staring straight at Doddie Weir, he bellowed, 'Who wants to take the seat in the middle? Who is going to be a leader today?'

Up jumped our hooker, Kevin MacKenzie – someone who embodied our new, assured air of self-confidence. 'I'm your man, Jim.' Jim looked somewhat dismayed. It was obvious he had wanted Doddie in the chair – maybe to make the point that as our most-capped player he had to take added responsibility on the pitch. Kevin didn't care and was happy to be our leader.

Before the French match, it seemed as if we were going to have a more standard talk as the chairs were set out in a customary fashion. We were dressed in our 'No. 1s' – smart trousers, blazer, shirt and tie. Suddenly he shouted at us to get down on our fronts, then on our backs, then on our fronts, and back up on our feet again. This routine went on for a few minutes. All the while, he kept repeating that we had to be switched on against the French, ready for anything. It felt bizarre at the time, but it seemed to have the desired effect – it was the best opening period of a match in my time with Scotland.

For the Welsh game, Jim placed the chairs in two lines, side by side. He called it 'the bus', and asked us all to get on board. There was one seat left spare at the front of the bus. Jim said this was going to be for the driver of the bus – the player who had been driving us to the top of the table in the championship. He said that this player was vastly undervalued by the media and had two things in common with himself – that he hadn't been contacted by Saracens (the big-spending club who seemed to be signing lots of international players) and also that he had a face only a mother could love. The man in question was Ian Jardine, a popular choice to become our bus driver.

In Cardiff our self-belief went up a further notch or two. We were even close to being over-confident, which was the only time I've ever experienced this sensation with a group of Scottish players. The team spirit we had built up had made us believe we were capable of anything. I always remember Basil cheekily sticking his tongue out to a passing television camera as we were waiting for the national anthems. We needed this belief, as we were far too loose at times when we should have been converting scoring chances.

For the 100th meeting between the two nations, Wales had named an unchanged team (the first time in thirty-one matches!). The half-backs – Rob Howley and Arwel Thomas – had been receiving rave reviews and it promised to be a closely contested game. We still attacked the Welsh with ball in hand, but sometimes this was from slow ball. I remember there was a photo in the papers the following day showing three defenders clinging onto me as I tried to go for a break. I don't think I had realized I was going to be marked as closely as I was that day. It was a vivid reminder that I would have to be more selective in choosing when to break in future.

Despite making many mistakes (I was a contributor here as I missed touch three or four times in a row), we were tied at 9–9 with less than ten minutes to play. I then managed to put Kenny Logan through a gap and we ended up with a scrum just to the right of the posts, five metres from the Welsh line. Rob Wainwright looked at me and I'm sure he was about to say, 'Drop-goal, please Gregor', but instead I opted for a move that I'd been waiting to call all season. It had previously brought me tries at Gala and it involved Basil looping open-side flanker Ian Smith before giving the ball back to me with a reverse pass. Rob let me make the call.

I made it through the first line of the defence and just managed to stretch out over the try-line to score. Despite Wales coming back to score late on, we had sealed a win and had set up a second Grand Slam match against England in as many years. On this occasion, however, we were the only remaining unbeaten team in the championship.

Despite some inaccurate kicking against the Welsh, I had played well in our three games. This was largely down to my temperament and the players I had either side of me. Basil's fast, accurate and long passing had me running onto the ball and taking on the opposition. Much is said of the importance of the half-back partnership, and rightly so, but for me, a stand-off's understanding with his open-side flanker and inside-centre are just as important as the link at 9 and 10. These were the two guys I looked to use if I was passing the ball or going for a break. In Ian Smith and Ian Jardine we had two excellent foils for an attacking game plan. It is amazing to think that neither Smithy, Jardie or Basil made it on the Lions tour a year later. They seemed dead certs after their perform-ances in 1996.

We knew that if we made as many errors against England as had been the case in Cardiff, there would be no chance of a Grand Slam. England had only lost once that season – a narrow defeat in Paris – and had a huge pack just like the previous year when we had lost to them at Twickenham. Jim Telfer's pre-match talk was much more low-key on this occasion, but captivating all the same.

He told us a story about how he had taken a walk that morning from the hotel towards the city. In the distance he saw what looked like a Saltire and thought it must be a proud supporter of the team. When he got nearer what he had presumed had been a Scottish flag, it was nothing more than two umbrellas crossed together on a porch. He had felt disappointed and cheated. He said that we too would feel cheated if we didn't go out and play to our potential and beat England. Our three matches had meant that a Grand Slam was in sight and it was now the moment to crown a great season.

Unfortunately, the game didn't live up to Jim's inspirational words. It's not often that an English side is criticized for stopping Scotland from playing open rugby, but that was undoubtedly the feeling as we succumbed to an 18–9 defeat. No tries and precious little attacking rugby from either side was on show. It was a poor advert for the game in the northern hemisphere.

That England were allowed to win the match by playing hardly any positive rugby was due mainly to the laws at the time. Our efforts of rucking to gain dynamic ball were penalized heavily while, on the other hand, the rolling maul, employed expertly by the English pack, resulted in them always retaining possession. Such were the now archaic-seeming laws in 1995, that whoever had the ball going forward, even if the ball was still off the ground, would get the put-in at the next scrum. It meant that England had scrum after scrum with number 8 Dean Richards – the most influential player on the field – picking up at the base and turning his back into us to set up another maul. It was dull, unambitious stuff and was the third year in succession that England had failed to score a try against us. But, crucially, it again proved to be effective.

Our fluid approach was the polar opposite and frustratingly before its time – but it would be foolish to say that it was just the laws of the game that had decided the outcome. We struggled at times in the set piece and also played into England's hands by kicking our restarts long, which went straight into the hands of Richards. I should have tried something different here, but I was more rueful about a sixty-yard break I made that ended in nothing. The score was 9–12 and we managed to steal lineout ball in our own 22. Smithy put me through a hole and I ended up very close to the English line. Frustratingly, England regrouped and our chance was gone. With it went the opportunity to win a Grand Slam. Our lack of clinical finishing against the French came back to haunt us as we ended up missing out on the championship title on points difference.

As irony would have it, our next two Test matches were to be played under new laws designed to open up the game more. Now, if the ball remained in a ruck or maul situation, it would be turned over to the opposition, unless it had made it to the floor. Even if the rules hadn't changed it wouldn't really have affected the approach of our next opponents – they had no desire to resort to a ponderous mauling style of play. We were about to embark on a tour of New Zealand and it would be a much better gauge of how far we had come since the beginning of the year.

The tour was a fantastic experience – the first time I'd visited New Zealand. The people were very serious and knowledgeable about their rugby and it was a place where you really had to excel to earn respect. I had arrived in the country after my best season at club and international level, but it was the month spent in New Zealand that I felt I showed what I was capable of. It was also here, playing against stand-off Andrew Mehrtens and centres like Walter Little and Frank Bunce, that I knew I had a great deal more to learn and work on if I was ever to get to their level.

If Australian culture is defined by sport, then in New Zealand the defining characteristic is rugby. Today, an estimated 317,000 play the game – that's approximately one in four of all males aged between fifteen and thirty-four. The All Black jersey is revered as the ultimate symbol of achievement for any New Zealander (or Fijian, Tongan and Samoan for that matter) and the depth of world-class players in the country is immense. In Michael Jones, Josh Kronfeld and Richie McCaw the country has produced the game's three best openside flankers of the past twenty years. Also, no nation possesses half as many quality, defence-breaking backs as New Zealand. I have played alongside three outstanding New Zealand centres – Tabai Matson at Brive, Norm Berryman at Castres and John Leslie with Scotland – all of whom were deemed not up to the requisite standards by the All Black coaches.

Although we'd had a terrific Five Nations, we knew that winning in New Zealand was going to be much more difficult. The inaugural Super 12 had begun three months previously and was already setting a new benchmark for attacking rugby, certainly in comparison to the northern hemisphere. There were some cynics in the British media who described the Super 12 as 'glorified basketball' and said it lacked a physical dimension. We were aware that this was nonsense and that the rugby players of the southern hemisphere were once again setting the course for where the future of the game was heading.

We gained respect from the locals for our attacking play in the early stages of the tour, but our inability to finish off some great build-up work against Waikato saw us lose out 39–35. Just as in the French match earlier in the season, we spurned at least three – it seemed – certain try-scoring chances. There was no way we should have lost the match, and the dubious try the home side scored in injury time merely rubbed salt in the wound. Despite the defeat, I'd made a good start to the tour, captaining the team against Wanganui and then playing my best game of the season against Waikato. Next up was the First Test at Dunedin.

The All Blacks were widely regarded as the best team on the planet at the time (when are they not?) and had even upped their game from the World Cup the year before. I think if we'd been told before the match that we would go on to restrict Jonah Lomu to just one try, we would have been quietly pleased. However, as Rob Wainwright so adroitly put it afterwards, 'Lomu is the devil we know. Cullen is the devil we're learning about.'

Full-back Christian Cullen, a devastating counter-attacker and supremely balanced runner, ran in for four tries in what was only his second cap. In his Test debut, the week before against Samoa, he had scored a hat-trick. This was some feat for the man known as the 'Paekakariki Express' (which must be a mouthful to say after a few beers). Cullen later went on to smash try-scoring records in the Super 12 and the Tri-Nations.

We did some record-breaking of our own at Dunedin – the thirty-one points we posted was the most the All Blacks had ever conceded in a Test match. Unfortunately, they racked up sixty-one points to comfortably win the match. It was a far cry from the tryless Calcutta Cup match. The new laws – which also decreed that flankers had to stay bound to the scrum – had helped unblock play, but it was really the attacking attitudes of both teams that created such an open game. The All Blacks were just a lot better than us at converting their chances.

The following week, it was a much more compressed Test match – a consequence of the torrential rain that fell at Auckland's Eden Park. We played into a howling gale in the first half and showed tremendous pride and determination to only be trailing 17–7 at the break. It could have been much closer as I was denied a try after a chip ahead, even though television replays showed I'd got to the ball just before Zinzan Brooke. Nevertheless, as we formed a huddle before the beginning of the second half there was an air of excitement building within the squad – we all believed we were going to be the first ever Scottish side to beat the All Blacks.

That we didn't achieve this was largely due to the powerful New Zealand scrum and their aggressive defensive line. Also, I didn't help our cause with my first action of the second half. My restart kick was carried over the dead-ball line by the strong wind, giving New Zealand an immediate respite from the deteriorating conditions and a chance to attack our scrum once again. We lost the match 36–12. I learned a lot that day about stand-off play from the imperturbable Andrew Mehrtens. He varied his alignment much better than me – I was lying too flat at times off slow ball – and he showed that to kick under pressure, you have to keep your arms stretched out in front of you. Although I had edged him in terms of attack in the First Test, I had much work to do in order to be able to control a game as well as he did. I was hoping the challenge of playing in the Premiership with Northampton would provide me with the ideal opportunity to do this.

However, my plans for the following season were put on hold when I received a phone call from the chief executive of Leicester Tigers, Peter Wheeler. He said he would like to meet – and that Leicester were very keen to have me as their new fly-half. As I was yet to sign a contract at Northampton, I thought there would be no harm in listening to what they had to say, so we arranged to meet in a conference room in a motorway service station midway between Northampton and Leicester.

Leicester were represented by Wheeler, coach Ian Smith and England and Leicester number 8 Dean Richards. The financial package they offered me was around 50 per cent more than what was on the table at Northampton, but that wasn't the thing I found most tempting. What really inter-

Left Me aged 18 months, a bit grumpy at having to wear blue dungarees.

Below Aged two, with my brother Craig.

Above An early family holiday by the seaside on the east coast of Scotland – notice the cool flares on my mum and dad!

Right A chunky Toony looking happy with life, aged three.

Right Trying to side-foot it over the bar at the Dunbar Under-9 mini-rugby tournament.

Left Starting to enjoy taking on the opposition with ball in hand, at the same tournament.

Right After persuading my folks that I was ready to play rugby at seven years old, I joined in with my brother's sevens team in winning the Under-10 Ward Sports at Netherdale. I'm the small one at the end of the back row.

Right The Galashiels
Academy Under-15 sevens
squad showing off their
trophies after a successful
campaign in 1988.

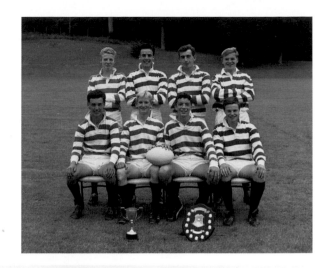

Above On this occasion I was picked in
my brother's sevens team on merit. At
fifteen years old playing for the Gala
Wanderers, I felt comfortable going up
against the older boys.

Left Being presented with a kitbag by
Sean Lineen for making the Scottish Schools
side in 1989. Sean has put in a lot of hard
work over the years to help Scottish rugby.

My first outing for Gala came at the age of 17 at the Kelso Sevens. It was a great experience even though we lost out in the final.

Right A nervous smile as I take to the saddle for the first time in my life while touring Australia with Scotland in 1992.

Below Stuart Bennet (Benzo) and I celebrate winning the Bayfield Cup with Warringah – after beating our rivals Manly in 1993.

Left Warringah captain Rob Blyth alongside Benzo and me at a rugby league game up in Newcastle, NSW.

Above Graduation day at Edinburgh University.

Left Lining up at Cardiff Arms Park – my first start for Scotland, 1994.

Above Looking happy with my Gala colleagues, Chris Dalgleish and Mike Dods, before setting off to Argentina in 1994. I wasn't smiling come the end of the tour though.

This was a change from those who believed that I gave my own team-mates heart attacks whenever I got the ball! Unfortunately, my weekend's work was all to no avail as I was once more selected at inside-centre for the first match of the Five Nations, at home to Wales. We were seriously outplayed and lost 34–19 to a much more enterprising Welsh side.

There was a clamour in the media for bringing in new players for our next match away to England, as our A team had hammered the Welsh 56–11. The selectors responded by making wholesale changes. Bryan Redpath and myself were reunited at half-back, Ronnie Eriksson won his third cap at inside-centre and Tony Stanger was brought in for his first start at outside-centre. Talk about a knee-jerk reaction. With our front-row of Tom Smith, Graham Ellis and Mattie Stewart only having three caps between them, it was suggested that our team had a look of lambs to the slaughter about it. Nevertheless, I was really pleased by the selectors' boldness. This wasn't just the fact that I was back at stand-off, but that the team had more ball players than before. Our game plan was to keep the ball alive and away from the touchlines, as we didn't want the huge English pack to get any easy starting points.

I was convinced that we had the right game plan – our previous two games against England had seen them dominate possession and we had created few try-scoring chances. We hadn't won at Twickenham since 1983 so it would have been foolish not to try something different. As with any strategy that involves taking risks, not everything will come off and mistakes will inevitably be made. This was exacerbated by my determination to prove to everybody that I was the right man for the number 10 jersey. It clearly wasn't the way forward and, in trying to force things, I made too many errors.

However, there was no denying that we opened up the English defence at times. I made a clean break from a midfield scrum and later Ronnie Eriksson ran in for a try after some good handling between forwards and backs. But for two controversial decisions from referee Paddy O'Brien, we could have ended the first half with a comfortable lead. Rob Wainwright had squeezed through a ruck near the English line to score what seemed like a perfectly legitimate try. To be fair to O'Brien, he wasn't allowed to use a television match official in those days and hadn't seen Rob place the ball over the try-line. Having said that, his decision to award England a penalty try late on in the first half was outrageous.

With England more than ten metres from our line, they tried to attack out wide. Before we could put in a tackle, O'Brien had already blown his whistle and was running towards our posts signalling a penalty try. We were astonished. He told Rob that he was forced into the decision because we had come up offside in the backs. This, itself, was debatable, but how does being offside mean that England would definitely have scored a try? From a position of strength we found ourselves trailing 16–10 at half-time. We never recovered and England's pack overpowered us in the final quarter, sending us home with a 41–13 defeat.

My game had certainly lacked control, but I knew it would improve the more I got used to playing stand-off again. Regrettably, I wasn't given another opportunity. Although the pack was left completely unchanged for our next game against Ireland, the selectors picked a revamped midfield. Craig Chalmers was recalled at stand-off, I was moved to inside-centre, and Alan Tait – recently returned from rugby league – was in at outside-centre. It was clear who was being made the scapegoats for the Twickenham loss. The coaches criticized my performance in the press and even distanced themselves from the attacking game plan we had used. I think it was around this time that I was no longer named as vice-captain. In fact, for the rest of my career I never regained the captaincy or the role of vice-captain. Nothing was ever said to me as to why this was the case but, together with being shifted around the backline, I was left utterly deflated.

We bounced back with a 38–10 home win over Ireland, but later crashed to a 47–20 defeat against the French. The match in Paris was another chance for the management to give me the brush-off. After Craig Chalmers went off injured, the coaches turned to replacement Duncan Hodge to play stand-off instead of moving me from inside-centre. It had been a disappointing Five Nations, and not just on a personal level. We had lost all the momentum we had built up the year before and it seemed that we had lost a great deal of respect as well. With only nine players in the initial Lions squad, we had the lowest representation from the four countries. (So much for the English journalist who had wanted all of our starting fifteen from the previous season in the final tour party!) Even though I'd played reasonably well at centre against Ireland, I knew there were a number of better centres than me in line for tour places. I was getting increasingly concerned that having only played one international match at stand-off in the previous twelve months might count against me.

I spoke to Geech at the after-match dinner following Scotland's last home game against Ireland. It was ironic that we discussed my concerns about my international career in Edinburgh, even though I saw him every day at Northampton. He could tell that I was somewhat apprehensive regarding the announcement of the Lions squad, which was now only a month away. Geech said that the Lions management knew what I was capable of in the number 10 jersey if I was given the chance of playing there. The glint in his eye suggested that I would make the final squad, but I wasn't going to take anything for granted. Besides, events over the final month of the season didn't put me at ease either.

First of all I had picked up a neck injury, which became more and more of a problem. I had a sensation like an electric shock going all the way down my arm whenever I was tackled with my back turned to the opposition – an impairment known as a 'stinger'. I kept on playing for Northampton, as the pain eased in a matter of minutes, but I knew there was bound to be some nerve damage in my neck. Geech's actions at the club weren't really filling me with too much confidence either. Even with Paul Grayson out injured, I was still being selected at outside-centre. In the *Daily Telegraph*, Stuart Barnes cheekily said that the front-runner for the number 10 Lions Test jersey was the third-choice number 10 at Northampton.

It was with a mixture of relief and joy that my name was among the thirty-five chosen. All five Northampton players selected – Matt Dawson, Tim Rodber, Paul Grayson, Nick Beal and myself – were informed at the club on the morning of the official announcement. Being selected for the Lions is the ultimate achievement for any international player from Scotland, England, Ireland and Wales. There is a magic quality about the Lions that captivates both players and supporters alike. Because the best of Britain and Ireland only come together every four years it makes it even more special. And it turned out to be a very special experience for all of us.

CHAPTER 7

Pride of Lions

*There's no limit to what a man can do or where he can go
if he doesn't mind who gets the credit.*

Ronald Reagan

*With the scores tied at 15–15, I could hear Neil Jenkins calling for me
to go for a drop-goal. As we entered the dying minutes, three points
would have been enough to win the match and the series. I turned my
head to take a look up at the goalposts, then watched as the Lions
forward pack drove deeper into the Springbok 22. Suddenly I noticed
a better opportunity had presented itself. Our forwards worked South
Africa so hard that their entire back-row were forced to join the
maul. And for a precious few seconds there was a space between the
maul and my opposite number, Henry Honiball.*

*As I advanced to a flat position I screamed for the ball. My two
Northampton colleagues, Tim Rodber and Matt Dawson, reacted brilliantly. First Tim held onto Andre Venter who was desperately trying
to leave the maul to plug the hole in the defensive wall (Tim got a nice
black eye from Venter for his troubles). Matt Dawson sent out a pass
as soon he could and, with the try-line less than ten metres away, I
surged onto the ball.*

*The South Africans countered the threat as best they could, scram-
bling back in defence. Because I had made it over the gainline, their
tackles weren't as effective as they would have wished and I was able
to stay on my feet. I could see the try-line, now only a few steps away.
I had to make a quick decision whether to go for it and risk losing the*

ball or to set up a ruck very close to the Springbok line. In the past there would have been only one solution: the higher risk option. This time I chose to go to ground, narrowly avoiding a late arriving South African forward. I was relieved to see Matt get his hands on the ball.

Relief turned to ecstasy as Jeremy Guscott had moved into the stand-off position and, from Matt's quick feed, he struck the sweetest drop-goal I have ever seen. It wasn't a difficult kick, but at that moment it meant everything. We were within touching distance of a 2–0 Series win. Our supporters were going wild but we knew we had to defend for another couple of minutes at least. From the kick-off South Africa won the ball back almost immediately and started to lay siege to our defensive line. Time and again they battered away but we managed to stand firm even though the Springboks kept recycling possession. Honiball had been the closest to breaching our defence but he could no longer see a way through. He decided that an up-and-under would settle the finale to what had been a pulsating match.

Honiball's last throw of the dice was similar to a 'Hail Mary pass' in American Football – a high hanging ball that puts its trust in luck (or, as the name suggests, divine intervention) for a positive result. Despite it being a desperate action, when Jenks fumbled his steepling kick it looked like being an inspired decision. Fortunately Austin Healy, who had just replaced Alan Tait, came from nowhere to safely touch down for a 22-m drop-out.

As Jenks was preparing to take the restart, the referee told us that he would blow the final whistle at the next stoppage. Martin Johnson had instructed Jenks to send it deep into opposition territory, but Scott Gibbs and myself were pleading with him to kick it straight out and thus end the game. This he did but for a few seconds there was no noise from referee Didier Méné. As both sets of forwards started to run back for a scrum, I bet Johnno was livid. However, he must have been delighted that Jenks hadn't followed his instructions when Méné – clearly a keen student of the dramatic pause – at last blew for the end of the match.

We were in delirium. It was undoubtedly the best sensation I had felt in my rugby career. It was even better than the emotional win in

Paris in 1995. We had worked extremely hard for over two months to complete this Series victory. My mum and dad were in the Kings Park stadium and I was overjoyed that they were here to share such a proud moment. And as I thought of Claire watching on television back in Scotland, the sheer magnitude of what we had just achieved hit home. Amid the scenes of jubilation on the field one thing stood out for me – players were hugging each other and saying 'It's been a pleasure playing with you.' This sense of mutual respect and sacrifice for the team was the overwhelming characteristic of the '97 Lions.

The Lions tour was a fantastic highlight of my career. In terms of the preparation, organization and profile, it was rugby's first real professional tour. It was also one of the last true tours, the final hurrah of the amateur game. We had the time of our lives, and we won. We had coaches who were at the height of their powers and a sensational group of players – some of the best ever to play the game. And as Ian McGeechan said to the squad before the Second Test, we created something special; a bond that enabled us to become friends for life.

In the UK, even though it was almost two years since the IRB had made the historic decision to 'open' the game, a culture of professionalism was still in an embryonic stage. The southern hemisphere rugby nations reacted much quicker to the opportunities presented by the professional game. With the introduction of a Super 12 provincial competition and a Tri-Nations series for their international players, a chasm was created between the north and south. What's more, coaches in these competitions favoured attacking game plans, which made for some spectacular rugby and left the more adventurous Five Nations players like myself looking on with envy. In terms of skill, pace and physique, the players of South Africa, Australia and New Zealand seemed to be a long way ahead of their counterparts in Britain and Ireland.

Only two touring international teams had ever won a Test Series in South Africa – the 'immortal' 1974 Lions and Sean

Fitzpatrick's 1996 All Blacks. As well as being crowned world champions in 1995, the Springboks had beaten all the home nations comprehensively in the preceding two years and we were completely written off before the tour. Lions coach Ian McGeechan described what lay in front of us as the equivalent to playing ten Five Nations games and three World Cup finals.

The coaching combination of McGeechan and his assistant Jim Telfer was a masterstroke and a key factor in the tour's success. In fact, together with manager Fran Cotton, they were proved to be right about every major decision they made. For example, appointing Martin Johnson as captain might seem a logical choice in hindsight, now that he has since led England to World Cup success, but in 1997 it was a surprising decision. Phil De Glanville was captain of England back then and the front-runners were Keith Wood, Ieuan Evans, Lawrence Dallaglio and Rob Wainwright. I remember an article earlier that year in a rugby magazine even claimed that I was the clear favourite to be Lions captain. I'm positive my mum had written the story under a pseudonym.

When Geech eventually announced Martin Johnson as captain he said he liked the idea of someone with a towering physical presence knocking on the Springbok door before the match. If Geech thought he might have been taking a gamble he needn't have worried – Johnno turned out to be a superb leader. His physical stature undoubtedly served him well in discussions with referees, but it was his unassuming presence – which commanded unilateral respect from his team – that most impressed me. Perhaps it was because of shyness or his intended style of captaincy, but he didn't say that much before a game. I prefer this approach as it naturally allows other leaders in the team to feel more involved. Moreover, when Johnno spoke everyone listened as he almost always had something important to say. Ultimately, he was a captain who led by example, and his performances throughout the tour made sure that his team were right behind him.

Geech and the rest of the management were also inspired in whom they chose to become the latest group of players to have the honour to wear the Lions jersey. Geech said that his selection policy was to try and counteract the fact that the Springboks were the best defensive team in the world. He correctly devised that the only way to achieve that was to choose players who were both thinkers and decision-makers, who could react to each other's actions and to what was in front of them. His choices for the final Lions squad included a number of surprises.

The rugby media mainly concentrated on the exclusions of those who had played for England in the Five Nations. This didn't mean that there was a dearth of English players as they contributed eighteen out of the thirty-five touring party. England's centre pairing of Will Carling and Phil De Glanville had been overlooked for Jerry Guscott and uncapped Will Greenwood. Both Matt Dawson and Neil Back had been picked even though they weren't deemed good enough for that season's English team. A general theme had been established: players renowned for their attacking abilities were to become the feature of the '97 Lions.

It was disappointing to see only five Scots in the final squad, given that the season before we had nearly won a Grand Slam playing the expansive rugby that Geech now wanted to develop in South Africa. I felt Bryan Redpath especially would have been a huge asset to the squad. As the tour went on to prove, players from the Celtic nations raise their level of performance when in the exalted company of other quality players. It is easy to get dragged into the notion that if England win a Five Nations then all their players must be of an equal standard and thus of Lions quality. While this is true in a number of cases, many players from Scotland, Ireland and Wales would be transformed given better ball and more intuitive team-mates. As it turned out, four out of the five Scots chosen played Test match rugby (with Doddie Weir having to leave the tour because of injury), while all four Irish players in the squad were picked in the starting fifteen for the First Test in Cape Town.

There was the same number of players chosen from my club, Northampton, as there were from Scotland. And Geech astounded many rugby writers by selecting the two stand-offs from the club side he coached. It looked like Paul Grayson and I would have to fight it out for the number 10 Test jersey as Neil Jenkins was listed as a full-back.

Geech is a coach who is constantly looking at the 'big picture' and is much more inclined to focus on overall strategy than working on individual skills. It was clear that he had thought out his tactics on selection carefully and it seemed that one of his main concerns was to make sure the '97 Lions would not repeat the mistakes of 1993, when the Test Series was lost 2–1 to the All Blacks. This was made abundantly clear during our first week together as a squad.

At our pre-tour base in Weybridge we spent a week doing all sorts of team-building exercises that helped the players get to know one another better. I tried my best not to be seen always talking to fellow Scots or clubmates from Northampton and found myself striking up instant friendships with the Welsh players like Neil Jenkins, Dai Young and Ieuan Evans. As there were so many English players on tour it was decided that the players from the Celtic countries would always share a room with an English player. At Weybridge, I was with Tony Underwood, a great guy and like me a first-time Lion. We absorbed everything like eager kids.

We combined as a group to produce the 'Lions Laws' – the core principles for the squad. It seemed that at the heart of every resolution was the premise not to repeat the mistakes that were made by the Lions in 1993. Both management and players were steadfast in their belief that there would not be a split between the midweek and the Saturday teams. There were guidelines about dress codes, punctuality and team selection – all designed to keep a hugely competitive squad a tight-knit group.

Players usually describe professionalism as meaning everything is catered for so you are free to concentrate on being the best you can be. Already the '97 Lions were looking like a professional squad – it was the first tour I had been on where nothing was left to chance. In fact, I realized that this tour would be a step up from anything I'd experienced before. Our open day for the media prior to our departure for South Africa saw the hotel grounds teeming with journalists and photographers. It brought home to the players that we were a part of something much bigger than playing for our respective countries.

Having missed the 1995 World Cup with injury, it was my first visit to South Africa. The tumultuous political changes in the country over the previous two years had held my interest, but I was unaware just how important rugby was to the South African people, albeit mainly the white population. I was to be impressed continually by their passion over the succeeding two months. Every game was played in front of sell-out crowds in some magnificent stadiums. An incoming Lions tour for the South Africans meant a great deal and they were adamant that they would prove themselves once more as the best rugby nation on the planet.

We installed ourselves at Umhlanga Rocks, which was a twenty-minute drive north of Durban (seven years later this was to be my home when I played for the Natal Sharks). Our first training sessions at Kings Park were not unfamiliar to me as a lot of what Geech introduced, I had already experienced under him at Northampton. I relished these sessions as they entailed moving defenders and hitting the ball at pace – natural ball players stood out in this environment. I saw at first hand how much quality there was in the Lions squad. Perhaps it was because I was used to the training drills, but I found myself at ease working with such illustrious company.

In fact at training I felt my skills were right up there with
those of Jerry Guscott, Rob Howley and Ieuan Evans, which
did wonders for my self-belief.

   One element of the training that was new to the majority
of the players was the defensive work. This was to prove a
contributing factor to the tour's success, especially as the Test
matches were very confrontational. While defence is 50 per
cent of the game, and now forms a substantial part of training
sessions for professional and international sides, back in 1997
it was practised rarely if at all. We trained wearing body
armour and routinely our sessions lasted for more than three
hours, but the players adapted quickly and an aggressive
defensive structure began to take shape. In our first week in
South Africa, I remember vividly one training session where
Scott Gibbs came flying at me on a crash ball – a terrifying
sight at the best of times. Fortunately I managed to put in a
good low tackle that sent him to the floor. I realized that my
neck injury could no longer be a problem if I was able to
tackle the Welsh juggernaut.

Eastern Province (Port Elizabeth)

*You've got the jerseys; you carry the responsibility, you carry the
challenge. What you've got now is four countries playing as one. The
mantle you carry, and the challenge that you have, is to put a marker
down in South Africa about the way we can play rugby.*

Ian McGeechan (addressing the players before our opening game)

Sport is all about momentum. This was all the more true for
the Lions, as players only had a limited time to build a mutual
understanding and find some form. I was delighted to get the
earliest chance possible to wear the Red jersey and show what
I could do. Probably any fifteen players Geech selected would
have been an exciting mix, but I was particularly pleased to
be paired with Rob Howley at half-back. I was his room-mate

when we played for the Baa-Baas against Australia the previous year and since then we had got on really well. Rob was the ultimate professional and we shared the same attacking philosophy – as well as an addiction to wine gums. In my opinion, he was also the undisputed number one scrum-half in the northern hemisphere and I knew that if we worked well together we could be the Test half-backs.

In front of a crowd of 30,000 we started the match as if we had all played together for years, before a litany of errors punctuated our rhythm. In the first half we showed glimpses of the attacking rugby that Geech wanted us to play, but we were far too loose at times for it to be effective. Neil Jenkins and myself had some careless kicks that didn't help things a great deal either.

Just after half-time we went 11–10 down and with the home support sensing an upset was on the cards, we reacted by playing some scintillating rugby in the last thirty minutes to win 39–11. We had responded to the pressure situation by playing attacking rugby with a style that would be a feature of our matches leading up to the Test Series. Although the local media concentrated on our deficiencies in the scrum, I think the backs started to realize that we had the skill to match the best of South African rugby.

Despite being disappointed with some of my kicking, I was delighted by my running game, particularly as I had played only intermittently at stand-off in the preceding few months. On the positive side, I had been involved in four of our five tries, which was pleasing. In fact I had found things much easier than playing with Scotland. This was undoubtedly due to the quality of players around me. It seemed that every time I went to attack the advantage line Will Greenwood was on my shoulder at pace continuing the move. He had a great game, and scored a deserved try late in the match. We had combined really well and, inside me, Rob had been excellent, always giving me quick ball on the move. Up front, the back-row of Dallaglio, Hill and most notably Scott Quinnell was impressive. Mind you, our scrum and lineout performance had been as inconsistent as my kicking.

I was a spectator for the second game, which was a much less free-flowing affair. We managed to continue our winning start to the tour, edging a scrappy match against Border 18–14 on a muddy pitch in East London. Again, we were 11–10 down in the second half and this time it was sheer determination rather than attacking play that saw us home. Considering the weather and the winning margins, it seemed that out of the opening two games, most of the squad would have preferred to play in the first match.

Ever since our time at Weybridge I decided to make the most of the opportunity to work with our specialist kicking coach, Dave Alred. Despite his ultra-confident manner, which put off some players, it was immediately obvious to me that he was brilliant at his job. Together with Jenks, Matt Dawson and Tim Stimpson, we trained very hard – so hard in fact that I tore my quadriceps. This injury ended up forcing me to miss the final Test match. The pain in my thigh seemed worth it at the time, though, as my kicking had improved substantially under the tutelage of Alred.

Whereas before the tour my kick-offs were of the lucky dip variety, a change of technique meant I now could get greater height on the ball. I also became much more certain of where my kicks were going to land. My goal kicking improved too, and I found that I enjoyed the drills we were doing – not least because I was privileged to be in the presence of the world's best goal-kicker, Neil Jenkins.

I remember we did a goal-kicking exercise, which involved taking thirty-three kicks from various parts of the field. It was far from easy and I was very pleased that I had been successful with twenty-three out of the thirty-three attempts. Alred told us that the best he had ever seen was Rob Andrew who had knocked over twenty-eight. Jenks smashed this record halfway through the tour, kicking thirty-two out of thirty-three. By the end of the session all of the squad had gathered to watch this kicking masterclass. Jenks had such an accustomed kicking ability that he was unaffected by what he had achieved and was actually upset that he had failed with one attempt. His modesty was also evident in 2003 after he had been successful with forty-four out of forty-four kicks at goal for the Celtic Warriors. He said at the time, 'It is my job – it is like praising the postman for delivering forty-four letters in a row.' It was typical of Jenks – a rugby legend but someone who didn't take himself too seriously.

Western Province (Cape Town)

With 50,000 crammed into Newlands, this felt like a real international match. The stadium reminded me of the Arms Park, although the surrounding area was far removed from Cardiff, as the sun shone brightly over Table Mountain. With Scott Gibbs not yet able to play in a Saturday match because of injury, Alan Tait was picked at 12 and I was once more at 10. The Scottish selectors had never picked this combination for some reason and I was looking forward to playing alongside Taity. Having been paired with him at centre against France and Ireland a few months before, I knew his angles of running would be similar to Will Greenwood. Taity and I hadn't immediately hit it off since he came back to the Scotland team from rugby league, but on tour we became good friends. I was his gym buddy as I joined in with the weights and boxing sessions he did to stay sharp.

As a squad we knew this match would be our first real examination – Western Province were classed as one of the five best teams in the Republic. We were due to play the other four over the following three weeks. The home media were unanimous in their belief that it would be during this stage of the tour that the Lions would get found out. The Province side contained some well-known players such as Springbok props Gary Pagel and Keith Andrews, flanker Corne Krige, and three-quarters Robbie Fleck, Dick Muir and James Small. At stand-off was Percy Montgomery, the rising star of South African rugby.

The game was hugely encouraging – we despatched Province 38–21 by playing some excellent rugby. Most of the team played well and I supplemented my good running and handling form with a much better kicking display. With all the talk before the game focusing on Percy Montgomery, I took some satisfaction from sidestepping him on the way to setting up our first try. As had seldom been the case earlier that season, I was enjoying every minute of the match, and at times I had to pinch myself when watching the quality of my team-mates. Rob Howley, Richard Hill and Taity were class acts, with Rob blazing through the defensive line late on in the game to send Ieuan Evans in for a try.

However, as the forwards had again struggled in the set piece, Jim Telfer decided that now was the best time for them to endure some punishing training sessions. I remember going to watch the end of some of these sessions after the backs had finished our practice. Two things jumped out at me: first, that there was no way that any sane human being would want to become a front-row forward in the modern game of rugby; and second, it was clear that these Lions forwards would do anything that Jim Telfer asked of them. This showed how much respect Jim had built up since we had left the UK.

Before the tour I had heard from my Northampton colleagues that the English players wouldn't stand for any intimidation, as they were aware of Jim's reputation of being a hard taskmaster. I'm sure that Jim was mindful of this and he probably knew that the likes of Tim Rodber and Lawrence Dallaglio would have to be handled unlike any players he had previously coached. He also seemed to put great thought into what he said. You could have heard a pin drop during his speeches. He spoke differently to the Lions players from the way he had done to the Scottish team – much quieter but with no less authority.

One reason I think Jim proved to be so effective in 1997 was that he had been named as the assistant coach. The previous year he had been manager of the Scotland team and it seemed to me that he was much more at ease dealing with purely rugby matters. Without having to worry about the press and other issues, he became very single-minded in his aim to make the Lions forwards the best they could be.

Jim has a brilliant rugby mind and has always been a totally passionate and enthusiastic coach. There were some who didn't appreciate his abrasive style but he has a charm and an honest manner that makes you want to open up to him. Later in my career his stubbornness and propensity to knee-jerk reactions would at times infuriate me, just as I no doubt frequently infuriated him. What Martin O'Neill once said about the late Brian Clough could apply to how many players thought about Jim: 'I've seen big men hide in corridors to avoid him. He can make you feel desperate for his approval. He was egocentric, sometimes a bully, often impossible but I wouldn't have missed a moment of being managed by him because, as a manager, he was magical.' After my playing days are over I am sure I will remember only the good times when Jim motivated me and was an inspiration to play for. The '97 Lions were extremely fortunate to have him on the coaching staff.

My clubmate Paul Grayson had to return home due to injury and Jenks was selected as stand-off in our next game against Mpumalanga. With his vast experience allied to his majestic goal-kicking ability, I was worried that the management would be impressed by his contributions in the number 10 jersey. Besides, Jenks was becoming my best mate on tour and I hoped we could both make the starting line-up for the Test matches.

The Mpumalanga match left the squad with a bad taste in their mouths as the nasty side of South African rugby reared its ugly head. Unfortunately for Doddie Weir it was to have dire consequences. A sickening stamp by Marius Bosman, which looked more like a karate kick, struck the outside of Doddie's knee as he was innocently standing at the side of a ruck. Doddie suffered a serious knee ligament injury as a result. Not only did he miss the rest of the tour – where he was in the running for a Test place – but there was a serious possibility that his rugby career might be over.

Despite this shocking incident, the Tuesday side carried on the high level of performance from the Western Province game, winning 64–14, with Rob Wainwright scoring a hat-trick of tries in the space of eight minutes. However, as the news of Doddie's injury began to sink in, there was a sombre mood in the camp as we got underway our preparations for Saturday's match in the traditional heartland of South African rugby.

Northern Transvaal (Pretoria)
My first ever game at altitude was memorable for mixed reasons as we suffered our first defeat of the tour. We began the match lacking the required intensity to win such a tough encounter. Whether it was because of the thin air at Pretoria or a general complacency following our great start to the tour is hard to say. Northern Transvaal had decided to take us on up front – and the performance of our forwards made their task a relatively easy one. Despite a well-taken Jerry Guscott try, we found ourselves trailing 25–7 just after half-time.

As a backline we hadn't seen much ball in the first half and, as a result, I decided to try and run at gaps if any possession came our way. Luckily the next ball I received was perfect off-the-top lineout ball, which Rob gave to me on the run. This had always been my favourite angle of running: trying to squeeze between the openside flanker and opposing stand-

off, who tends to line up to tackle the inside-centre. With
Taity again outside me in the number 12 jersey, a late dummy
pass to him was enough to take me through the defence.
Instinctively I veered to my outside to get to their full-back,
and link up with the rest of our backs. Jerry was spot-on in
his reading of the situation and as I got near the full-back I
gave him an inside pass and he cruised in for his second try.

Ten minutes later another delayed pass from me would
again result in a try. This time, however, it was for Northern
Transvaal. My interception pass as I was trying to create
something from deep in our half had me feeling what it must
be like to score an own-goal in a FA Cup Final. For the first
(and last) time on tour I had fallen into the trap of passing
into where there was a gap in the defensive line, and not
where my team-mate had decided to run. This is something
that I've tried over my career to restrict to the training
ground, even though I know in the back of my mind that if
a team-mate has also noticed the space then a line break will
be made.

Geech had said of me before the tour that at times I had
'become too predictable', in contrast to the general impression of most rugby people that I was a rather unpredictable
player. What he meant was that I would almost always try to
do something with the ball. I suppose this was a fair assess-
ment and it was true that playing a patient game did not
come easily to me. There had even been occasions where I
preferred getting bad ball from my scrum-half because it was
more challenging to try and make something out of nothing.

Having made the mistake that allowed Northern Transvaal
to lead 32–20 with only twenty-five minutes to go, there was
no way I was going to go into my shell. Perversely, there was
some part of me that enjoyed this scenario, having to both
chase the game and make up for an individual mistake. We
gave it a real go and once again our superior fitness levels saw
us finishing the match strongly. Jerry and Taity combined to

put me in for a try, which left me absolutely knackered as I had to run over sixty meters – playing at altitude really does push you to your limits. This try together with my overall performance left me reasonably satisfied with my game despite the pain of letting my team-mates down with the interception pass. We had come very close to winning and we were attacking right to the final whistle, losing 35–30.

With the benefit of hindsight, the defeat in Pretoria proved to have a galvanizing effect on the squad. It also brought home to the selectors that they would have to look at other options for the front five. Tour novices Tom Smith, Paul Wallace and Jeremy Davidson were the guys in form and had to be given a chance in the Saturday team. After the match Geech said that the way we reacted to the defeat and how we trained would determine how good a touring party we really were. For the next month our training sessions were of the highest quality and some of the rugby that was played by both the midweek and Saturday team after leaving Pretoria was sublime.

We moved from Pretoria to Johannesburg, the largest and most populous city in the country. It was here I found out more about the real South Africa. Johannesburg also encompasses Soweto to the south-west, a vast urban area constructed during the apartheid regime specifically for housing African people who were then living in areas designated by the government for white settlement. There was a request put in to any Lions players who wanted to visit the area and help out at a coaching clinic with some local kids. While there were only a handful of us that agreed to go, I was glad I had said yes. The experience was as memorable as anything I had gone through so far on tour.

Soweto has a population of a million people and comprises around thirty townships. Driving through one of the poorest areas of the world, where thousands upon thousands of tiny corrugated huts are massed together, was deeply affecting.

There was a stunned silence on our bus. Having witnessed this poverty, I was expecting discontentment and anger when we arrived at the playing fields right in the heart of Soweto. Instead we were greeted by smiling faces. In fact the day turned out to be tremendously uplifting. You could feel the hope and sense of community all around you. The assembled youngsters, some in their bare feet, were enthusiastic and eager to learn. We felt privileged to have been able to help them in some small way.

Our next game against Gauteng (the new name for Transvaal) was marked out as one of the hardest on tour and was to be played by our midweek side. Coming after the defeat against Northern Transvaal and a tour-ending injury to Scott Quinnell – a certainty as the Test Number 8 – there was a great deal of pressure going into the match at Ellis Park.

The midweek team's performance underlined the overall quality of the squad as they beat the Gauteng Lions 20–14. A combination of superb defending, higher fitness levels and clinical finishing had put the tour back on the rails. Jenks had come on as a replacement and knocked over some crucial kicks but the match-winner turned out to be winger John Bentley who scored an amazing, long-range, solo try. Bentos had turned out to be a real character of the tour, and although he only won three caps for England, his score against Gauteng was one of the abiding memories of the tour.

With one Saturday match remaining before the First Test there were many players pushing for selection. We all knew the starting fifteen against Natal would be an indicator of who the coaches wanted to play against the Springboks.

Natal (Durban)
The media dubbed the match against reigning Currie Cup champions Natal as the unofficial fourth Test and the massive home support at Kings Park were confident of a victory for their team. The selectors once again mixed things up – Rob

Howley and myself were now the only two players to have started in every Saturday game up to that point. Taity and I were the only non-Welsh players in the backline. Taity was moved to the wing to allow Alan Bateman to link up at centre with Scott Gibbs. I liked the look of our backs and was eager to bring the two talented Welsh centres into the game.

Up front, Tom Smith rightly deserved his selection as he had improved immeasurably on tour. His skills in the loose were being matched by some impressive scrummaging for a player with only two international caps to his name. Elsewhere it was interesting to note that there hadn't been any outcry from the media at the fact that only four English players had made the starting line-up. With Natal coach Ian McIntosh promising a fluid, fast-paced game, it had the potential to be a cracking match.

The home side started well and the match was played at a very high tempo. After twenty minutes we were trailing 6–3 and had to soak up a fair bit of pressure. During this period we had injury problems as both Rob Howley and Martin Johnson were forced to leave the field. With Johnno soon back on the pitch, we struck back. Keith Wood kicked ahead and I was first to the ball to nip in for a try. Our defensive shape was excellent and Natal were being tackled time and again behind the advantage line. Scott Gibbs was at the core of this aggressive defence and he was also proving to be a handful in attack, knocking Springbok prop Ollie Le Roux on his backside on one occasion. I remember Gibbsy joking later as we were watching TV back in our hotel that evening that it might be the CNN 'play of the day'.

Once more we had upped our game and it was our most complete performance of the tour so far, which augured well for the Test Series. We felt more and more in control as the game wore on, eventually winning 42–12. It was probably my best game of the tour and I even managed to knock over a drop-goal in the second half. I think almost everyone in the team played well and anybody who didn't get picked for the Test match the following week would have had to be considered desperately unlucky.

However, we knew that we couldn't get too carried away as Natal were missing their Test players and the following week would be a different game altogether. The Springboks had shown their power that weekend, crushing Tonga 74–10. Also, our victory celebrations were somewhat muted as we lost another key player, Rob Howley, who had dislocated his shoulder very early in the Natal match. To be injured only one week before the Test Series must have been heartbreaking for Rob. He had been tremendous so far on tour and I am positive that he would have been even better in the Test matches. I was so delighted by our partnership at half-back that I was seriously considering joining him at Cardiff the following season.

First Test (Cape Town)

This is your Everest, boys. Very few ever get the chance in rugby terms to go for the top of Everest. You are privileged. You are the chosen few. Many are considered but few are chosen. It's an awesome task you have, an awesome responsibility.

Jim Telfer (speaking to the forwards on the morning of the game)

After the midweek side recorded a 51–22 win over the Emerging Springboks, the squad was informed that each player would find a letter under their door by eight o'clock the next morning. Inside would be a note of congratulations on making the Test squad or one of commiseration. This was one of the 'Lions Laws' we had decided together back in Weybridge.

On any tour there will always be disappointed people when a side is announced. When dealing with highly competitive international sportsmen, it was necessary to make sure this didn't affect the harmony of the squad. Instead of the shock of a team announcement in front of the whole squad, what had been proposed was that each player would receive prior notification stating what position they were selected for in the team, or if they hadn't made the squad. This gave individuals time to vent their anguish in the confines of their hotel room. We had also agreed that it was up to the players not selected to congratulate those who had been chosen ahead of you. There were a number of players who struggled to sleep that night, as many believed, rightly, that they had done enough to make the Test team. I actually didn't have any trouble getting to sleep, although the movements of my room-mate, John Bentley, did wake me once or twice. Bentos left his bed on a few occasions to see if a letter had been placed under our door and ended up interviewing himself on camera out in the corridor.

As it turned out, the team announced by Fran Cotton to the players the following morning included a number of players from all of the four nations. There were three Scots (Tom, Taity and myself), three from Wales and five from England, but the biggest surprise was that all four Irish players in the touring party – Paul Wallace, Keith Wood, Jeremy Davidson and Eric Miller – were selected. (Eric was later struck down with flu on the eve of the match and was replaced at number 8 by Tim Rodber.)

Matt Dawson and I were chosen as half-backs and we were together a lot in the days leading up to the Test. The night before the game we were the last to leave the team room as we stayed up until 1 a.m. discussing tactics, playing darts, watching video analysis – anything to put off the inevitability of having to wake up on match day. Matt had played well on tour and had looked comfortable in the win against Natal. The South African media had concluded that the Lions would no longer have a breaking scrum-half now that Rob was back home, but I knew Matt was a very dangerous runner in heavy traffic.

With a 5.15 p.m. kick-off, the build-up to the game seemed to last forever. We finally turned up at Newlands to find that the rain that had been forecast had not yet arrived. We were soon aware that there were thousands of Lions supporters within the ground. As the Springboks sang their moving anthem 'Nkosi Sikelel' iAfrika', I knew that nothing in my rugby career would be as important as this night. I was going to try and enjoy it.

There wasn't much between the two sides and the match was evenly poised until the last five minutes. As expected, there was much more kicking than in any other game so far on tour. Despite constant pressure from scrum-half Joost van der Westhuizen and openside Rubin Kruger, I felt relaxed and had probably one of my best-ever kicking games. I was helped somewhat by Andre Joubert, the Springbok full-back, having an off-night. Our lineout, where Jeremy Davidson was tremendous, set a good platform for us to pressurize the Springboks. From this base we varied our tactics, either driving the ball forward or launching Scott Gibbs who was devastating on the switch ball.

Our defence really shocked the Springboks. On many occasions their key ball-carriers were floored by big hits. Tim Rodber and Gibbsy led by example in this domain. I worked closely in defence with our flankers Richard Hill and Lawrence Dallaglio, and I once even managed to knock back the imposing figure of Henry Honiball, the Springbok stand-off. In attack we were closed down throughout the match as the Springboks tried to negate our planned tactic of moving the ball wide. Nevertheless, their renowned defence was embarrassed by the dummy of the century by Matt Dawson.

From a scrum on the halfway line, Matt had called a move where he would break to the right and link up with Ieuan or kick for the corner. Honiball had followed me to the left but there should have been sufficient cover to look after Matt. His feigned basketball hook pass stopped three Springboks in their tracks and he strolled in for a try. It meant the game would go down to the wire. We had always finished strongly throughout the tour and the confidence we had built up gave us the edge going into the last few minutes.

I gave Gibbsy a scissors pass and he made huge inroads into the Springbok defence. Quick ball followed and two wide passes later Taity was doing his gun-slinger celebrations after scoring the match-winning try. Soon after, the game was over – we had won 25–16 – and the elation amongst the team and our supporters was unconfined. I wasn't able to jump for joy myself as I had just suffered a knee in my ribs (from Jeremy Davidson of all people), which had left me in agony. I walked off the pitch with James Small and I tried to shake hands with as many Springboks as I could before slumping down in a happy heap in the corner of our changing room. What we had achieved was phenomenal but I couldn't stop thinking that it would mean nothing if we didn't win the following week. I also needed reassurance that my sore ribs would not prevent me from being involved in the match in Durban.

Before we had time to focus on the Second Test, our midweek team had the unenviable task of playing Free State. Fortunately, the match at Bloemfontein was as stunning as the victory over Natal – in fact, it was much more impressive given that it was basically our second-string side that dismantled the Super 12 team 52–30. Neil Back and Eric Miller were outstanding and manager Fran Cotton declared the result 'one of the all-time great Lions performances'. Yet again, though, there was an incident that would take some of the shine from the victory. This time Will Greenwood suffered an injury that left him unconscious for over fifteen minutes. This was an extremely worrying time to be out cold. Thankfully he made a full recovery but he had also dislocated his shoulder, which ended his tour.

The fourteen players that hadn't been selected in the twenty-one-man squad for the match at Bloemfontein had stayed

behind in Durban as the spotlight turned to the all-important
Second Test. The nature of the win against Free State brought it
home to all of us watching the match on television that
anything was achievable if we wanted it badly enough. The pain
in my ribs had improved but I was now worried that my thigh
injury would stop me from playing again on tour. Luckily for
me the Lions had Scotsman James Robson as doctor.

James was aware how desperate I was to play but he also
knew that my leg was not in a good state. My main problem
was kicking, as that was how the injury had originated. I said
that Jenks could take the majority of the kicks to touch and
with padding on my thigh I would be able to last the full
eighty minutes. Not for the last time in my career, I was enor-
mously grateful to James for his trust and good judgement.
The Second Test became even more important for me as I now
knew that, no matter what, it would be my last game on tour.

Second Test (Durban)

*There are days like this when many rugby players never have it, never
experience it. It is special. These are the days that you'll never believe
will come again. But it has ... When you come to a day like this, you
know why you do it all. You know why you've been involved; it's been
a privilege – it is a privilege, because we're something special. You'll
meet each other in the street in thirty years time and there'll just be a
look, and you'll know just how special some days in your life are.*

*We've proved that the Lion has claws and has teeth – we've
wounded a Springbok. When an animal is wounded it returns in
frenzy. It doesn't think – it fights for its very existence. The Lion waits
and, at the right point, it goes for the jugular, and the life disappears.
Today – every second of the game – we go for the jugular. Every tackle;
every pass; every kick – is saying if you're a Springbok, you're dying.
Your hopes of living in this Test Series are going.*

*Go out and enjoy it. Remember how you got here and why, and be
special for the rest of your lives. Good luck.*

Ian McGeechan (two hours before the Second Test)

A speech packed full of emotion and intelligence and spoken with the humble authority that Geech has quietly projected throughout his coaching career. I could listen to a thousand other coaches and there wouldn't be another pre-match speech that would ever come close to these inspiring words – the squad was captivated before heading into the cauldron of Durban's Kings Park stadium for the crucial Second Test. We had all the motivation we needed to make history for ourselves.

With the huge amount of criticism since the First Test still ringing in the ears of the Springboks, there had been much soul-searching and introspection in the opposition camp. As a consequence, the South African game plan was a return to their traditional strengths, which meant taking us on in the set piece and contact areas. It was also soon evident that they intended to kick high and deep in order to target Jenks in his unaccustomed role at full-back.

The Springboks caught the first kick-off and immediately stormed up the field. The pressure they exerted early on was immense. This was just as we had expected but initially, it seemed like we couldn't cope with the onslaught. In defence, we started the game missing the same aggression as the previous week. Also, we weren't able to keep hold of the ball, either because we were kicking possession away, or through our own mistakes.

We weren't even very successful with the small amount of possession we garnered in the first half. Instead of hitting Scott Gibbs on a short ball, which had brought us success in the First Test, we were convinced that the Springboks would try to close down this channel of attack. So the move we devised was to pass the ball behind Gibbsy in order to give Jerry Guscott some space from first phase ball. This rugby league type move is commonplace nowadays, but in 1997 only the Wallabies had used it. Unfortunately, Guscott wasn't the right player to make the most of this move. Alan Tait or

Alan Bateman would have been perfect, but Guscott, who didn't relish taking on an aggressive defence, ran onto the ball too tentatively and was driven back behind the advantage line.

Geech later said that Alan Bateman was the unluckiest player on tour, although Eric Miller or Rob Howley might argue with him on that point. Alan was the only back (apart from Rob) who played against Natal and didn't make the starting line-up for the Test matches. After Ieuan Evans picked up an injury before the Second Test, the selectors apparently deliberated over playing Bateman at outside-centre and moving Guscott out to the wing before selecting John Bentley. That would have been my preferred backline. It would have meant four centres and two stand-offs occupying the six outside-back positions – a potent combination of ball players and decision-makers. With the excellent Will Greenwood being the fifth centre in the squad, this illustrated the high level of competition for certain positions on the tour.

Maybe the Lions players knew that we had finished every game on tour very strongly, or were genuinely taken aback by the rampaging start the Springboks had made to the match, but for whatever reason we were on the back foot for most of the first half. In attack, we weren't nearly ambitious enough until the latter stages of the match, which became more and more frustrating for me. I remember calling handling moves at certain scrums but number 8 Tim Rodber told me to kick downfield instead. Perhaps Tim didn't trust my game management after our time together at Northampton or believed that kicking would get us back into the game, but as we continued to kick away first phase ball it was obvious that this policy wasn't going to bring us success.

Geech came out with a brilliant line in the press conference after the match: 'We won it through fifteen-man rugby, it was just that we didn't have the ball.' He wasn't wrong. Admittedly, the Springboks dominated the early proceedings, but they struggled to breach the advantage line once our defence recovered the intensity of the First Test. We became stronger and stronger as the match progressed, inspired mainly by Scott Gibbs who had the best tackling game of any player I have played with. Despite this, the Springboks did manage to score three tries. However, it must be said that two of these were gifts, due to uncharacteristic errors by two of our ex-rugby league players.

Taity was the first guilty party. He threw a reverse pass to the opposition just after he had recovered the ball in our 22, allowing Percy Montgomery a free run to the line. His fellow wing and Newcastle team-mate, John Bentley, was at fault for the third South African try. Bentos had at times throughout the tour lifted the confidence of the squad by his self-assured nature and his conviction that we were better players than our South African counterparts. He had also displayed great attacking ability, scoring that remarkable solo try against Transvaal. However, Andre Joubert exposed the defensive part of his game by brushing off his attempted tackle to score in the corner.

It wasn't until Joubert's try midway through the second half that we finally had a go at the Springboks with ball in hand. At 15–9 down, we had no choice but to force the issue. By doing this we coerced the opposition into giving away the penalties that proved crucial to our Series victory. Legendary American football coach Vince Lombardi used to preach that the harder you work, the harder it is to surrender. We had worked extremely hard for nigh on two months – it was time for payback. And, even though my thigh was close to seizing up once and for all, it was in the last twenty minutes that I felt I could at last have some influence on the outcome.

Moreover, it was in the latter stages of the match that the influence of the leaders of the team, notably Dallaglio, Gibbs, Wood and Johnson, proved too much for the opposition. After we had played our way back to a 15–15 scoreline, Keith Wood chased down his own kick superbly and won us a lineout ten metres from the South African try-line. It was an unbelievable effort from a player whose body had been pushed well past its limits throughout the tour. Like many of the team, he was playing on adrenalin as the game reached its closing stages. It was from this lineout that Guscott knocked over the drop-goal that put us in the lead for the first time in the game.

The match winning three-pointer was the perfect reward for what had been a monumental collective effort ever since we had come together as a squad. What compelled players who were more used to playing against each other to work so effectively together was, I believe, the goal of winning respect from their team-mates. This is a sentiment that motivates all rugby players and is the starting point for any team in creating team spirit. I think there are four main components that make a successful team: skill, strategy, sacrifice and self-belief. They all need to be combined to turn a team of champions into a champion team. Team spirit is the glue that holds it all together, and it is what you rely on in pressure situations.

Former Scottish footballer Steve Archibald once said that team spirit is an illusion you only glimpse when you win. While it was true that the united harmony of the squad might have been disrupted had we lost some earlier games, the players worked harder to generate team spirit than any other group I have been involved with. With Martin Johnson leading the Saturday team to hold tackle bags every Sunday to help the midweek side prepare for their matches, and the midweek doing likewise the day after they played, it really was a total squad effort.

If we had earned praise for our attacking abilities in the games leading up to the Tests, it was our defence in the Test matches that won us respect from the Springboks, albeit through gritted teeth. Other factors were also important to our success. Our discipline in the Second Test, when we had to defend for long periods, was incredible. We were penalized only once in the second half. Also, the confidence that we had built up by playing some great rugby earlier in the tour gave us a collective belief that a Series win was achievable. Ultimately, though, it was an unrelenting determination not to be beaten in the final minutes of the Second Test that drove us to victory.

We were aware that our win in Durban was generating huge interest back home, never mind the reaction we were getting from the thousands of travelling Lions supporters in South Africa. Fran Cotton showed us a letter sent by Tony Blair, who had been elected as Prime Minister just before we set off to South Africa:

> On my return from Hong Kong I wanted to send my congratulations to you and the Lions squad on your magnificent triumph at the weekend. It has truly been a team achievement and every one of your squad can feel enormously proud of its success. The team spirit you have so clearly fostered is priceless on the pitch, as you showed on Saturday. Under the greatest pressure the team held its nerve and pulled off another stunning victory to delight us all back home. To the great Lions team of Willie John McBride of 1974 must now be added the team of '97. I shall be holding a sports reception at Downing Street later this summer and would be delighted if you and the Lions squad were able to come. Well done again. Now go and win three–nil. The whole country is behind you.
>
> Tony Blair

I missed the Third Test in Johannesburg, as my torn thigh wasn't able to hold out any longer. It was a pity – this Test was the only one that involved sustained attacking rugby from both sides, as the pressure to win was much less tangible. The Springboks salvaged some pride, winning 35–16, against a Lions team missing five players through injury who had played in Durban.

The 1997 Lions tour was already being called a watershed for international rugby in the northern hemisphere. Professional rugby had at last arrived and there would be no turning back. Once I began to come down from the incredible highs of the tour, I was determined to make sure that the experience would also act as a watershed for my career. Having played winning Test match rugby at stand-off against the world champions, I knew I had to be playing week-in week-out in the number 10 jersey.

CHAPTER 8

Recurving

Good judgement comes from experience, and experience –
well, that comes from poor judgement.

A. A. Milne

After my exertions with the Lions, I was forced to take some time off from rugby to rest my torn thigh. I had proposed to Claire in Cape Town and we celebrated our engagement by travelling around southern Africa and on to Zanzibar. The euphoria of Durban was still fresh in my mind and I found myself reflecting on where my career was heading. Despite playing in the two victorious Test matches at stand-off for the Lions, I had only been selected for Scotland at number 10 on one occasion in the previous twelve months. My club coach, Ian McGeechan, also seemed resistant to moving me from the outside-centre position. Something had to change.

I am sometimes asked, why the big concern over playing at centre? Well, there are two main reasons. First, I thought that stand-off was my best position and I believed I had the potential to be the best I could be as a rugby player in the number 10 jersey. Second, although I didn't dislike playing at centre and had performed well there in the past, I knew deep down that, because of my physique, there was a limit to what I could do in the role. I might have been wrong, but I saw a trend for more power and size in the position. That season I'd come up against some very strong and physical centres like Newcastle's Va'aiga

Tuigamala. The changing professional game meant that playing at centre seemed to be much less about creating things – my strength – and more about breaking the advantage line.

During the Lions tour, Rob Howley revealed that Cardiff were keen to sign me and that they knew that I wanted to establish myself as a stand-off. Cardiff chairman Peter Thomas was staying in the same hotel as us in Johannesburg and I met him in the lobby the day after the Third Test. He didn't want to discuss any specific details as he realized there was still a lot of celebrating to do, so we agreed to meet up back in the UK as soon as I returned from holiday. But this was not the only club that I was preparing to visit. I had already discussed my future with a certain Clive Woodward who had recently been named Director of Rugby at Bath.

Dear Gregor,
It was a pleasure to meet with you last week – bad luck on Saturday against Wasps.

I do not want to over-sell the idea of coming to play at Bath as I hope I covered all the key points in our meeting. To put it simply, however, it would obviously be marvellous for the club, the current players and our continued commitment to excellence in every aspect. I also think this would be a superb move at this time in your career.

Clearly if you want to play international rugby as fly-half, then you must be playing it week-in week-out. It is too specialised a position to be swapping and changing, especially at international level. As I clearly said in our meeting, I would never guarantee any player a position on any side. However, all I can say to you is that I believe your best position to be fly-half and I believe that is the position that would suit you best at Bath. End of story.

The potential backline you would be joining includes Nicol, Catt, Guscott, Adebayo, Geogeghan, Perry (probably the best of this lot!) and De Glanville. I passionately believe we can win the European Cup with our current team, plus three extra signings – I hope that you will be one of these signings.

I think you are a player who will play even better when surrounded by the best players in Britain. The challenge of a change of club, change of environment and change of coach is something I feel you will need and rise to, once the 'highs' of the Lions Tour are over.

The club is now putting far more investment into full time fitness, full time physio/medical, and an upgrading on our training facilities that will give all our players the opportunity of performing on the absolute highest level, with no excuses. Our aim is to win the European Cup.

Lastly, though I was pleased to see this was not your top priority, are the financial rewards. I am not sure what you are currently on, but your basic salary would clearly need to be substantially more than that. I have no doubt your earning potential from outside sources would vastly increase as a high profile Bath player.

No more selling! Anyway I do hope you give this serious consideration. I fully understand the implications re: Lions etc. but I would appreciate some feedback prior to departure so as we can look forward to the end of the Lions tour for further discussion or to leave you out of our thoughts immediately as time is of the essence for next season.

I obviously look forward to speaking with you again shortly and if you are interested it is important that you come down and meet with all the key people in the club including Andrew Brownsword (Owner), Tony Swift (Chief Executive) and Andy Robinson (the 1st XV coach), and get a real feeling for what the club is now doing.

Good luck in South Africa but I hope we can talk again prior to you going. Please do not hesitate to contact me if there is anything that you need to discuss with me, or in order to take this further.

Yours sincerely
Clive Woodward

I also think that the colour of the shirts at Bath will suit you as well!!

Woodward's enthusiasm and positive energy was infectious – I didn't think it would take much to be persuaded by him to move to the most prestigious club in England. As time was of the essence, I agreed to meet both clubs on the same day. I hoped that I would be swayed decisively by either Bath or Cardiff as I was certain that I had to leave Northampton if I was to continue my development as a stand-off.

My meeting at Bath started very well and I had discussions with their acclaimed fitness coach, Jim Blair, as well as head coach Andy Robinson. I was struck by the professionalism at the club both on and off the field. I felt at ease in Clive Woodward's company and his ambitions for Bath were exciting to say the least. It was obvious that the club would continue to be at the forefront of the English game in the new professional era. However, just before I set off for Cardiff, I was to leave Bath with much less encouragement than I had when I arrived.

Andy Nicol – Bath's scrum-half, but also my Scotland colleague and a good friend – tried to help me meet some of the key individuals at the club, and invited his team-mates, Jerry Guscott, Phil De Glanville and Mike Catt, to join us for lunch. Unfortunately, this trio didn't share Andy's own eagerness for another Scotsman signing at Bath. Perhaps it was only natural that they weren't overly enthusiastic – my arrival would certainly have added extra competition for a starting place in the Bath midfield. Maybe I read too much into their reaction – because at the back of my mind I was already beginning to search for signs that joining Bath wouldn't be a good move.

The reality was dawning on me that leaving Northampton for another English side would have been extremely problematic. My contract still had a year to run, but there was a clause that stated I could leave at the end of any season provided that I joined a non-English club. This was ostensibly to keep the door open for a return to Scotland, as I had originally intended to leave Gala only for a couple of seasons to gain some business experience in London. However, in the new professional era, returning to Gala was no longer an option. Scottish-based players were now contracted to four professional sides (Caledonia, Glasgow, Edinburgh and the Borders) and clubs like Gala had remained amateur entities.

As word spread of Bath's interest, Northampton owner Keith Barwell threatened a court injunction if I entered into an agreement with another English club and placed a hefty transfer figure on my head. Both Clive Woodward and Tony Swift insisted that they could deal with legal threats and were prepared to negotiate a transfer fee, but I knew that things could turn acrimonious between the two clubs – especially as Keith Barwell had announced to the media that any potential transfer fee was to be no less than £500,000!

So, after being impressed by the organization and ambition of Bath, I headed westwards to Cardiff. Welsh and British Lions legend Gareth Edwards showed me around the Arms Park and, during meetings with owner Peter Thomas and chief executive Gareth Davies, I was made to feel very welcome. The only downside was that there was uncertainty over where Cardiff would actually play. Political crisis reigned in both England and Wales, primarily between the national unions and their respective clubs. The English clubs had announced that they would boycott the Heineken Cup while Swansea and Cardiff were planning to leave the WRU and join the English premiership.

Despite these doubts, things felt right at the club and the possibility of linking up with Rob Howley was a massive incentive. Cardiff also showed they cared for my career by setting a maximum amount of games that I was allowed to play, in order that I be as fresh as possible for Scotland. Just before I set off back to Northampton, I made my decision. I informed Cardiff that I would accept their contract offer and would join up with them within the next two weeks to begin pre-season training.

However, on the train journey home, I couldn't help but dwell on all the good things I would be leaving behind at

Northampton – the terrific atmosphere at Franklin's Gardens, the warmth of the fans, the friends I'd made and, of course, my coach Ian McGeechan, who was in many ways my mentor for both club and country. Just as I began to lose myself in nostalgia, my mobile phone buzzed in my hand with 'Geech' flashing on the panel. I stifled the impulse to ask him if he'd added telepathy to his many talents. His voice was concerned and urgent as he asked me to come to meet him at the club that night. Obviously word had spread that I had been speaking to Bath and Cardiff. He asked me if I would give him a chance to hear him out.

Geech knew that following the Lions tour I had my heart set on playing as a stand-off, which probably wasn't going to happen if I stayed at Northampton. He had been pursuing my Lions colleague Scott Gibbs but had been put off by Swansea's demands for a huge amount of compensation, which perhaps explains the £500,000 figure that Keith Barwell had demanded for me from Bath.

Barwell was close to three senior players at the club who in turn had a strong influence on his rugby decisions. Scrum-half Matt Dawson, stand-off Paul Grayson and number 8 Tim Rodber formed a powerful clique and I knew that they were also pushing the club to sign Gibbs. I suspected that I was the expendable part of the deal. Obviously Paul wasn't that keen on the idea of me playing stand-off on a more regular basis and Tim saw me as an outside-centre through-and-through, even though I had played alongside him at stand-off for the Lions in South Africa. I never had any confrontations with Tim about it, but everyone at the club recognized he had a major say in team selection. As I was picked at centre on a regular basis, it didn't take a rocket scientist to guess his input on my best position. I remember on the Lions tour, after we had watched a video of the First Test, he had said to me that the way I was playing was so different to how I played stand-off at Northampton. He was trying to be complimentary, but at the time it just confirmed my suspicions that after two seasons at the club he didn't trust me in the number 10 jersey.

I arrived at the club later that evening, making my way across a muddy car park to Geech's office. The building, which was sandwiched between the main ground and our training fields, looked deserted. The only light was coming from Geech's office as the other staff had gone home a long time ago. I told Geech straight away that I'd decided to join Cardiff – he looked shocked and was obviously unaware that things had reached the point of no return. He then spoke with real emotion on how central he saw my development to the future of the club: 'Gregor, you know how I feel about you as a player – I want to build the team around you. And that means I want you at stand-off. We've signed Andy Blyth to cover outside-centre and, if needs be, Grays has the ability to play at full-back.' I nodded my head, trying to be as noncommittal as I could. Geech continued: 'We are trying hard to sign Gibbsy, and I know how you liked playing beside him in South Africa. With Tim and Daws inside you both, I think we can really challenge for the league title.'

I thought I'd prepared myself for this – I knew the club's best interests were his sole priority and with Paul still injured he didn't want another stand-off being unavailable for the start of the new season. At the same time, something was chipping away at my resolve and I began to question whether moving to Cardiff was the best option after all.

Geech went on: 'I see you're still not convinced that you'll be playing at 10. To prove it, how about I get Keith [Barwell] to insert a letter in your contract that states that you will be considered only as a stand-off?' This didn't feel right. I could never envisage putting my personal ambition to play at stand-off above the good of the team, but I felt Geech was now paying more than lip service to my desire to develop in the position.

After another hour or so of listening to how he now viewed me as the starting number 10 in his Northampton squad, I found myself being persuaded that the better option could be to stay under his tutelage for another season. I had much to thank Geech for as he had helped me reach the pinnacle of my rugby career by selecting me for the Lions tour. I realized that the final decision had to be made there and then – I put my trust in Geech and agreed to stay on at the club.

Of course, going home that night I knew I had just agreed to play for two clubs for the next season (even though I hadn't actually signed with either of them). The shame of knowing that I would have to tell the good people of Cardiff that I had changed my decision was weighing heavily on my mind. Things got worse when I got home to check my answer machine for messages. As I listened I could hear the soft Welsh accent of Gareth Edwards, who was once voted the best ever rugby player in the game's history: 'Gregor, I just want to say that you've made a fantastic decision to join Cardiff and we're all looking forward to you joining the club. I think next season we will now move up a level.' There was some muffled noise as he spoke to someone away from the phone receiver. 'This is what it means to your new team-mates.' The answer-machine's speaker crackled and distorted as it strained to contain a massive roar. It was the whole Cardiff squad cheering my decision to join. This was a wonderful touch but I was mortified that I would now have to go back on what I had told them earlier in the day.

Despite the bad news, Cardiff accepted my explanation with the decency they had shown me in all our dealings and were very understanding of my predicament. It had been a tough few days trying to sort out my future and I decided that it would be the last time I negotiated my own rugby career without an agent. I suppose in life everyone has regrets – I was hoping to end up with the right regrets. However, I can't deny that nagging doubts lingered in my mind as I recovered from my torn thigh to start the new season with Northampton.

As I'd feared, I was used only sporadically at stand-off, and with Paul returning to fitness less than a month into the season, I was back playing at outside-centre once again. Geech explained that the reason behind this was that the team had to include a reliable goal-kicker. I had kicked badly in our opening game of the season against Harlequins, but I thought he could have used Matt Dawson as kicker – he had performed well in that role when he had taken over from me. Paul's return at stand-off coincided with a run of victories for the team, so I knew this would be the preferred starting line-up from then on. I accepted my fate and never reminded Geech about the plans he had outlined for the side with me at stand-off. There was no use in expressing my discontent – once a season gets underway, individual concerns have to be ceded to a large extent for the good of the team. However, not being able to develop at number 10 as I'd planned convinced me once and for all that a move from Northampton was my only option.

I operated mainly at outside-centre and even made three appearances at full-back near the end of the season, which went much better than I'd anticipated. Geech, did try Paul at full-back on a few occasions, and I played at stand-off in our wins against Bath and Leicester. However, these were rare occurrences and as a result the confidence that I had built up with the Lions took a pounding.

I tried my best to look at the positives: at least Scotland selected me at number 10 for the autumn internationals against Australia and South Africa, which hadn't been the case the year before. However, it was getting increasingly difficult to play centre at club level and switch to stand-off for international matches. My disappointment at not being a regular number 10 at Franklin's Gardens translated into some distinctly average performances at stand-off for Scotland.

Scotland suffered three defeats in a row, including a record home defeat to South Africa. The last of these losses, away to Italy, saw the sacking of the coaches, David Johnston and Richie Dixon. I was sad to see Richie go as he really cared for the team and had worked wonders with a young side back in 1996. He also realized that Scotland needed to play a fast-moving game and hadn't been afraid to implement it. However, his assistant coach, David Johnston, was a burden to him.

Since my first experience of being coached by Johnston in 1992 it was obvious that he never really rated me as a stand-off. In 1997, while I was performing well in South Africa with the Lions, Johnston (Scotland backs coach at the time) proclaimed in the press that Craig Chalmers should have been chosen as stand-off for the tour. When he later resurfaced as a media pundit, he didn't waste any time before criticizing me. Even during our championship-winning season in 1999 he slated the selectors' decision to pick me in the number 10 jersey. There was an irony about Johnston airing his tactical views in a newspaper column, as he had spent little time communicating them to me when he had been my coach.

Johnston was a relic from the amateur era – which in itself is no bad thing. However, rugby (especially in terms of preparation and analysis) was fast becoming a science. Johnston had a laissez-faire approach to coaching that was by then an anachronism. On one occasion, I remember we assembled for a midweek get-together at Murrayfield where instead of working on skills or team plays, Johnston took the backs for a game of football. It had been a wasted journey for those of us based in England who had caught an early flight to travel to Scotland for what we thought would be an organized squad session.

To be fair to Johnston, his limited input might have been a consequence of the fact that he held down a full-time job as a solicitor. Perhaps, with his background in the law, he would have been more suited to a management or administrative role. It seemed that he himself would have preferred such a role – on the tour to New Zealand in 1996 he spent most of his time writing a paper called 'The Future of Scottish Rugby'. He appeared to enjoy antagonizing the SRU, and Jim Telfer in particular, more than coaching the Scotland backs.

Just as a new manager in football gets a result from players who had previously underperformed, our new coaching regime of David Leslie and Roy Laidlaw had the desired effect, at least in the short term. Roy, in particular was a breath of fresh air. He was approachable, honest and set out the areas I needed to work on while reinforcing to me the strengths of my game. He even worked one-on-one with my kicking and distribution after team sessions had ended.

Unfortunately, another Five Nations went by with me playing at outside-centre as Craig Chalmers was recalled at stand-off. We reverted to a tight game plan, which initially yielded some success as we sneaked a rather undeserved 18–17 win in Dublin. The win was what those in the world of commerce would call a 'dead cat bounce'. This is a description of the FTSE when there is a temporary recovery from a prolonged decline, after which the market continues to fall. Our limitations were badly exposed in our next game, going down 51–15 at home to a French side who themselves had lost 52–10 to South Africa two months previously.

We opened up our play in a cracking match with Wales at their temporary home of Wembley Stadium, but for all our enterprise in a closely contested game, we fell short, and our one-point win over the Irish was to remain our only victory of the 1998 Five Nations. I managed to play the final twenty minutes of the Calcutta Cup match at stand-off and there was some satisfaction as we scored two long-range tries in the closing stages of our 34–20 home defeat. This brief cameo, and the thrill of scoring a try on Wembley's hallowed turf, had been the only highlights of another frustrating season for me at international level.

It had been a long and unrewarding year. Also, my third season at Northampton had probably been the first of my career where I had seen no overall improvement in my game. Worse than that was the fact that from being Lions stand-off in 1997, the following season I was still unable to play in that position on a regular basis for either Scotland or Northampton. There were even sections of the Northampton crowd that began to heckle me as it became apparent I was set to leave the club. Changed days from when the fans used to sing my name (much to my embarrassment!).

My form was, at times, atrocious, but I toughed out the season, being an ever-present in the side. Sky Sports produced a table of British players who had played the most games in the past year. Lawrence Dallaglio was on forty-three, Paul Wallace forty-one, and I was third, having played forty games. It had been a test of endurance given that we had toured with the Lions in the summer. Also, the English Premiership had stepped up a notch or two in terms of its physicality. Newcastle – with players like Pat Lam and Gary Armstrong – and big-spending Saracens had changed the face of elite club rugby in England. It had become truly professional.

My last game for Northampton was an inconsequential mid-table clash with Gloucester. On a sunny April afternoon, I arrived at Franklin's Gardens with a heavy heart. In the changing rooms before the match I was on the verge of tears knowing that a wonderful chapter of my life was coming to a close. Once again the atmosphere within the ground was electric and I was touched to see that a group of supporters had brought a banner expressing their thanks for my three years at the club. Written underneath was the line 'Scotland's BriveHeart', a nod to the next destination for my rugby career – France.

At the time I was reading *Generation X* by one of my favourite authors, Douglas Coupland. In the book he coined a term called 'recurving', which meant leaving one job to take another that pays less but places one back on the learning curve. I knew I had to do some recurving of my own to kick-start my stalled career. There were many times during the season when I wondered what might have been if I had gone to Cardiff – playing at stand-off on a regular basis would have helped not just my development and confidence, but also my chances of playing much better for Scotland in the number 10 jersey. I felt it had been a mistake not to leave, but I suppose staying at Northampton opened the door to playing in France.

I viewed my rugby career as a chance to seek continual improvement. I had always learnt and improved the most when I left my comfort zone – playing a season of club rugby in Australia in 1993, for example – and I believed that the demands of French rugby would challenge me sufficiently to become a better player. Having made my intentions known that I wanted to play in France, I was approached by three clubs – Toulouse, Bourgoin and Brive.

The last of these three proved to be my most eager suitor and I hoped that moving to France would be the catalyst to improving my game and cementing my place at stand-off in the Scotland team. However, with French caps Christophe Lamaison, David Vendetti, Olivier Campan, Argentine Lisandro Arbizu and New Zealander Tabai Matson in the Brive backline, there were no guarantees that I would even make the side, never mind starting for them at number 10. In my mind, though, the worst-case scenario was that even if I didn't force my way into the Brive team, the experience itself would make me a better player.

It was hard to know what others really thought of my decision to go to France. My friends and family were naturally very supportive and they knew it was something I'd had my mind fixed on for a while. My team-mates at Northampton wished me well, but at times it was an uneasy atmosphere towards the end of the season. No rugby player likes to see someone leave their club and I began to get the cold shoulder treatment from some of the more senior players. Others weren't sure that I was doing the right thing. Leaving the confines of a stable and ambitious club to take a step into the unknown didn't appeal to many of them. That was probably the sentiment of my Scottish team-mates as well, but a year later, a number of them were on the phone to me enquiring how they too could sign up with a French club.

So many things about the move appealed to me: playing rugby in better weather in front of huge crowds; the chance to learn a new language; and experiencing a different culture with a renowned quality of life. Ultimately, it was the marked differences of French rugby that most interested me, primarily because I assumed that playing a distinct type of rugby would be both challenging and help broaden my knowledge of the game. The subtleties of Australian rugby, when I played for Warringah, improved my handling skills and enhanced my awareness of attacking the advantage line. Looking from the outside, the French game seemed to be unique in its angles of running and width of passing. By immersing myself in this, I was convinced that I could only improve.

In the summer of 1998, as I prepared for my move to France following my marriage to Claire, French sport was on a high – *les bleus* had just won the football World Cup and France were the undisputed kings of northern hemisphere rugby after securing their second Grand Slam in a row. Some of their play had been breathtaking, especially in their final away match of the season when they demolished a Welsh side packed with British Lions 51–0.

During the same period as the French national side's reign in the Five Nations, Brive had dominated European club rugby. In 1997 they had completely overwhelmed Leicester in the European Cup with an irresistible combination of power and pace, and they had been just as impressive throughout the following season. For the second year running Brive had reached the final, once more facing English opposition. However, an 18–17 loss to Bath had narrowly denied them the chance to become the only side to retain the Heineken Cup.

Conventional wisdom suggested that French rugby was spiced with wonderful attacking play but was let down by intermittent periods of brutality. Brive seemed to epitomize this reputation. The season before my arrival, they had been involved in an explosive match with Pontypridd. The violence wasn't just restricted to the game – later that night local police had to storm a café using tear gas to split up warring players from the two sides. Neil Jenkins had described the battle of Café Tulzac to me on the Lions tour as being like something from a movie – a Western set in rather more quaint surroundings – with chairs being cracked over people's heads and a multitude of bottles flying across the room. It seemed that while Brive had won the match, Pontypridd had come back to win the bar brawl. My new team-mates Philippe Carbonneau and Christophe Lamaison refused to elaborate on this – it was clearly a night they'd rather forget.

Just after I signed for Brive, Thomas Castaignède had his cheekbone broken in a bruising championship match for his team Castres. I was acutely aware that I wasn't just leaving the comfort zone in terms of rugby and language – playing in France would be more than anything else a test of my character.

My first weeks at Brive eased me into the vagaries of French rugby and also gave me a chance to appreciate the slow pace of life in deepest France. Brive-la-Gaillarde (to give its full name) is a town of 49,000 situated in the Corrèze, on the northern edge of the Dordogne – a picture postcard of the beautiful French countryside. Initially, I stayed in a hotel in the charming village of Donzenac, ten miles north of Brive, and, thanks to the wonderful cooking from the hotel's legendary owner Madame Salesse, I very quickly put on an extra kilogram or two.

Madame Salesse had a close link with the club – this was where we met for our pre-match meal before going out into Donzenac's main square for our final meeting with the coach. She had looked after many Brive players over the years, especially those from abroad. Throughout the hotel there were photos of Australian lock Peter Fitzsimons who had spent four seasons at the club, and Nick Farr-Jones who had been Brive's coaching consultant while he was working in Paris for a year. I understood why everyone talked so warmly of Madame Salesse, who was now in her eighties. I was pampered from dawn to dusk by her and she was upset if I didn't have three meals a day in her restaurant. She was very easy to oblige, as the food was exquisite.

I had tried to learn the language on my honeymoon, but my French was still very rudimentary when I joined up with the rest of the squad for our introductory *stage*, a pre-season training camp that every French team endures, usually somewhere in the mountains. Brive had chosen the medieval village of Saint-Flour as their base, which is perched on top of some of the highest volcanic outcrops of the Massif Central. Hard training in the midday sun was interspersed with canoeing and long runs over the hills. I shared a room with French flanker Olivier Magne, a lovely guy who was fortunately able to speak a few words of English. Nonetheless, it was difficult to get to know my fellow team-mates as I couldn't really engage any of them in conversation. In the end I found myself chatting mainly to Argentine Lisandro Arbizu, who, luckily, spoke very good English.

Although there were some forlorn moments in having to adapt to the language and new team, I had prepared myself for this, and knew that after two months things would improve immeasurably as Claire was due to arrive after finishing her law traineeship in Edinburgh. However, a couple of unexpected mishaps made me at times wonder if my move abroad was destined to be a disaster.

I had returned from a brief weekend visit to Wales for the wedding of my Lions half-back partner Rob Howley, catching the last flight to France out of Heathrow on the Sunday night. It was nearly midnight as I stood in the deserted car park at Toulouse airport. I was over 130 miles from Brive – and I was stranded. My car, a black BMW that Alain Penaud – the man I had replaced at Brive – had driven the year before, was gone. After more than half an hour of searching I had to admit defeat. I eventually asked a security guard. He shrugged indifferently and explained that it was probably stolen. 'It happens all the time,' he said. 'They take them to Spain.'

I had no option but to haul my bags over to a nearby hotel and dig in for the night. After dragging my reluctant body out of bed very early the next morning, I made my way to the police headquarters in Toulouse. Thereafter, I played a long, drawn-out game of charades in my attempts to explain my predicament to the gendarmes. I did, at least, manage to learn a new French phrase: *ma voiture est volé*, which of course means 'my car has been stolen'. Late in the afternoon I was informed that the car had been recovered – close to the Spanish border in fact – but I was never to see it again.

The club must have thought that it was somehow my fault as the replacement vehicle they organized was a rusting wreck that broke down at least once a day. This was some downgrade from the BMW they had given me when I signed. The next day I went to see head coach Laurent Seigne to ask him when I could get a better car. I obviously chose the wrong time to see him – as I walked into his office, his face looked like he'd just found a half-eaten cockroach inside his baguette. Later I was to discover that this was Seigne in one of his good moods.

'I see you like the French life, no?'

'Yes, it's fantastic,' I replied.

'You were not fat when I saw you playing for the British Lions.'

'Yes, that's right,' I said, wondering what this had to do with my replacement car.

'Now, you are fat – I think you are eating too much.'

'Okay, then. About this car ...'

He put his hand out towards me, as if to say that he wasn't there to discuss the car. 'You have to stop eating as much. I am not happy with it. You have a lot of work to do to win a place in this team.'

With that, he picked up the phone and dialled a number. Our conversation was over. I didn't bother bringing up the subject of the car again. You could safely say that my honeymoon period at the club had officially ended. I kept my head down as we prepared for our first game in *le championnat*, a derby match away to Périgueux.

During our pre-season games – against Stade Français, Montferrand and Italy – I noticed that Brive's playing jerseys were very similar to that of Warringah (white with thin horizontal back stripes). It wasn't the only similarity between the two sides: both had never won a championship final. With four final defeats, only two teams had been in more finals than Brive without winning one – Montferrand (seven) and Dax (five). Although the Heineken Cup triumph had given them something tangible to be proud of, there was great expectation that we had the players to at last break the club's duck in the French championship. To mark the new season the club launched – much to my disappointment – a new playing jersey. This time it was thick black and white vertical stripes, an exact replica of the Italian football team Juventus.

I was picked at centre for the Périgueux match and, probably for the first time in my career, there was no twinge of disappointment. In fact I was rather relieved to be in the number 13 jersey – the three games I'd played at stand-off in pre-season had been a struggle due to my poor French. Despite a frenzied atmosphere, the game was rather uneventful and with little of the famous French 'champagne rugby' that I had hoped to see. This would be a recurring theme of my five years of playing in France. We won comfortably against spirited but, ultimately, average opposition.

While I hoped that it would not be long before I was ready to challenge for the number 10 jersey, I soon found that being able to play in a number of positions was a common feature of French rugby. In the UK, moving between positions is often viewed negatively – and nobody likes to be classed as a utility player. At Brive we had a number of these flexible players, especially in the backs.

In fact many French teams have props that also play hooker or second rows that are able to move seamlessly into the back-row. Toulouse even base their game plan and recruitment policy on adaptable players. Jean-Baptiste Elissalde and Frédéric Michalak frequently interchange between scrum-half and stand-off and the likes of Clement Poitrenaud and Yannick Jauzion cover a variety of positions in the backline. I've always thought that we could better utilize our playing resources in Scotland by selecting our best ball players, even if it meant a change of position. It's plain to see that Scotland scrum-half Mike Blair has many qualities to be able to play at stand-off – hopefully he will get the chance to play there at some time in his career.

Whilst it is almost a given that certain teams in France do not lose at home (fortunately Brive were one such team), away victories were rare even for the top sides and, following our success at Périgueux, there was a positive vibe at the club. I thought I could finally relax and be able to show what I could do. This enlightened state of mind only lasted until our training session on the Wednesday evening.

I had discovered that training at Brive was very different to anything I'd experienced before. In general, coaches preferred to practise game scenarios rather than focus on technical areas such as rucking or body positions in contact, which had been the case with Scotland and Northampton.

Training sessions fluctuated between touch rugby and full contact – some clubs even brought in a referee to make it more realistic. There would be times where I made more tackles on a Wednesday night than I did during a match on a Saturday. The Wednesday training game after the win at Périgueux proved to be much tougher than our opening match of the season.

Going in to make a tackle, Christophe Lamaison had swung round accidentally (I hoped) and smashed his head into my nose. Through the streaming blood and wincing at the shooting pain, I touched what was left of the bridge of my nose – it had been a clean break. I was taken to see a doctor later that night and he tried to push my broken bones back into position. While this was a far from pleasant experience, I knew it had to be done as the nose would quickly set in place.

Unfortunately, when I went to see a specialist in Toulouse the following day, he informed me that my nose had not been properly set and that he would have to re-break it in order to fix it correctly. Words alone cannot describe what a horribly painful procedure this was. The doctor strapped me into a seat and then proceeded to administer around a dozen injections all the way up inside my nostrils – or at least he tried to. Each time he threaded the needle up my nose, I couldn't help but grab his arm to stop him going any further. He explained to me that the injections were absolutely necessary – it was local anaesthetic that would numb the pain when he set about realigning my nose later on. I couldn't believe that re-breaking my nose could ever be as sore as those excruciating injections.

I think I was close to passing out by the time I heard the crunching noise of my bones being put back in place. The doctor had been right – the local anaesthetic had made things better, but I wasn't convinced it had been worth it. He then pushed lengths of cotton up my nostrils – I always remember the French word for it was *le mesh* – secured the bridge of my nose with strapping and told me that I would be able to take the cotton out the following morning. That night, my eyes were watering and it felt as if I had a migraine such was the throbbing pain in my head. Unable to get any sleep, I went against the doctor's wishes and pulled out the cotton. Such was the quantity he'd squeezed up there that it took several decent yanks to clear each nostril. Removing *le mesh* had an immediate, wondrous effect – my headache quickly subsided and at last I was feeling like normal. The nightmare was over – or so I thought.

As the next day was Friday, I proceeded gingerly to the Parc des Sports to watch my colleagues at Brive go through their final team practice. After the team run, Laurent Seigne asked me how I was feeling – I was definitely in a better state than the previous day but I didn't envisage taking any contact for at least another week. So I was somewhat surprised and suddenly extremely concerned when he informed me that he had selected me to play against Colomiers the following evening.

He claimed he had played with a broken nose before and said I would be okay if I strapped on a protective cast. I thought that this would bring unwanted attention to my injury which might tempt one of the Colomiers forwards to break my nose for a third time in the space of four days. I said I didn't want any protection and, in discussing match preparations, I now felt there was no way I could call off the following day's game. Seigne was obviously setting me a test to see how much I was willing to invest in my new club. I was desperate to make a good impression so I thought the best thing to do was to say I was up for the game. Luckily for me my nose was only struck once in the match, and I even managed to score my first try for Brive in our relatively easy home win.

The French championship is not just renowned for its physicality but also its length. Today, with fourteen teams in the first division, it must rank as having the longest domestic season in world rugby. Back in 1998, there were twenty-four teams in the top flight – it was amazing they managed to fit all the games into one year. This huge number of competing clubs was viewed as a successful structure, as only six years before that they had had an incredible eighty clubs grouped together. And people say Scottish rugby has had its problems getting its house in order!

The twenty-four teams were split into three pools of eight with the top sixteen qualifying through to the next stage, which would involve four pools of four. Brive and Toulouse were the pacesetters in pool A and, as my confidence grew with the new language, I felt I was now ready to control a game from stand-off. The incumbent, Christophe Lamaison, hadn't been playing that well and, after six games in the centre, I was given the chance in the number 10 jersey in our home match against Pau. Despite having to adjust to the different demands of French rugby – the hardest of which was having to increase my passing length – after three months in France I was convinced that my skill level was as good if not better than that of my team-mates.

The atmosphere for the game was excellent with around 10,000 supporters in the ground – not too bad for a town that had a population of 50,000. A brass band set a pulsating rhythm, mixing traditional French music with other more bizarre tunes such as 'The Lion Sleeps Tonight', 'Yellow Submarine' and, most bizarrely, 'She Wore an Itsy-Bitsy Teeny-Weeny Yellow Polka Dot Bikini'. With the referee being whistled at remorselessly by supporters if any decision went against their beloved team, it was a stage not far removed from a Five Nations match at the Parc des Princes – an environment in which I thrived. It was with this self-belief that I took the game to Pau, playing my best rugby since the Lions tour. The crowd responded to some terrific team play and we raced into a twenty-point lead at half-time. Unfortunately, things soon came to a shuddering halt for me.

During the second half, I broke through the first line of defence and closed in on the Pau full-back Nicolas Brusque.

However, instead of taking him on, I turned to look for a support player, hoping to draw Brusque and add to our try count. I looked left and right but to no avail – no one in a black-and-white jersey was anywhere near me. This gave Brusque a chance to be aggressive in defence. He drove me back in the tackle and I landed on the ground with my full weight on my right shoulder. I knew immediately that it was dislocated – which meant an enforced lay-off of six weeks. Apart from leaving me back at square one with Brive and the demands of French rugby, this blow also left me playing catch-up to get back in time for Scotland's autumn internationals.

Uncharacteristically, a few weeks after my injury, Scotland coach Jim Telfer had told me that if I could prove my fitness then I would be selected at stand-off. In my desperate attempt to regain the number 10 jersey for Scotland, I made myself available for Brive in their European Conference game away to Bridgend. The match in Wales was only seven days before Scotland took on the New Zealand Maori, the first of four games in succession at Murrayfield. Although Brive had already qualified for the next stage of the European Conference, Bridgend outplayed us, winning 20–15. It had been a poor team performance and my own game was nowhere near like I had been playing before my injury.

However, I believed that my form would return as soon as I felt confident with my shoulder. I was kidding myself, but I didn't want to turn down the chance to play for Scotland and I was delighted to be picked at number 10 for the Maori game. After all, the selectors had been at Bridgend so were well aware that I was still finding my feet since my injury. On the Wednesday evening Jim Telfer arranged a practice match against Melrose, which took place behind closed doors at Murrayfield. Although he informed the squad that it was an opportunity to try out some new moves and structures, I knew that this was a final chance for me to test out my shoulder.

Well, I made it through the training game despite pain every time I put in a tackle. I convinced myself that this pain was manageable. Big mistake! My performance the following Saturday was well below par and it brought home to me that I was at least one or two matches away from full fitness – not something that I could hide against a team as accomplished as the Maori. We lost 24–8 and I had been substituted midway through the second half.

I was foolish to play in the Maori game. It isn't unusual for rugby players to declare themselves fit even if they are well below 100 per cent and there have been several occasions when I've played carrying an injury – I remember once when standing for the anthems before a Calcutta Cup game my neck was so sore I couldn't look over my left shoulder. But to go into a Test match having only played once in the previous two months was asking for trouble. Why did I do it? I can only think that having told the coaches that I would be alright for the autumn internationals I didn't want to let them and the team down, but I ended up letting the team and myself down with my performance. It was the wrong thing to do, but it is particularly difficult to make yourself unavailable and watch somebody else take your place.

Worse was to come the following Monday when the side was announced to play South Africa – I was dropped from the Scotland team for the first time in my career. I suppose there was a degree of inevitability about it as Duncan Hodge had played well as my replacement, but I still felt thoroughly disappointed. I had pushed myself to the limit to be available and had then been dumped after only my second game returning from injury. My disappointment was exacerbated by the feedback I received from ex-Scotland stand-off and backs coach John Rutherford.

I had enjoyed working with John in his time as coach to the Scottish Students and he had taught me more than a thing or two about playing number 10. However, on this occasion I couldn't believe it when he told me that it might be in my best interests to move somewhere else in the backline. Suddenly I felt I had become a bad player overnight – this was surely a knee-jerk reaction to a one-off performance.

As luck may have had it, it was not long before I found myself playing in another position as Derrick Lee picked up an injury in the first five minutes of the match against the Springboks. I came on for the first time in my international career at full-back and despite us losing the game 35–10, I had upped my performance from the week before. For the next two matches – non-cap World Cup qualifiers against Spain and Portugal – the selectors retained me in the number 15 jersey.

However, I continued to hear stories from others that the coaches thought I was no longer a reliable option at stand-off. I felt claustrophobic and angry by this sudden air of negativity surrounding my game and I longed for some positives as I returned to France. I should have known better. Following my poor display against Bridgend the month before, I was dropped for Brive's next few championship games. Unwanted by club and country, this was one of the loneliest times in my rugby career.

A couple of weeks later I was to get confirmation in the French sports newspaper L'equipe that the Scottish selectors had no intention of playing me at stand-off. Brive were in Paris playing Racing Club de France and I had been selected at centre. After Racing had dominated the first half, I was moved to stand-off. We fought back to win the match by a point and I had noticed that John Rutherford had been watching from the stands. I had been pleased by my game but it obviously hadn't been as impressive as I'd thought. John's quotes in L'equipe the following morning read: 'Even though Gregor played in two positions tonight, neither of these are where we consider his international future now lies.'

So, after playing in every championship game since my debut in 1993, I feared that the last ever Five Nations – Italy were to join to make it Six the following year – would take place without my active involvement.

After my performance against Racing, coach Laurent Seigne selected me at stand-off for Brive's next match, away to Bourgoin. The match was the semi-final of the European Shield, a big game for the club. I knew this might be my only chance to win back some respect and the coveted number 10 jersey. I was back to full fitness and I was extremely focused all through the week. I knew self-confidence would be a key factor in my performance. Experience tells you what you should do in any situation in a game; confidence allows you to do it.

To regain confidence, I've found that I need to get my hands on the ball, or more accurately, have the mindset that I want the ball to come to me as much as possible. Being passive merely allows doubt to set in. It is amazing how easy decision-making becomes when you want to be put in areas to make decisions.

At Bourgoin, I played my best game of the season, although we lost 26–23. Losing so narrowly was really disappointing but when I returned to the changing rooms, I was surprised to discover a celebratory atmosphere. Coaches and players were smiling – it was as if we'd won the game. I slumped down and must have looked pretty glum as my scrum-half Philippe Carbonneau came across to chat to me: 'Greg, why are you upset? You had a great game today.'

'Thanks Carbo, but we still lost. We could have made it into the final if we'd taken our chances.'

'But this a great result for the club, Greg. When we were here last year, we lost 35–3.'

While I struggled to work out how a semi-final defeat was a great result for the club, a wave of satisfaction began to envelop me – I knew I had taken a massive step forward with the way I'd played. After my injury troubles and the sometimes brutal introduction to my new environment, I felt like I'd climbed a mountain. And now it was time to enjoy the view that French rugby provided.

CHAPTER 9

Vive la différence!

*How can anyone govern a nation that has
240 different kinds of cheese?*

Charles de Gaulle

For lovers of good food, wine, history and culture, it would be hard to find a better place to live than France. It's not without good reason that it's the world's leading tourist destination. The excellent weather also makes it a great place to be a professional rugby player – it seemed a world and a lifetime away from the long, bleak winters of my youth, training on Gala's muddy fields. Moreover, as I quickly discovered, the game in France was far more popular and intertwined with daily life than anywhere in Britain.

Such is the dominance of rugby in the south-west of France that the vast swathe of territory is known as *l'ovalie* – the land of the oval ball. Starting along its northern edge at Bourgoin, Clermont and Brive, it stretches out to La Rochelle and Biarritz in the west, and takes in the Pyrenean towns of Pau and Tarbes as well as the Mediterranean cities of Perpignan, Montpellier and Toulon in the east. With the rugby-mad city of Toulouse as its focal point, I found that French rugby still thrived in the multitude of villages and towns that make up the *Midi*. To play rugby in France is to enter a different world – a world where tradition and violence collide (or more likely go hand in hand), where your own coach is often more dangerous than the opposition players and where smiling or singing can be a sackable offence.

In fact there are so many differences in French rugby that it is sometimes unrecognizable as the same game I'd played in the UK. Although often incredibly frustrating, I still found that the quirks made France all the more appealing. Despite many lows in my five years of playing there, I fell in love with the uniqueness, the colour, the passion, the traditions and the importance of rugby to the fabric of French society. I hope one day to write a book on the history of French rugby, which is rich in incident, anecdote and achievement. Until then I have compiled a rough guide to the vagaries of playing in France that will hopefully help anyone keen to sample a unique rugby – and life – experience.

The Backpacker's Guide to French Rugby

Learn the language

It's amazing how many of your new team-mates are fluent in English, but you will only discover this fact when your French gets to a conversational standard. The irony is that once you master how to speak French, they all want to speak English with you. It would also be best to learn the nuances of this wonderful Latin language when speaking with figures of authority, as I nearly found out to my cost.

In my second season at Brive I was named captain in our away game at Montauban. Early in the match I thought I should try to speak to the man in the middle (as captains do) after we had just been penalized. I was shocked that he took offence to my polite questions. Luckily my open-side flanker, Loïc Van der Linden, overheard what I said and quickly pulled me aside. He informed me that instead of saying 'Monsieur L'arbitre' – which means 'Mr Referee' – what I had in fact pronounced was 'Monsieur La bite'. This, I later found out means 'Mr Penis'. (I blame my mouth guard, but maybe I had made a Freudian slip in French?) Fortunately the game was being officiated by one of the few referees in France with a sense of humour and, instead of sending me off, he had a chuckle to himself.

Another language faux pas I remember occurred when I was playing for Castres – although thankfully it wasn't my error this time. *Spéciale* is a French word that does not have a direct English translation. It can mean peculiar or dodgy but we would probably use the term 'something not right'. What it certainly does not mean is the English word 'special', as Scottish winger Shaun Longstaff found out to his cost when he joined the team. He was asked to say a few words at a pre-season supporters function. Trying to remember whatever French he had learned at school, he announced that he was delighted to have joined such a *'spéciale'* club as Castres. What this translated to the supporters, players and management was, 'I think Castres is a pretty dodgy club.' He was surprised and disappointed that his first ever public-speaking effort in French was greeted with disdain from those present.

Learn the traditions
I've heard it said that politics is everywhere in French rugby, but that surely applies to every rugby-playing nation (with South Africa edging Scotland from the top of the list). No, it is tradition that is the distinguishing feature of French rugby. And the first tradition you have to get used to is shaking everyone's hand on a daily basis. If you forget to do this or, even worse, shake someone's hand for a second time on the same day, expect a barrage of abuse coming your way.

Another tradition is that every French club meet up at least seven hours before a match so that the team can focus as one – I think it was really so that the coach could control his players for as long as possible. There were even times when we would meet up at 9 a.m. for a night game. Killing time became the order of the day, which usually meant playing endless hands of cards. Of course, it would be a rather humourless game at times, as we were warned not to smile during the day.

Yes, being laid-back before a match is not encouraged. The look that Brive coach Laurent Seigne gave Olivier Magne and myself for giggling on a bus before a match was one that said, 'If any of you two even think about smiling again before a game, I will rip your teeth out with my bare hands.' Even in my last season in France, coaches were still taking the build-up to a game (and themselves) far too seriously. At Montpellier we were informed that in addition to being totally focused on game day, we weren't even allowed to smile the day before away matches when we were together in a hotel.

In my years in France I tried to perfect my 'game face' – a stony, introspective expression, along the lines of an anti-hero in a François Truffaut movie (something I inexplicably found easier when wearing black polo necks). At the same time I also worked on an insouciant Gallic shrug (pouting lips and upturned palms included), intending to convey to referees my complete innocence and incomprehension whenever accused of any penalty infringements. I am not sure I was ever very successful at either.

The enemy within – or how to survive the psych-up à la Français

By reputation, French rugby has a violent edge, but I had always thought that this was confined to the field of play. That was until I witnessed some extraordinary scenes in the lead up to our home games. The excitable Brive coach Laurent Seigne, like a bull in search of a china shop, took it on himself to 'motivate' his players. This usually meant he would prowl around the changing rooms picking a fight with anyone he met. Luckily for me, it was more often than not the forwards that he targeted. There were many occasions where Seigne and some forwards would be bleeding or have had their T-shirt ripped to shreds as we were being called by the referee for the start of the game.

Unfortunately, the fateful day came when I was once forced to join in with the pre-match psych-up. Seigne would often say that the centres had to be as hard as the forwards and decided to call over Lisandro Arbizu (my Argentine centre partner) and myself to join up with the Brive pack. We were then told to lie on the floor so the other eight players could carry on with their match preparations by running over us. When some of them didn't stand on us, Seigne would intervene and do it himself, telling the forwards to make sure they stepped hard on the two centres. Lisandro and I didn't know whether to laugh or cry.

On another occasion, Laurent Seigne asked us all to find a partner for tackling practice – just before we were about to leave the changing room to go out onto the field. Having recently recovered from a shoulder injury, I quickly tried to put on my shoulder pads. By the time I had done this, however, there was no one left with whom I could pair up. I looked around to see my smiling coach standing looking directly at me – Seigne stepped in to be my partner for tackling practice with worrying eagerness. He went back almost to the other end of the room to begin his run-up. As he was doing this I watched other players tamely going through the motions of tackling technique. Why oh why did I have to go and look for my shoulder pads?

As he began to charge at me I realized how a matador must sometimes feel in a bullring (except I had no cape or men on horses with spears to help me out). Amazingly, I hit him exactly where I wanted to, driving my shoulder under his waist and lifting him from the ground. This action had saved me from pain and also won me much praise and respect from my pumped-up coach.

This warm-up was tame, however, compared to the treatment our winger Pascal Bomati received before one game. I was outside at the time, passing with scrum-half Philippe Carbonneau, but when I came inside I noticed that Pascal had blood gushing from a head wound. I immediately knew what had happened. Pascal later confirmed my suspicions – Seigne had initiated a clash of heads that was by no means an accidental occurence.

I am relieved to say that I only experienced this anachronistic match preparation in my first season in French rugby, although I have heard that it wasn't confined to Brive. At Beziers the coaches believed that switching the lights off and on in the changing room just before the game sent the players into a frenzy. This strobe light effect seemed to have had some success, as Beziers dominated French rugby in the Seventies and Eighties. I have also been told that at Stade Français while current France coach Bernard Laporte was in charge, another interesting ploy was used to psych-up the players. After the team had finished their warm-up they returned to the changing rooms to find that the showers had been on at full heat, which created an area of impenetrable steam. Then the coaching staff apparently switched the lights off and encouraged the players to have a free-for-all to get them in the right mood for the game.

I had to laugh when I saw comments from All Black players who had watched the video *Living with Lions* (the documentary charting our successful series win over South Africa in 1997). They said they were very surprised by all the shouting that went on in the changing rooms before Lions matches in South Africa – they found it far removed from their own quiet, focused preparations for Test match rugby. Fortunately for them they weren't aware of what happened in the build-up to Brive's matches – I think that video-documentary would have struggled to get an 18 certificate!

While I viewed these match preparations as outdated machismo, surprisingly few French players seemed to mind them. In fact, I think many French players preferred that someone psyched them up for games. It wouldn't be unusual to see a few of the forwards so emotionally charged that they had tears streaming down their face as we left for the kick-off. In Donald McRae's *Winter Colours*, esteemed French rugby writer Richard Escot described why he thought French players have this different approach to the game:

> *You have to understand the particularity of French rugby. We need a tough warm-up – for we are like children sometimes. Perhaps, after all, French rugby is most reminiscent of childhood. There is a lot of joy in the play and I would say that most players in France want to entertain themselves, their friends and their family.*

It's true that French players are treated like schoolchildren at times and for a rugby nation that prides itself on expressing themselves on the field, individuality is not as encouraged as much as I had imagined it would be. Many in France view rugby as war in all but name, and as such the players have to behave as if they are in the army. When head coach Laurent Seigne was sacked at the end of my first season at Brive, he blamed the poor end-of-season performances on too many players questioning his authority. He said that in an army regiment, no one is allowed to question the leader and you have to follow orders. That was what we had failed to do, which he said was why we lost our last four matches, when only one win would have seen us qualify for the championship quarter-finals.

Professionalism has eroded much of this need to be dictated to, as coaches have become aware that obtaining knowledge and advice from players is a better strategy. Empowerment and collective responsibility have proven to be much more effective ways of getting the best out of a rugby team in the professional era. However, I have to say that I have sympathy with French coaches in their efforts at getting the best out of their players. Maybe it is a consequence of their fantastic quality of life or because, as Escot believes, they are like children, but the work ethic and attitude of many French players when it comes to training leaves a lot to be desired. The longer I played in France, the less I cared if the coach went a little bit crazy, as long as it had the right response from his charges.

French flair is a myth

Although it is undeniable that there are some incredibly talented individual players in France, very few club sides promote attacking rugby as a playing philosophy. The majority of the coaches in the club game do not adopt the movement, timing and angles that I associated with the French national team.

For me, the distinctive character of the French game at international level is one full of movement, intelligence and artistry, whereas at club level it is more often than not a hard-nosed approach based on physical confrontation and a strong set piece. When I joined Castres we had six international props and spent much more time on scrum practice and driving lineouts than anywhere else I've experienced.

Toulouse are a side that seem to have no restrictions on what their players are allowed to do, but this could be due to the fact that with a budget of £10 million they have so many wonderful attacking players. Yet, there is no denying that their side is first and foremost a physical threat to the opposition. This spirit of rugby being a battle – *le combat* – is what really underpins the playing culture of French rugby.

Rules, what rules?

The French believe intensely in *les regles de vie* – how a team must conduct itself, respecting the traditions and values that have been established over generations. However, just as French citizens praise the influence of a strong state, they are also ardent individualists, proud of flouting the law. In general, I found the French took pleasure in the fact that they ignored petty regulations like paying for parking, or restrictions on urinating wherever they pleased.

However, in a team environment, ignoring rules can be detrimental to a side's development. For example, no one seemed to mind if players cut corners during fitness testing or smoked a few cigarettes before a match. Likewise, retiring ten metres from penalties didn't seem worth bothering about. It amazed me that coaches wouldn't criticize players who got yellow-carded after taking out scrum-halves who tried to run quick penalties. It seemed exceptions had to be made for the Latin temperament and they viewed consistency as Anglo-Saxon (and therefore boring).

With sides like Biarritz and Stade Français increasingly playing more disciplined, controlled rugby than even Wasps and Leicester, it seems that professional rugby is slowly beginning to turn French players into upstanding, law-abiding Anglo-Saxons once and for all. (*Quelle dommage.*)

Anything goes in a fight

While I never felt the game in France was much 'dirtier' than I'd experienced in England – where 'cheap shots' were an increasingly frequent feature of the play – French coaches continually likened rugby to war. Sometimes the actions of the players weren't out of place with a guerrilla ambush. It was during an intense derby match for Brive away to Montferrand that I got first-hand experience of this.

After being held up in the tackle, I was surprised that the Montferrand open-side flanker let go of his grip of the ball. I then found his fingers pressing into my eyes – it was my first experience of the gruesome act of eye gouging. Fortunately, no damage was done to my eyes, but I was incensed – and for the next ten minutes I tried to smash my assailant in the tackle as hard as I could. However, during the second half the same player did the same thing to me once again. This time, instead of getting angry, I asked him if it made him happy to have to resort to eye-gouging. At least I tried to. My French at that stage was still rather basic, so what I said to him translated as, 'Are you happy?' He smiled, pointed to the scoreboard – Montferrand were leading by twenty points – and replied 'Oui.'

Get ready to be blamed for everything

'It is very disappointing to hear these things being said by the coaching staff in the press.' So said Australian rugby superstar Joe Roff, who had followed up winning the World Cup in 1999 by playing an integral role in Biarritz being crowned French champions in 2002. However, despite his outstanding ability and his clear influence in taking an unfancied side to the summit of French rugby, he was publicly blamed by the coach and president of Biarritz after they lost a game earlier in the season. Some Biarritz supporters also left abusive messages on his answer machine at home following the public criticism.

Unfortunately for foreign players, this is sometimes par for the course in France. I remember former Scotland wing Tony Stanger being blamed in the media by the Grenoble president for his team's failure to score more tries, which was ludicrous – Grenoble played ten-man rugby. Unless you can consistently perform at a high level, as a foreign player you will undoubtedly be blamed at some stage if your team suffers some losses. I remember arguing with my coach at Castres when he dropped our centre and former All Black, Norm Berryman, despite the fact that he had been playing some outstanding rugby for us. But the coach explained to me that, as a foreign player, he must be better than the French players at all times and set an example or his place in the side could not be justified. Although it's a frustrating and self-defeating premise, I am pleased to report that if you can stay in France for more than one season, you no longer are viewed as a foreigner who must continually out-perform the locals!

Never lose a home game

Two traditions of the French game seem to me to be inextricably linked. This concerns the inability of teams to win away from home and likewise the dominance of most clubs on their home ground. It's not just the fact that French sides mess up their preparations for away matches or 'aren't up for the game'. What I found is that playing at home pumps up the players so much that they play to a standard they couldn't possibly be able to repeat the following week on their travels. It's as if sides play at 120 per cent at home and 80 per cent away from home.

Throughout my four seasons at Brive and Castres, we only lost three times at home in *le championnat*. Even this small number of defeats was viewed as a disaster for the supporters of the respective clubs. I remember leaving the field at Brive after losing against Agen and witnessed supporters ripping up their season tickets in front of the players' faces. At Castres, a home loss was met with the cry from the stands, 'We don't pay to see defeats!!'

You have been warned.

Kissing another man and being heterosexual is possible

While shaking hands is a daily ritual, I discovered that a few of my team-mates greeted each other by planting a kiss on each cheek, which increased to three kisses in Montpellier. I found out that players who knew each other well moved on from shaking hands to kissing. The only time kisses were shared around was after victories, which wasn't the best introduction for me to this unique French tradition. I had to join in, though, and I tried not to look too aghast as sweaty, unshaven forwards grabbed me for a celebratory kiss or two. I must have got in touch with my feminine side by the end of my five seasons in France, as I didn't mind this kissing lark, and even started doing it on a daily basis!

Get to know your president

Presidents in France hold a power equal to their counterparts in Spanish football and their actions can have a direct effect on their team's performances. I remember after a crushing loss to Brive's oldest rivals, Montferrand, our president charged into the changing room and spoke to the players. He said that if we wanted Laurent Seigne to be sacked he would do it immediately, never mind the fact we only needed to win our last home match to qualify for the championship quarter-finals. (This similar knee-jerk reaction to defeat has seen a number of managers at Real Madrid look for alternative employment over the years.) In a secret ballot the following day the players decided that Seigne could remain until the end of the season, but it underlined the decisive role a president holds in French club rugby. In the four seasons I spent at Brive and Castres, the head coach was sacked on three occasions.

At Brive we had co-presidents – one with the aforementioned power to sack the coaches, the other, Patrick Sébastien, an emblematic figure for a popular club. Just like the flamboyant Stade Français president, Max Guazzini, Sébastien's popularity helped transform the media image of rugby in France. He was a television presenter-cum-film director as well as a singer in his own right, a Gallic cross between Rod Stewart and Jonathan Ross. Not a pleasing combination I admit, but this didn't affect his popularity within France. As a former Brive back-rower, he cared a lot for the club. The players appreciated his input, and no doubt everyone at Brive loved the fact that their small town of 50,000 people had showbiz connections. Patrick even managed to turn a championship match into a gathering of the rich and famous.

He had held his wedding – his fourth – on the Brive pitch just before our crucial home game against Toulouse. Some 18,000 supporters crammed into the ground for the occasion, witnessing a parade of French TV and film stars and more importantly a narrow win for their beloved *Brivistes*. More memorable for me, though, was the reception later that night. With half of the guests being a 'who's who' of French celebrities, it was an interesting evening watching them interact with a team of drunk and rebellious rugby players. The highlight was our guitar-playing Maori prop, Kevin Nepia, singing along with some of the best-known musicians in France. Unfortunately his actions didn't go down that well with coach Laurent Seigne – two days later he was informed that he was no longer rated by Brive and could join another club straight away.

In addition to a powerful president, there are certain clubs in France that have benefactors who provide the majority of their budget. Castres were one such club, their main funding coming from a pharmaceuticals multi-millionaire, Pierre Fabre. For a town of 50,000 and a club that has one of the lowest crowd attendances in the top flight, Fabre's money was the sole reason that Castres continued to compete with the best of French rugby. Although he was something of a reclusive figure and had no official role within the club, he loved his rugby and seldom missed a home game. He even went out of his way to watch ten minutes of a pre-season friendly against Montauban – my first game for the club. The unusual thing about this was that he viewed it from his own private helicopter, which circled overhead for the opening quarter of the match. It occurred to me then that Castres wouldn't be affected by financial worries as long as Fabre was involved.

Players have lots of power too
The French players union must be the most powerful in world rugby. They have a representative who gets a say on how the season is structured (which is one reason why it is so long, with set holiday periods throughout the year). A ten-day rest

over Christmas is still obligatory and I recall the disputes that raged until this was finally agreed, as the players union had originally demanded a two-week break. Every player in France was given a T-shirt with *'Non'* emblazoned on the front that we had to wear for training sessions and pre-match warm-ups.

In a club setting there was just as much militancy, especially when players didn't get on with the coach. The two seasons I spent at Castres were viewed as having been very successful for the club, reaching the semi-finals of the French championship and repeating this the following season in the European Cup. But during this time two head coaches were disposed of. Player involvement was rumoured to have had an influence in Alain Gaillard's departure, as he had dropped two players who had close ties to the president. He was sacked the following week. His replacement, Remy Tremulet, was fired the Monday after we lost to Munster in the semi-finals of the Heineken Cup. Castres' achievements in Europe that year were unprecedented in the club's history, but it didn't stop two senior players organizing a petition to have Tremulet removed. Also at Grenoble, the playing squad refused to board the team bus for their away match in Toulouse unless head coach Dean Richards was sacked.

If there was one game that encapsulated for me the different animal that is French rugby, it has to be when I travelled with Castres to play Agen. It was a game that captivated and infuriated me in equal measure, leaving me with only one thought – 'Only in France'.

As league leaders, we started the match against second-placed Agen confident of continuing our winning run. The ground at Agen was packed out, which created a seething, hostile atmosphere – something I relished. Having weathered the inevitable early storm, we started to impose our game on our pumped-up opponents. I was loving every minute of it –

the noise, passion and intensity wasn't far removed from a Test match. We were playing well, too, making inroads by attacking them out wide. Unfortunately, it soon all went pear-shaped.

The red mist began to descend over one or two of our players who took exception to Agen's muscular approach. If you want to win an away game in France, you have to make the referee your best friend, as they have a tendency to side with the home team. Obviously, nobody had explained this to our openside flanker, Arnaud Costes, who hurled the ball towards the back of the referee's head after another decision hadn't gone our way. He didn't miss, but managed to talk his way out of a red card, saying he hadn't done it on purpose.

A short while later, however, our Argentine prop, Mauricio Reggiardo, wasn't so lucky and was sent off, just after returning from ten minutes spent in the sin bin. The writing was now on the wall that we were going to lose the match. We quickly lapsed into chaos and ill-discipline. From leading at half-time we went on to lose the match by twenty points. This wasn't too surprising, though – by the end of the game two more of our players had been sent off. Our biggest game of the season and we had self-destructed to be left with a team of only twelve players, which would have been one less if Costes had also been shown a red card. *Plus ça change* ...

Since the game turned professional in 1995, I have ended up playing almost half of my career in France – although this had never been my original plan. I suppose I stayed there because the unique environment I discovered gave me many pleasurable moments, even though playing there had taken a while to get used to. There are imperfections and anachronisms in the French game that would test the patience of a Trappist monk, but when things are going well, there isn't a better place in the world to be playing rugby.

CHAPTER 10

Le beau jeu

In the middle of difficulty lies opportunity.

Albert Einstein

'Claire, do you think we should wake up Grimesy?'

'No, let him sleep off last night.'

'But look they're still in with a chance. They could do it.'

'I don't think he'll thank you for it.'

'Grimesy!'

'Leave. Me. Alone.'

'Grimesy!'

'This had better be good.'

Oh this was good all right. The euphoria of the previous day and night may have been leaving the body at the same time as the alcohol, but watching Wales battle it out with England was starting to get the juices flowing once again. As Stuart Grimes wandered through from the bedroom, still wrapped in his duvet, he dropped heavily onto the couch beside me, and turned one bleary, baleful eye my direction.

'What?'

'Wales are holding on. England haven't killed them off yet. They could do it. And then we'd be champions!'

'Aye right. Dream on.'

After two years of professional rugby, the Celtic nations were struggling to keep pace with France, England and the three southern hemisphere giants. The Springbok coach Nick Mallet summed up what many rugby people thought about the Five Nations: 'There are only two serious sides in it now – France and England. In fact I would say that there are seven or eight Super 12 sides who could beat Wales, Scotland and Ireland easily.' A harsh judgement, but the evidence was damning – the French and English had shared the title between them over the previous four years. It was undeniable that, both in terms of results and style of play, the Celtic nations were playing at a vastly inferior level.

My own optimism had been badly bruised both by our performances over the previous two seasons at Test level and the mess that was being made to introduce a professional domestic structure to Scotland. I was interviewed by the writer Donald McRae in the summer of 1998 for his book *Winter Colours* and I told him that it was a struggle to see how any of the Celtic nations could be competitive in the near future: 'We know we're some way behind the top five countries. We can't just ignore the fact that Scotland and Ireland lost to Italy this year. I sometimes worry that the gap between us and the French and English might widen rather than narrow in the next few years.'

In Scotland things looked very bleak indeed. Since our tremendous run in the 1996 Five Nations we had lost thirteen out of sixteen Test matches. As a result, our coaching team of Richie Dixon and David Johnston had been sacked. In fact, our stock had fallen so dramatically that bookmakers gave us odds of 100-1 to win the 1999 Five Nations Championship.

But who could blame the bookies? Scottish rugby wasn't just in disarray; it had descended into full-blown civil war. As the SRU and the leading (amateur) clubs faced-off across the domestic battlefield, both made rallying calls to the famous faces of the game. And in that goal, the clubs were winning. The last four Scotland captains – Jim Aitken, David Sole, Finlay Calder and Gavin Hastings – campaigned across the country against the SRU's decision in 1996 to have four professional teams based on the districts of Edinburgh, Glasgow, the South (Borders) and North and Midlands (Caledonia). A bitter and divisive enmity grew between this formidable gang of four and the SRU Director of Rugby, Jim Telfer. The argument for a professional system based on club teams seems more misguided – and financially impossible – with each passing year and never saw the light of day. However, the campaign did create a great deal of damage, which hasn't ever been repaired.

At a time when Scottish rugby should have been attracting a new and enlarged audience, negativity was everywhere. I believed that the district route was the right way to proceed – sustaining eight or ten club teams would have been financial suicide even in the short term. Already in England, London Scottish and Richmond were facing bankruptcy. Ireland was one of the few countries that were making a success of professional rugby, based on a system of four provincial sides. Crowd numbers were beginning to increase in Munster and Leinster, and Ulster had just won the European Cup.

Yet despite the internecine quarrelling, after two years of the district structure, there were tangible signs of progress in Scotland – which, of course, was just when the SRU hit the panic button and decided to strip the number of sides from four to two. They described this as a 'natural progression' and believed it would greatly help amateur rugby with some sixty players returning to the club game. Whether it did this or not is a moot point and also irrelevant in the era of professional rugby. Every season since 1995 the gap between professional and club rugby has widened. The fact that sixty players were now excluded from training full-time only boosted the amateur game in the short term while at the same time removing a large number of future Scotland internationalists now unable to fulfil their potential. What is certain is that this one decision created distrust, disharmony and anger from those who had committed to professional rugby only to see their contracts terminated without warning. The events of 1998 have had repercussions that still resonate today as many people refuse to support professional rugby because of antipathy towards the SRU.

In truth, it was clear that competing against the millionaire sugar daddies that had invested in the leading English and French club sides was extremely difficult for an organization such as the SRU (particularly as they had just spent vast sums of money redeveloping Murrayfield stadium). Mind you, it wasn't as if there weren't opportunities for them to share the financial burden of running the professional game. However, with the SRU refusing to give up any control, they were doomed from the start.

An attempt to form a British League failed in 1998 because of a lack of compromise and a lack of will. And in 1999, Scotsman Brian Kennedy met the SRU and leading Scottish players and presented a marketing plan to take London Scottish back to Scotland. The players loved the plan – it would have seen them competing in the English Premiership with home games in Edinburgh – but this, too, fell through on political grounds. The fact that Kennedy then took over Sale and transformed them into English champions with regular crowds of 10,000 merely rubbed more salt into still seeping wounds.

So, by the end of 1998 the omens were far from good, and I could see why nobody in the rugby world would give us a cat in hell's chance of making any impact in the last ever Five Nations. However, sport can be incredibly fluid and unpredictable at times. Despite my pessimism at the turn of the year, as the weeks drew on I began to find myself believing that – contrary to all expectations – there was a chance that this Five Nations might not be a two-tier competition after all. The Celtic nations had been just as competitive as France and England during the autumn international series. I hoped that being positive wasn't just wishful thinking on my part.

Although France had won two Grand Slams in a row, there was still heated debate within French rugby circles over how the national team should play going into a World Cup season. Viewing things from my base in Brive, it seemed that club rugby in France at the end of the twentieth century was characterized by two opposing styles of play, epitomized by Stade Français and Colomiers.

Week in, week out, Stade Français produced winning performances by playing a very direct, almost English style game based on discipline and set-piece dominance. On the other hand, Colomiers, who weren't even ranked in the top ten of French clubs, played in the classical French style by moving the ball wide and trying to play out of the tackle. This continued to be the game that worked for the big one-off matches, which had already taken them to the European Cup Final against Ulster.

At Test level the French side had recently mixed both styles to devastating effect – their scintillating running angles and unshakable defence in the 51–0 victory against Wales at Wembley the previous season had been frighteningly impressive. However, there were concerns about the physicality of their midfield backs, which was evident in the recent defeat by Australia in November. Although very gifted ball players, the likes of Thomas Castaignède, Stéphane Glas and Frank Comba were lightweight in comparison with most international backlines.

England's preparations hadn't been without difficulty. Their domestic game was in turmoil. The English clubs had boycotted that season's European Cup and the RFU came very close to being forced to pull out of the Five Nations over financial issues with the Celtic nations. Moreover, a disastrous summer tour to Australia and New Zealand, albeit with numerous key players missing, had dealt a significant blow to coach Clive Woodward's World Cup preparations.

At first glance, it appeared that Scotland hadn't made progress in the months leading up to the 1999 Five Nations.

We had toured Australia in the summer with a squad that might have been selected by Mother Hubbard such was our lack of experience. British Lions Alan Tait, Gary Armstrong, Doddie Weir, Tom Smith and Tony Stanger were all unavailable for the trip. Although we were badly beaten in the first Test match against the Wallabies, it was a tour that would bring dividends as we had been encouraged to play attacking rugby. A number of aspiring players had stepped up to the plate.

My excitement with our new playing style and being selected at stand-off in Australia had turned to disappointment by the autumn. After suffering a shoulder injury and then appearing at full-back against the Springboks at Murrayfield in November, I had been desperate to get back to France and establish myself as a stand-off. (Frustratingly, I had only been selected in my preferred number 10 jersey on two occasions in the previous eight Five Nations matches.)

I stayed at full-back for the two World Cup qualifying matches for Scotland, against Spain and Portugal, but at least managed to reclaim the number 10 jersey for Brive. I felt that my form and confidence were back in abundance, but for the Five Nations opener against Wales I was selected at outside-centre, and found myself having to adjust to yet another position. At the same time, I was relieved to have made the side – with Alan Tait on the bench the competition for centre was intense, so at least the selectors had shown faith in me as a rugby player.

The Welsh side were alive with anticipation for a great season. It seemed that almost every rugby commentator was tipping them to make a major impression in the championship. The strange thing was that their team consisted of almost exactly the same players who conceded over 110 points in two matches the previous year. How could they have improved so much?

A large amount of credit was rightly given to their so-called great redeemer, Graham Henry. He's a hugely experienced coach, and seemed to understand the needs and motivations of the Welsh players. He had breathed new life into Welsh rugby, reinvigorating a team and a nation. They performed heroically against South Africa before Christmas – a scintillating blend of passion and skill as they tried to attack from anywhere on the field. On paper, Wales had the best backline in the championship and had several players who had played so well for the Lions in South Africa. Rob Howley, Neil Jenkins, Scott Gibbs, and Alan Bateman were on top of their game and, with Dafydd James and Shane Howarth also hitting form, we knew we would be tested out wide.

Wales

Our strategy was to attack the Welsh as much as possible in the set piece, but we knew this would be difficult as they took quick lineouts and moved the ball wide at any opportunity. We also had a plan to target Welsh winger Matthew Robinson. He was a dangerous runner, but was winning his first cap after recently switching to union from rugby league. We thought his positioning might be suspect, and John Leslie was charged with the task of putting him under pressure right from the beginning of the match.

Our coaching staff must have been giving themselves high-fives as we made a dream start to the game. John fielded Duncan Hodge's reverse kick-off brilliantly and stormed on to score a try after only ten seconds, equalling the record for the fastest-ever international try. Had John not run on unselfishly for a few seconds after crossing the try-line to get as close as possible to the posts before touching down, he could have held a record that would have been virtually unbeatable. Even worse, the gesture was in vain as Hodgey missed the conversion.

Our opening few seconds were the solitary highlight of a first half that was spent mainly on the back foot, as Scott Gibbs and Scott Quinnell in particular powered Wales forward. Early on in the game Alan Bateman had exposed me defensively at outside-centre, but I was soon getting used to playing at 13 again and was beginning to make some half-breaks. However, Wales were in command, and after forty-six minutes we were 13–8 down with a defeat looking the likely outcome.

Two events transformed the game within the space of a couple of minutes – and my own season was to be transformed by them as well. First, Duncan Hodge, who had been playing well, suffered a leg injury and had to leave the field. I moved to stand-off and almost immediately had a slice of luck as I picked up a dropped Welsh pass and ran in a try from halfway. Despite my embarrassing effort at diving over the try-line, the noise from the Scottish crowd gave me the spur to produce what I thought was an authoritative performance. It had been years since we had had such a good atmosphere at Murrayfield. The noise level increased even further when, with ten minutes remaining, Alan Tait – who had come on to play at outside-centre after my shift infield – was at my shoulder to take my offload out of Alan Bateman's tackle to go over for a try. It took the score to 20–20.

It was a pulsating match with both teams playing well, but we held the edge up front, especially in the lineout. It was fitting then that the superb Scott Murray scored our last try as we went on to win 33–20. After the game I received glowing reviews for my controlling performance at stand-off and my kicking game, although I personally thought that the latter aspect of my performance wasn't as good as it could have been. It was true that I'd felt much more secure playing at number 10 for Scotland. The ultimate reason for this was that I had been back playing regularly at stand-off for my club side – the first time in four years.

The confidence of a winning start to the Five Nations did wonders for the players' belief and attitude. We suddenly approached our next match away to England with some eagerness instead of the usual trepidation. Scotland had last won at Twickenham way back in 1983. Our victory over Wales had even changed the media's perception of the squad. At last there were some positive articles being written about Scottish rugby.

England
Clive Woodward insisted that his side would try to play attacking rugby, and he was true to his word – we were almost blown away in the opening quarter. England's huge pack continually made inroads and after eighteen minutes we found ourselves trailing 14–0. In an intimidating arena like Twickenham, with an English team clearly on their game, I think that even our most optimistic of supporters feared a record defeat was on the cards. However, the self-belief that had been created with our win against Wales drove us onwards.

Alan Tait scored two terrific tries, both of which were great examples of taking the game to the opposition. His first score came after Eric Peters had won back a loose ball in the line-out. Realizing that there might now be a gap in the defence, I got as flat as I could and Gary Armstrong quickly put the ball out in front of me. I managed a half-break and was just able to pass out of the tackle to Martin Leslie. He sucked in more defenders and offloaded to the supporting Scott Murray. Taity, the master finisher, had sensed that the ball might come back outside where there would be no English players left to stop the move. His timing onto Scott's pass was spot on and he was at full speed to score a try full of class, pace and angles that were so well judged they would have made Pythagoras proud.

Taity's second try just after half-time brought us to within three points of the English and right back in the match. This time his score was an immaculately executed first phase move. We had come up with the move on the training ground earlier in the week and it gave Taity just enough space to breach England's defensive line. That was all he needed to display his finishing prowess once more, sidestepping the desperate English cover defence to touch down for another try.

I had been desperate to call the move during the match and a lineout just outside the English 22 provided me with an ideal opportunity. Quick off-the-top ball from the tail of the lineout meant that Gary could pass to me on the run. He needed to do this, as he was to get the ball back from me on a loop. My aim was to fix the open-side flanker Neil Back. Gary now was once again in possession of the ball and the timing of Taity's run outside him was to be the critical factor for opening up the English centres. We had practised it on many occasions at training, but against an aggressive defence there was much less room for error. John Leslie ran a decoy line so that it appeared that it was he who would get the ball from Gary. Both Jonny Wilkinson and Mike Catt were drawn in to defend John and Gary, which created a hole between them and outside-centre Jerry Guscott. Tucked in close behind John came Taity who received Gary's pass behind John's back and accelerated through the English defence.

In the professional era I've found that when such a move is successful, coaches tend to be reluctant to let their players repeat it in subsequent matches. They are convinced that opposing sides will have analysed their team's moves and organized their defence accordingly. I disagree. Sticking to what works should form the basis of any winning strategy. Why put yourself under unnecessary pressure by trying something that hasn't worked for you before?

Also, I believe that any move should have at least two options – it is the players' responsibility to adapt and decide to attack where the defence is weaker. In other words, if the defence is ready to check Plan A, you go for Plan B. What makes for a successful move is that it should be executed at pace and with skill – and not determined by whether the opposition have done their homework.

If there is already fear in the minds of an attacking team that the defence can never be broken down, then players will no longer be thinking about running hard and trying to find space. Instead, they will concentrate on protecting the ball in contact rather than concentrate on trying to offload or create quick ball. This attitude of mind leads inevitably to a systems-based game plan, with a succession of pre-determined phases. Many coaches prefer this approach, because it seems to remove the element of uncertainty, while enabling them to think they are more in control of what happens on the pitch. Only the Australians have enjoyed success with this style of play and to my mind it doesn't suit Scottish teams.

Scotland tends to produce lighter players than our counter-parts, but in terms of fitness, dynamism and commitment we can still be ranked with the best international Test sides. These attributes have led Scottish coaches over the years to look to the All Blacks as our best role models. The All Blacks are uncompromising at the breakdown and constantly look to get quick ruck ball. Thereafter they prefer not to play to any pre-planned system and attack with width and pace, nowa-days with a focus on breaking the gain line from first phase ball. During the 2005 Six Nations, Wales successfully imple-mented this style of play. Their strategy was on securing quick ball and attacking space, rather than hitting the ball up for a few phases to grind down the opposition defence. In 1999 the Scottish coaches knew that a similar game plan might bring reward as it would be playing to our strengths.

In the second half both England and ourselves scored rather lucky tries from dropped passes. I found myself in the right place at the right time for the second game running as I managed to steal ball from Mike Catt and run in from the halfway line. We had just gone 24–14 down and I decided that we had to take some risks if we were to come back and win the match.

England set up an alignment from a scrum with Dan Luger at stand-off and scrum-half Kyran Bracken standing wide of number 8 Lawrence Dallaglio. I gambled that Luger would be a decoy runner and that Bracken was going to pass behind him to stand-off Mike Catt who was lying wide and deep. I decided to sprint up to tackle Catt, ignoring Luger who was really the player I should have been marking. I was reasonably certain that Luger wouldn't get the ball. If he had he would have had a free run through our backline defence.

As Bracken was getting a long pass from Dallaglio I knew I could put Catt under some pressure, at best tackle him man-and-ball. I never once thought there was a chance of me recovering the ball, but that was what happened. As I raced to within a couple of yards of Catt, his arms were outstretched in anticipation of Bracken's pass. Just as the ball arrived I was right next to him and he looked at me instead of the ball, which was to then ricochet between us. As I was driving forward, I managed to grab the ball and kept going all the way to the try-line.

I had a clear run to the posts and was confident I wouldn't be stopped. In the middle of such an explosive moment, I found that my mind was racing. For a few instants, the crowd had gone quiet apart from some small pockets of Scottish supporters cheering me on. Suddenly a surge of defiance began to build up inside me. My mind went back to 1995 when a group of English supporters had barracked us before our Grand Slam match at the same ground. At the time we were incensed that a few drunken louts had shouted a torrent of abuse at our captain, Gavin Hastings. They made it clear that we weren't fit to lace the boots of the English rugby players. I wanted this Scottish side to get the respect they deserved.

My rage was no doubt also a reaction to the criticism I had received that season and even that morning in the Scottish press – former backs coach David Johnston had chosen the morning of the Calcutta Cup to proclaim why he thought I shouldn't have been selected at stand-off. Something in my mind was telling me that I either had to show the Twickenham crowd some sort of contempt or be as nonchalant as possible when scoring my try. I really wanted to spike the ball in the in-goal area like they do in American football. In the end I settled for carrying the ball in one hand rather than showing any disrespect. It was the first time I'd felt such emotion scoring a try and – with adrenalin approaching overload – I was determined that we would leave Twickenham with a win.

England were rattled and looked a shadow of the side that had started the game so confidently. However, we weren't able to get back in the English 22 and all our efforts and good play in the last ten minutes were restricted to our half of the field. They clung on for a win, although I was positive that if the game had been extended by five more minutes then we would have won. We had put in so much effort and to lose 24–21 was an incredibly frustrating result. Although the media blamed Kenny Logan for missing three penalties – which was in contrast to Wilkinson's 100 per cent return – it would have been hard to argue that we were robbed of a victory. Ultimately, we had let England build up too much of a lead early in the match, but in scoring three tries we showed that we were a talented side capable of breaking a highly organized defensive line.

To play so well at Twickenham and not win was, to me, much more disappointing than the injury-time loss we suffered against England in 1994. Maybe it was because winning at Twickenham would have been much more special or that back in 1994 beating England wasn't such a rarity. I think all the team realized that we would probably never have as good an opportunity to win at Twickenham throughout the rest of our careers.

Nevertheless, the defeat did nothing to dent our burgeoning self-belief. Furthermore, our next two games were to be at Murrayfield, which we hoped would give us the springboard to build on what we had already achieved. Next up was Italy, who were still a year away from being involved in a new Six Nations tournament. The match didn't live up to its 'friendly' billing, though, and the Italians were lucky to only have one player shown a red card. We won 30–12, but our performance hadn't reached the heights of the English and Welsh games. This was largely due to the spoiling tactics of the Italians who have always proved a tough team for Scottish sides to break down. Although Italy unquestionably deserved their place in an extended championship, there wasn't the same build-up or atmosphere as in our two previous Five Nations outings. We couldn't wait to get back into that environment with the visit to Murrayfield of a buoyant Irish side who had just beaten Wales at Wembley.

Ireland

I still feel that this match was my best all-round performance in a Scottish jersey. The four fundamentals of a stand-off's game – passing, kicking, running and tackling – were at a standard with which I was particularly pleased. I said in the press conference after the match that it was the happiest I'd felt playing for Scotland. This wasn't strictly true – the 1996 season had been more enjoyable – but it was unquestionably the best Scottish team I'd played in. We were playing intelligent, precise, attacking rugby and it was a joy to be at the heart of it. Although the midfield trio of John Leslie, Alan Tait and myself were getting a lot of the plaudits, Cammie Murray and Glenn Metcalfe were also excelling in the backline.

Our forwards were now consistently producing quick ball and in Scott Murray and Stuart Grimes we had two of the best second-rows in the championship. Scott again dominated in the lineout and Grimesy displayed tremendous work-rate and no little pace in taking the scoring pass for our last try – the culmination of a sweeping move that had started in front of our own posts.

Ireland themselves played well and showed glimpses of what a strong side they would become. With arguably the best front five in the competition, they had under-achieved in the previous two or three seasons. When Brian O'Driscoll broke into the team the following year, their credentials as potential Six Nations champions were firmly established. However, despite Keith Wood, Dion O'Cuinneagain and David Humphrys urging their team forward, we seemed to hold the edge in all facets of play. The winning scoreline of 30–13 might have been similar to our result against the Italians, but our play was at a much higher level.

The game also included a try from myself, which meant I'd scored a try in each of my last four matches for Scotland. If only the games against Spain and Portugal had been granted Test status I would have had six in a row! I knew the try run would dry up soon enough and I'd been fortunate so far that my tally had included two interceptions. I was also very conscious of the fact that the try in the Irish match almost didn't happen – a split second before receiving the scoring pass I was busy looking in the other direction.

After a drive from our forwards, Gary Armstrong had made a sniping run and seemed to be in the process of setting up a ruck close to the Irish try-line. As I thought the ball would come back slowly, I turned round to Cammie Murray who was on my outside to tell him that I would do a switch move with him. I was unaware that Gary had flicked the ball back from the ruck and that John was now running forward with the intention of giving me the ball. Luckily I looked back over my shoulder just in time to get my hands up to receive John's pass. As I had barely started to run onto the ball, I thought the only solution open to me was to go forward myself. Somehow I made it through Keith Wood's tackle and stretched over for a try.

Our impressive win had generated an irresistible momentum that raised our expectations going into the final game of the championship. However, we knew that playing France away was probably the toughest fixture for any side in the competition. Despite a memorable day in 1995, that win remained our only victory in Paris in thirty years. To lose two games in the championship would have been scant reward for the season's efforts. Also, in terms of building confidence and preparation for the World Cup, we knew that our performance in Paris had to at least match that of the Ireland game. Moreover, we were acutely aware that anything less would almost certainly see us losing the contest. With key players Tom Smith and Eric Peters dropping out injured, playing the French in Paris looked like being even more of a challenge than usual.

France

It was the first ever France–Scotland match at the magnificent new Stade de France – scene of the football World Cup final the year before. In front of 80,000 partisan supporters and with the sun on our backs, we immediately tried to attack the French with ball in hand. However, we were nervous going forward and were guilty of a number of errors early in the match. I probably made more mistakes in the first five minutes than I'd done in my three previous games. Even more worrying for us was that the French had scored a try within two minutes of the kick-off. For any French side playing at home, going into the lead early in a match is usually a cast-iron guarantee that they will pulverize the opposition.

Instead there followed a period of breathtaking rugby by Scotland. Within twenty minutes we had scored five cracking tries and could have easily added one or two more. Everything seemed to fall into place with almost all of the side playing well. A number of players like Glenn Metcalfe, John Leslie, Martin Leslie, Stuart Reid and Gordon Bulloch played their best ever games for Scotland. Added to our attacking style of play, this was a potent mix.

We managed to get back into the match in the ninth minute with a try from the excellent Martin Leslie following a break by Kenny Logan. At the next restart, the French decided to take a deep kick-off and I called a wide attacking move. There was some element of risk because we would be moving the ball in our own 22 m, but the rewards were there if we were accurate under pressure. The bold call paid off spectacularly. Teams chasing a long kick-off tend to rush up close to the resulting ruck or maul since they expect their opponents to kick for touch. This may result in a gap being left in the wider channels. Our move was simple enough. All it involved was a miss pass from me to Taity who would then pass to Glenn (missing out blindside wing Cammie Murray who positioned himself outside our centres).

As expected, the French centres came up fast and nearly knocked us down not far from our own line. But this let us turn a hazardous situation into a positive one as Taity managed to get his pass away to Glenn just as he was being tackled. Glenn had picked a great line and ran through the gap that the move had created. His impressive speed carried him on a further seventy yards before finally being tackled. At the ensuing ruck, the ball was moved to Taity who had got himself back in position to score another top-notch try.

We only had to wait three minutes before we scored our third try, and although it was much less spectacular, it provided me with a moment of absolute euphoria. After John Leslie took a flat pass from me and was tackled in the middle of the field, I was presented with an ideal opportunity to take on the defence. I moved out to the right-hand side of the pitch, just outside the French 22. Quick ruck ball meant that the French defence was not as organized as they would have liked to be. I saw what I hoped could be a gap between Raphael Ibanez and my Brive team-mate Philippe Carbonneau. At worst I thought I would suck in the two Frenchmen and get an offload to Cammie, unmarked on the wing. Carbonneau probably did the right thing by drifting wide to take Cammie, so my chances of scoring depended on whether I could get outside Ibanez. He managed to get his fingers on my jersey but it wasn't enough to halt my progress.

I had made it over the try-line and it suddenly occurred to me that I'd achieved something that before Christmas, when I had been dropped from the side, would have seemed impossible. Scoring a try in every Five Nations game put me in a group of only four other players who had achieved the feat and the first British player to do it since 1925. I had also been fortunate enough to score a try in each of my previous five games, which was a Scottish record. Every try I scored for Scotland gave me a tremendous buzz, but this was special – this was my proudest moment on a rugby field. Making my way to score behind the posts I could hear the many Scottish supporters who were in that part of the stadium. I was so excited that I almost kissed the ball before touching it down for a try!

The madness continued for another fifteen minutes as Taity scored his second try of the match. Although Taity's score came from another brilliant break by Glenn, it was John Leslie who had created the initial damage by once again offloading out of the tackle. John played better that day than any inside-centre I've played alongside, better even than Scott Gibbs for the '97 Lions in the second Test in Durban. John's fitness level was staggering and, despite taking some huge hits at times, he kept taking the ball to the French and created space for others to play in.

It was his initial thrust from a midfield scrum that enabled me to take a scissors pass and nearly score a second try. Unfortunately my attempted side step of Émile N'Tamack was too elaborate even for me and I tumbled to the ground agonizingly close to the try-line. Almost immediately Marty Leslie arrived on the scene to take my pass and dive over for our fifth try of the match – with only twenty-seven minutes gone the score was: France 12, Scotland 33.

By half-time France had reduced the deficit to 33–22 but they were on the receiving end of a multitude of whistles and abuse as we ran back to the changing rooms. Despite the French crowd's anger, we could have rightly been aggrieved ourselves to be leading by only eleven points. We had dominated proceedings but had let Christophe Dominici in for a soft try just before the break.

Inevitably, the excitement and desire to attack was to be diluted somewhat as we sat in the changing rooms reflecting on what had happened in the opening forty minutes. The coaches were as pumped up, and no doubt as surprised, as the players were. Senior players kept urging the rest of the team that we couldn't sit back and try to defend our lead. We were all aware that it would be much harder to put our words into actions. It was a given that France would come out in the second half much more aggressive and attack from everywhere.

The fact that the French weren't able to score any points in the second half showed that our attitude, discipline and application were unaffected by the crazy events of that first half. It was a magnificent collective effort, but it must be said that at times the French still looked shell-shocked from our twenty-minute blitz earlier in the game. Although we kicked more in the second half, poor finishing denied us an opportunity to score forty or even fifty points. Taity had a try disallowed for a forward pass that would have given him a hat-trick and we were only inches from the French line when the referee blew the final whistle.

No one was complaining though – we had held our nerve to record a stunning 36–22 victory. After the game we went out to salute the 5,000 or so Scottish supporters in the ground in scenes reminiscent of our win at the Parc des Princes four years earlier. I was interviewed by French television on the halfway line, unaware that it was being broadcast live to everyone in the stadium. As I thought that my comments were only going to be heard by the French I tried to say something about the game that they would relate to, something with a bit of poetic licence. *Du beau rugby* is an expression that is often used in France. I would later get some stick for saying it, but calling our performance 'beautiful' still seems an appropriate description.

Champions

Thinking back to the match now seems almost like a dream. (In fact I'm sure that during the match itself there was a dream-like quality to what was unfolding.) The twenty-minute spell in which we scored five tries reminds me of the first half performance of the All Blacks against England in the 1995 World Cup semi-final. It was said after the match that France had never ever been beaten so comprehensively at home in the Five Nations, even by the great Welsh sides of the Seventies. I don't think even the most optimistic Scottish supporter could have envisaged such a result. After all, we had conceded over ninety points to the French in our previous two meetings.

To be a part of what was probably the best ever rugby played by a Scottish team in such an important match was incredible. The thirty-six points we had notched up were the highest on record for a Scottish side against France. The fact that the record was achieved away from home made it even more special. I had thought the Irish game was Scotland's finest performance since 1990; our win against the French could be ranked as one of the best ever Scottish displays.

It had been a cracking Five Nations – there were no one-sided games and France were the only team that had not improved from the year before. With England to play Wales at Wembley the following day, our win had propelled us into top spot in the championship on points difference. As we celebrated the night away in Paris none of us held out too much hope that England would fail in their quest for a Grand Slam. Since our narrow defeat at Twickenham they had beaten France and Ireland. Surely two massive upsets couldn't happen in the same weekend?

The following morning's train journey from Paris to Brive was four hours long and, with a whopping hangover, it seemed to last an eternity. We eventually arrived just in time to watch the English match. Stuart Grimes and his girlfriend Trish were staying with us for a couple of days and as I'd claimed the sofa, he went to bed for the first half of the match. I thought he'd made the right choice as England were dominating proceedings, leading 25–18 at half-time having scored three tries to nil. I was sure they were on course for an easy win, but when Grimesy finally got out of bed I told him optimistically to watch the second half as Wales could still win the match. In fact the Welsh did improve and with five minutes to go they were only trailing 31–25.

There then followed a moment of pure joy for Welsh and Scottish supporters around the world – from nowhere Scott Gibbs broke three tackles to score a wonderful try. The only Welshman who wasn't celebrating was Neil Jenkins – as he still had to kick the conversion to put Wales into the lead. Grimesy and I were suddenly jumping up and down but we had the agonizing wait to see if the final kick would be a success. If there was one man you wanted to take a kick that would make Scotland the last ever Five Nations Champions it was Jenks. He didn't falter and Wales held out for a 32–31 victory.

The champagne corks started popping from the balcony of our apartment in the centre of Brive. The previous day's elation was resurrected and Grimesy and I met my Brive team-mates Olivier Magne and Francois Duboisset who had managed to get a bar in town opened, on a Sunday, just for us to celebrate the occasion. Plans were being made for the squad to meet up in Scotland that night at the Three-Quarters, a sports bar in Edinburgh that I co-owned. It was also being arranged that the Five Nations trophy would be presented to the squad at Murrayfield the following day.

Unfortunately, being stuck at Brive, Grimesy and I had to miss both events. The public turnout at Murrayfield after such short notice was amazing, as more than 10,000 people watched Gary and the rest of the boys parade the trophy. I suppose this spontaneous positive reaction showed that there were many that cared about Scottish rugby, and the national team had given them something to be proud about. To believe in something and never waver through the lean times – to see that faith repaid when everyone else said it could never happen, that is the ultimate achievement.

The foundation of our success in 1999 was, in my mind, put together during our summer tour to Australia in 1998. Although the team would be much changed going into championship, the Australian tour gave Glenn Metcalfe, Cammie Murray, Gordon Bulloch, Scott Murray and Stuart Grimes valuable Test match experience. Also, against New South Wales, we played our most expansive rugby since the 1996 season. Our 34–10 win in Sydney saw incisive running off quick ball – a hallmark of what we would later demonstrate in the Five Nations.

What we needed were three or four players to take the team to another level. They arrived from New Zealand in the form of the Leslie brothers and the return from injury of Alan Tait. However, it was more through luck than any grand design that the team finally came about. Injuries were a contributing factor to how the side was moulded: Bryan Redpath, Duncan Hodge, Derrick Lee, Jamie Mayer and Doddie Weir all started in our match against South Africa in December, but were to later miss out through injury.

Also, two of our best players – Tom Smith and Eric Peters – picked up serious injuries prior to our final match in Paris.

These were two of the bravest people I have met – and not just in a sporting capacity. Tom had become one of the best props in the world, his performances enabling him to play in all six Test matches on the Lions tours of 1997 and 2001. This was realized despite suffering from epilepsy, which shows what can be achieved with bucketloads of courage and dedication.

Eric had suffered a horrendous injury between the Irish and French matches playing for his club, Bath, in the English Premiership. His kneecap had been shattered which required complicated surgery and many months of rehabilitation. During this period Eric was diagnosed with testicular cancer, meaning he had to battle against serious illness and serious injury. Amazingly, he fought back to resume his playing career, coming very close to playing once more for Scotland. Amongst the euphoria and celebrations it is worth remembering the sacrifices and hard work that go into a winning performance. Tom and Eric had gone an extra mile and were desperately unlucky not to have been involved in the French match.

One of the first people I called after Wales beat England was Bryan Redpath. Having myself missed out on the 1995 World Cup, I knew exactly the conflicting emotions he must have been feeling. He had been our captain during the Australian tour and in all our matches before Christmas. He had been an excellent leader and his game would have been ideally suited to how we had played during the Five Nations. Although he said he was really happy for the squad, it was obvious that he was deeply disappointed not to have been involved.

There wouldn't have been many teams that could have replaced Basil as scrum-half – and captain – with an experienced performer like Gary Armstrong. In many ways Gary was similar to Basil – a down-to-earth Borders lad who was universally respected by both players and coaches alike. His courage and commitment had already made him in many eyes the bravest player to have worn the Scotland jersey. Off the field he was very much one of the boys and had always been the joker of the squad. When we were in camp, Gary would always be trying to sabotage someone's hotel room. His favourite tricks were to spread Vaseline over phone receivers, cling film across the toilet seat, coffee granules under the bed sheets or to hide the mattress itself in another room.

Gary's game was also very different since the 1996 New Zealand tour, which was the last time we had been partnered together at half-back. It was obvious that playing and training as a professional for Newcastle had made him a more rounded player. He no longer played like a ninth forward and his first option was to quickly get the ball in my hands. He would always pose an attacking threat to the opposition but didn't overplay his renowned running game. This balanced approach came to fruition in our final match in Paris where his contributions were immense.

Gary was fittingly one of only two players that had played in the championship-winning sides of 1990 and 1999. The other player was our hugely underrated tighthead prop Paul Burnell. Paul was never one who sought the limelight and his contributions to the Scottish team during the Nineties have gone largely unreported. Both players can take much satisfaction and pride from the fact that winning two championships must be one of the best records for any Scottish rugby player throughout the game's history.

Another significant factor in our success in 1999 was the role of John Leslie. His Super 12 experience and the fact that he had no previous dealings with the coaches were to have an important effect on how the management treated the squad. John combined a very stubborn personality with a desire to play attacking rugby. He would win frequent arguments with the coaches over proposed complicated lineout moves or a kicking game plan. On top of the fact that we worked very well together on the field, I also now had an ally in trying to play an attacking game.

Once the confidence of our win against Wales gave the squad some momentum, the coaches wisely let the players make as many decisions as was feasible. Our coaching staff of John Rutherford, Hugh Campbell and Jim Telfer began to realize where our strengths lay and created an environment for decision makers to emerge. Our training sessions were still fairly structured and hard work, but the players were now running our final training run the day before the match, something unheard of in Scottish rugby at the time but which proved to be highly successful. By the time of the Irish and French matches, our Friday sessions were the best training runs I'd ever been involved in – quick, intense and error free. Consequently, the number of decision makers in the side began to increase, resulting in greatly improved interplay between backs and forwards.

The year 1999 was not only my best season in a Scottish jersey – that year's team was the best Scotland side I played in, and its style of rugby came close to my ideal vision of how the game should be played. Despite the fact that we didn't achieve a Grand Slam, I hope that 1999 can stand alongside 1925, 1984 and 1990 in the annals of Scottish rugby. We had managed to score 120 points in our four matches, which included sixteen tries. Although this compares very favourably with Scotland's Grand Slam seasons, 1999 will probably never receive the same recognition, as it didn't include a win against the Auld Enemy. In fact it seemed that the following season's victory over England was more memorable to many Scots than our Five Nations triumph.

The Calcutta Cup game was to be the only highlight in 2000 in an otherwise depressing year for rugby in Scotland. From a personal point of view, the rollercoaster that had been my career now propelled downwards, as I was to experience a desperately frustrating season both at club and international level.

CHAPTER 11

Feeling Blue

*I've failed over and over again in my life
and that is why I succeed.*

Michael Jordan

It was embarrassing. In front of the rest of the players the new Brive president, Jean-Jacques Madrias, called me aside and asked me to join him. He put his arm around my shoulder, which I knew would give onlookers the impression that we were best buddies. That was certainly how Madrias felt.

'Gregor, I need your advice on who we should be signing for next season? Do you know of any more Scotland players that are available?'

The club had already signed hooker Steve Brotherstone and prop Tom Smith – it was clear that Brive couldn't get enough Scotsmen in their ranks. I told him that most of the players in Scotland were already signed up for next year and some of them – Bryan Redpath, Stuart Reid, Paul Burnell and Tony Stanger – had joined other French clubs.

'What about Shaun Longstaff or Adam Roxburgh?'

'No chance,' I replied.

Shaun had come to Brive a month earlier and went through some rigorous fitness testing – but a week later he injured his knee. He felt the safer option was to remain in Scotland so he had re-signed for Glasgow. Roxy had impressed Brive for the Borders the previous year – one of the four professional sides in Scotland at the time – and he had a similar style of play to the club's own Olivier Magne. He would have been a great signing, but he too had opted to stay in Scotland.

Madrias then asked my opinion on one or two Brive players that he was thinking about releasing, which put me in a very awkward situation. I couldn't wait to get back to my team-mates who had just finished playing a pre-season friendly against Bègles-Bordeaux.

Ah, the summer of 1999 – heady times indeed. My days were filled with lounging out in the glorious French sunshine on my balcony in Brive, going on an around-the-world holiday with Claire and helping launch the *Champions* video about our Five Nations triumph. I had missed Scotland's development tour to South Africa in order to rest a shoulder injury from earlier in the season, but I felt refreshed and raring to go as we began our preparations for the World Cup. Little was I to know that my knee would break down at training and that I would soon find myself out of favour, not just with the Brive president but the coach as well. By the end of the autumn, my optimism had fallen faster than the leaves from the trees.

My first appearance at a World Cup was a bit of an anti-climax for a number of reasons, but at the time I was mightily relieved just to have experienced the event – a knee injury less than a month before the big kick-off almost forced me to miss my second tournament in succession. Gary Armstrong had landed on me in training a few days before our warm-up matches against Argentina and Romania. The severity of my injury was misdiagnosed at first and I wasted a couple of valuable weeks trying to get back to full fitness.

Luckily, the team physio, Stuart Barton, urged me to get an MRI scan on my knee – he was positive that there was some internal damage that hadn't been picked up by the other medics. However, the scan didn't show anything that warranted further investigation. By sheer chance, I was back in Brive for a few days while a visiting consultant surgeon was also at the club. I showed him my scan results and straight away he pointed out an abnormality – according to him I'd torn my meniscus, which forms part of the knee cartilage. I returned to Scotland and was operated on the following day. This mishap left me with just twelve days to go before Scotland's last warm-up game against Glasgow. Considering I hadn't played for nearly five months, I was in desperate need of some rugby.

It was a close call but I made it just in time for the Glasgow game and was declared fit for the World Cup. Unfortunately, our opening match was against the reigning champions, South Africa. We were very rusty – none more so than me – and we were beaten 46–29. My own game was far too loose and clumsy. I can't use my injury as an excuse, though, as I committed some basic errors that weren't due to a lack of match practice but to a lack of concentration. We did play our part in producing an exciting, open game and managed to score two tries. It was the only match in which the Springboks conceded a try throughout the tournament, even though they played the likes of England, Australia and the All Blacks.

It would have been nice to have started with Spain or Uruguay (our two following matches), but the organizers chose to pit the world champions and the Five Nations champions together in the first round of matches – a miscalculation (certainly from our perspective!) as the group's positions were pretty much decided from then on.

The World Cup was a pretty dismal affair for the northern hemisphere nations – Ireland crashed out at the group stage and France were the only team to make it past the quarter-finals. We were drastically under-prepared for the Springbok match and, in retrospect, we could have done with more games in our build-up. We played only two Test matches in the six-month gap from our Five Nations win until the World Cup – against Argentina and Romania – while the southern hemisphere countries had the intensity of some incoming tours and the Tri-Nations to get them battle-hardened. If we'd played South Africa in the summer, or a month after our win in Paris, it would have been a very different proposition.

Another blow to our morale was the injury to John Leslie. I remember joking with John in the showers at the Stade de France at the end of the previous season. It was the last time I saw him before the World Cup build-up began, as he was going to Japan to play for Sanix. 'Make sure you don't pick up an injury out there!' I said.

'Don't worry, mate – I'm never injured,' was the reply.

It was true that John had hardly missed any games during the previous ten years of senior rugby, but the ankle injury he suffered in the second-half against the Springboks was a turning point, not just in the match itself but also for his career.

Deep into the second-half, we were trailing by only three points when John had collected my chip ahead and was careering to the try-line. I was unmarked on his outside but he probably didn't need to use me as it looked like he was going to score himself. A last-gasp tackle by South African winger Deon Kayser (who would later be a team-mate of mine at the Sharks) denied us a try and also forced John from the field. He was out of action for five months and never again produced the form he had displayed so wonderfully that year.

Our remaining pool games were desperate affairs. Just over 9,000 people turned up for the matches against Uruguay and Spain – less than the amount that had spontaneously arrived at Murrayfield on a Monday night in April to see the Five Nations trophy being presented. The main reason for this apathy was due to the poor organization of the tournament. Fixtures were arranged on weekday afternoons and ticket prices were much higher than for normal internationals. I also think that there

were still many people in the country eager to make a statement of displeasure at the SRU's running of the game. Either
way, it was incredibly disappointing for the players.

I thought naively that our championship win would galva-
nize support for the game within Scotland and persuade the
SRU's critics to start looking positively at what could be
achieved. Instead, a fantastic opportunity to grow the game
was wasted (which contrasts sharply with the reaction and
buzz created in England after the 2003 World Cup). Realisti-
cally, winning the Five Nations was the equivalent to a World
Cup victory for a country like Scotland. And yet, six months
later, we had pitiful crowds for three of our World Cup
matches and more than 10,000 empty seats for our quarter-
final match against New Zealand.

Before the All Blacks game, we faced Samoa (again at
Murrayfield) in a play-off match. The Samoans always seem
to turn it on for World Cups – they'd made the last eight on
their previous two appearances – and had already beaten
Wales in a pool game. Only 15,000 supporters were there to
see us play our best game of the tournament as we took the
direct, physical approach that had worked for Scotland in the
1991 World Cup, winning 35–20. It was also my best
performance of the competition by miles – I felt like my knee
operation was a distant memory.

The play-offs had been another organizational error –
thankfully addressed for the World Cup in 2003. By having
five pools instead of four, it meant that only the winners
progressed directly to the last eight. England, Argentina and
ourselves all had to play a match four days before the quarter-
finals. Unsurprisingly, none of us made it into the last four.

We played very near to our potential in the quarter-final
and the important thing for me was that we kept up our level
of performance throughout the whole eighty minutes. I
remember sitting in the changing rooms at half-time and
going over for a quiet word with Jim Telfer.

'I don't think we can play much better than that, Jim.'

'I know, but we've got to keep it going.'

We were both aware that even our best wasn't going to be good enough against the All Blacks. Their first-half display was as close to perfection as was possible, especially given the wet weather at Murrayfield. It had been a fairly even opening period, but they had the class to put points on the board whenever they had us under any kind of pressure. We trailed 25–3 at the break.

Our second half was an outstanding team effort – we 'won' it by 15–5 and scored two tries through Cammie Murray and Martin Leslie. It was a fitting send-off to three players who were retiring from international rugby – Gary Armstrong, Alan Tait and Paul Burnell. It was also supposed to be Jim Telfer's farewell as coach, but he couldn't resist the challenge of helping the Scottish cause and came out of retirement two years later.

I didn't have much free time after our exit from the World Cup, as the French championship had already started. My first game back for Brive was against Narbonne – who had my Scottish colleagues Stuart Reid and Bryan Redpath in their ranks. I managed to get a try in our home win. I was then made captain for the second half of our next match against Montauban, but this was to be the end of the happy times at Brive. In France's dramatic World Cup semi-final win against the All Blacks, my club-mate Christophe Lamaison had starred in the number 10 jersey. As soon as he returned from the World Cup, I found myself out of the picture. The president, who only a few months before had embraced me like his favourite son, never again spoke more than two words to me.

I had a lot to thank Brive for – not just for the fact that I had been able to play regularly in the number 10 jersey. My handling skills and defence had improved immeasurably in France, and backs coach Francis Leta had devised an ingenious way of helping my kicking. He had got the club to invest in two poles as tall as the goal posts, which he placed five metres apart in varying places along the touchline. My accuracy at kicking to touch from penalties was much better as a result. Despite some early problems adapting to French club rugby, my game had been of a consistently high standard. Regrettably, my second season in France was a particularly distressing time.

I knew I'd have a challenge on my hands for the stand-off jersey as Christophe had performed so well for the national side. However, he rarely hit the heights for Brive. Try as I might – and I put in some really good performances – I found myself more often than not sitting on the replacements bench.

Lamaison was by no means a 'team player' and he would frequently have a go at others at training and during games, even though he was struggling for form himself. This made it even more frustrating for me – his play and attitude should have prevented him from being anywhere near the starting line-up, but it was clear that he was first choice stand-off, no matter what. Leta, the backs coach, tried his hardest to persuade new head coach Serge Laïrle that I should start, but it was all to no avail – a few months into the season, Laïrle brought in another backs coach, effectively sidelining my only supporter on the coaching staff.

Serge Laïrle had managed to upset quite a number of players at the club. For some inexplicable reason he had our brilliant scrum-half prospect Dimitri Yachvili playing for the 2nd XV (and on some occasions he wasn't even deemed good enough for that level). It was no surprise that Dimitri later left France to further his career at Gloucester and then Biarritz. Laïrle obviously seemed to like going against conventional wisdom – when we played Agen he picked our full-back at scrum-half and our number 8 (and future French cap) Elvis Vermeulen at prop. Poor Elvis – he looked white as a sheet before the game, as it was the first time he had ever played in the front row. I remember Laïrle slapping him on the face and saying, 'I played in the front row, second row and the back row when I was your age, so give yourself a shake and get stuck in out there.' He left the field after only twenty minutes with a neck injury that, luckily, didn't turn out to be serious.

For our last match before the Christmas break I was given a starting spot away to Stade Français. Despite losing, we had played well and the coaches said to us that whoever put work in during our ten-day break would play in our next match against Toulouse. Now, I would never profess to being the fittest player in the world but, after training hard on my own over Christmas and New Year, I recorded the best results in the club at the fitness testing we did on our return. It didn't make a difference – I was named on the bench once more for the Toulouse game. I lost the little faith I had left in the trustworthiness of the Brive management, and I realized that leaving the club was my only option. I wasn't the only one thinking this way – eleven out of the twelve internationalists at Brive left the club at the end of the season. Tom Smith was the one who remained, a season that saw Brive relegated from the top flight and coach Laïrle removed from his post following a petition by the players.

I looked forward to joining up with Scotland – it appeared that I now had much more chance of playing for my country than for my club. Our first match of the inaugural Six Nations tournament was away to Italy, and it will be forever remembered as being a tremendous day for the new side or a humiliating defeat for the champions, depending on whether you are Scottish or not. It wasn't the finest hour in the history of Scottish rugby and it must be a game that our coach, Ian McGeechan, would like wiped from his memory.

That Geech had taken over as head coach following the World Cup which was hailed as a coup for the SRU, as the RFU had been very close to persuading him to take charge of the England team. I, like many others, welcomed the appointment – at the time Geech was still one of the best in the business and an inspiration to listen to and play for. However, he didn't make the most auspicious of starts to his second reign with Scotland.

Everyone involved at the highest level of sport has an appreciation of the ephemeral nature of success and how painfully precarious it is to repeat. On the odd occasions Scotland has reached the summits of international rugby, in 1984 and 1990 for example, each triumph has been followed by a season of under-achievement. It probably wasn't the best time for Geech to take over – right after we had won the championship – and we didn't help him with a passionless display in Rome. It was as if we had seen the banana skin in front of us and serenely walked right onto it.

The momentum we had created the previous year disappeared in an instant and we struggled to rediscover our form throughout the rest of the campaign. There were a few reasons for this. First and foremost we failed to gain parity up front in our opening two games. It is much more difficult to play on the back foot, as we were forced to do in Rome and then Dublin, and the quality of ball we had was nothing like it had been the year before. Also, the retirement of Gary Armstrong, Alan Tait and Paul Burnell left a gaping hole of experience in the squad. But it was the handling of John Leslie that most hampered our focus going into the Italian match.

Geech had made the controversial decision of installing John as Scotland captain. It was the first time that Scotland had named a captain who had been born, and played almost all of his rugby, in New Zealand. His father, Andy, was a former All Black captain and John's appointment caused a right stink. I didn't think he was the right choice as captain – after all, Bryan Redpath had been a terrific skipper before he missed out on the 1999 Five Nations through injury. Also, like many Scots, I felt it was a slight on players who had been involved for many years in Scottish rugby.

John was a strong character with forceful views and had quickly become an important figure within the squad. He tended to question authority and always looked at ways of doing things differently to the set instructions given by the coaches. I believe he was too questioning to be a captain but was of great value as a dissenting voice without the obligation of position – an excellent foil for a captain, but ill-suited to the top job. He also didn't care much for the Scottish media, which later became apparent when he had to attend press conferences with the coaching staff. For all these reasons, Geech should never have made him captain – but more crucially, John should never have been included in the team for our opening game.

John had only arrived back in Scotland the Monday before the Italian game after getting married in New Zealand that weekend. It turned out that he hadn't been able to play a match for his club in Japan, Sanix, following his ankle injury during the World Cup. That Monday, he told me, was the first full training he had managed to do since then. No one can go into Test rugby without having played at least one competitive game in the previous three months. Perhaps he thought (like all of us no doubt) that the wonderful rugby we had played the year before would just happen as soon as we got back together again. We were in for a rude awakening.

We certainly weren't lacking in confidence and we actually started the match the much better side. Unfortunately, Kenny Logan missed four kicks at goal and then, after only fifteen minutes of play, John Leslie hobbled off injured. We lost our shape and soon after that, our hopes of winning the match. The ultimate 34–20 defeat was one of the worst results from a Scottish team in living memory.

Suddenly, we were under tremendous pressure for our next game, away to Ireland, in what had recently become an extremely tough fixture. Even though I'd not had that much game time since the World Cup, I'd actually played reasonably well against Italy, and I thought that by being back at stand-off my form could only improve.

Our tremendous run in the previous year's championship proved that confidence is contagious. We soon discovered that in sport a loss of confidence can also reach epidemic levels. Experiencing incredible highs and staggering lows is part and parcel of an international rugby career, but at Lansdowne Road I went through the full gamut of emotions in eighty minutes. If only the game had finished on a high, the pain would have been easier to bear.

We actually looked to be back to our best early in the match. My own game was going really well and my kicking couldn't have been better. In the corresponding fixture a year before, Stuart Grimes had finished off one of the best ever Scottish team tries. After twenty minutes we scored another cracking try against the Irish. After Scott Murray had caught an up-and-under, we counter-attacked with Budge Pountney and Glenn Metcalfe making crucial inroads. After recycling quick ball, this sweeping move ended with me floating out a wide pass to the unmarked Kenny Logan to run in for his first ever try in the championship. Kenny made no mistake with the touchline conversion.

The match was my first exposure to the magnificent Brian O'Driscoll. And he ripped us to shreds. For years, Ireland had always been strong up front, but what they desperately needed was a world-class player in their midfield. In O'Driscoll they had just that, and more. A supremely talented and competitive force in attack and defence, for me he ranks as the best centre I have seen in the game in the last twenty years. He would also be among the top five attacking players I have played against, the others being – Tana Umaga, Rupeni Caucaunibuca, Jonah Lomu and Christian Cullen.

After half an hour we were leading 10–3 and seemingly in control of our destiny. The concluding fifty minutes saw us concede forty-one points, as we crashed to a 44–22 defeat. It was a painful and lonely experience for those of us in a blue jersey. As soon as we went behind I tried to force things to get us back in the game, but my efforts had a decidedly low success rate. Despite the fact that I was attacking the line well, a poor pass of mine led to a score for Ireland.

I remember trying to bring Stuart Grimes into the game with an inside pass – but he ran outside. The ball dropped loose and David Humphreys kicked on. I lay helpless on the ground as Ireland surged forward for yet another try. I could imagine David Johnston sitting at home in his front room, smiling to himself: 'What did I say all along? Townsend cannot be trusted in the number 10 jersey.'

Not for the first time I was reminded that the pain of disappointment – whether through losing form, losing a match or non-selection – is much worse than any physical pain one endures in a rugby career. We lost our next match 28–16 at home to the French and, although we had performed much better, the opposition had been there for the taking. Failure plays such havoc with your senses that sometimes you doubt your ability to perform even the most basic of tasks. I knew I had to change my worries into positive thinking and my anxiety into creative action.

I managed to block out the disappointment of losing with Scotland during Brive's trip to Clermont, where we were due to play a quarter-final match of the French Cup against Bourgoin. Instead of worrying about the negatives of Scotland's start to the Six Nations and the fact that I'd not played that much for Brive, I focused on why rugby gave me so much pleasure. It came down to the fact that I loved running with the ball, finding where there were holes in the opposition defence and making the correct decisions. All I could prepare myself for was willing the ball to come to me, safe in the knowledge that I would do whatever was the right thing to do in any given situation. I found space that night and took control of the game.

With Lamaison out injured for a couple of months, I managed to get a run of games at stand-off for Brive. We recorded some notable victories, making it all the way to the French Cup Final against Biarritz. It is never easy telling yourself you have what it takes to perform at the highest level immediately after you have lost while representing your country. Your first emotional response is a sense of shame that you have let down so many people. But you can't let negativity cloud your judgement and aspirations. I had won the battle inside my head and felt ready to take on the world.

However, I knew from my previous experiences that my improved, but ultimately uninspired, display against France wasn't going to be enough for me to keep my place at stand-off. I was moved to centre for the Welsh match, the occasion of winning my 50th cap. Whilst I was grateful to have kept my place in the starting line-up, I still felt somewhat frustrated as I felt I had finally regained my form playing for Brive.

Our trip to Cardiff had seen us lose again, this time 26–18, to a Welsh side that had been forced to drop New Zealanders Shane Howarth and Brett Sinkinson because of doubts over their eligibility. We hadn't been able to capitalize on their internal problems, producing yet another mediocre performance.

It was tradition for the SRU president to address the players after an international, prior to the after-match dinner. That season, Harvey Wright, our amiable president, had tried to remain as upbeat as possible following defeat after defeat. At the end of every speech he reminded us that the most important match of the season was our last – at home to England. He said that he knew we would be victorious. These turned out to be prophetic words indeed.

In contrast to our played four, lost four stats, England – with four successive wins under their belts – were overwhelming favourites to end the season with a Grand Slam. They had just beaten Italy in Rome 59–12, whereas we went into the match without our injured captain John Leslie, who had previously returned to the side for our games against France and Wales. After Lawrence Dallaglio had scored early in the match, and with England leading 10–3 at one point, there was no reason to believe that we were going to pull off a shock result.

I have to hold my hands up – Dallaglio's try was partly my fault. With England wheeling our scrum, I called full-back Chris Paterson over to defend against his opposite number on the left-hand side of the field. This had left quite a lot of space on the other side of the scrum for Dallaglio to go past Andy Nicol. Fortunately, Andy was smiling at the end of the match – he became the first Scottish captain to lift the Calcutta Cup in ten years. He had led the side well and put in a courageous performance at scrum-half.

We were clearly 'up for it' as they say. We more than matched England in terms of physicality and there was a fair bit of niggle throughout the game. Despite Jim McLaren being yellow-carded in the first half, it was England who lost their discipline and with it any composure they once had. We went on to win 19–13.

There is a simple recipe for success in international rugby – forward dominance, solid defence and an elimination of errors. For the first time that year we managed to do all three. The horrendous conditions at Murrayfield made it hard for attacking rugby – something the English fatally failed to realize – so it came down to who wanted to win the most and which side made the more effective use of the deteriorating weather.

The match was a personal triumph for Duncan Hodge, who scored all nineteen points. It was the happiest I'd seen him playing for Scotland. Hodgey was very popular throughout the squad and I don't think there could have been a nicer guy to be in competition with for the number 10 jersey. He recently said in an interview that if he was to come back in another life he wouldn't want to be a stand-off, as the pressure is so great. I can empathize with that. Still, the memory of beating England must have made it all seem worthwhile. Hodgey played the conditions much better than Jonny Wilkinson that day and it was a tremendous end to our season. I was also delighted for Geech, who had taken flak for the way we had performed that year. It must have been pleasing for him to get one over on the side he turned down in order to coach Scotland.

The result generated an amazing response throughout the country, which I actually found a bit undeserving. By the public's reaction it was as if we'd repeated the heroics of the 1990 Grand Slam team. I for one wasn't going to forget the four matches we had lost. Still, we weren't going to complain too much and were quick to help the SRU promote the DVD of our glorious win. It was a cathartic moment for the players at the end of what had been a trying season for us all.

In the summer we toured New Zealand and I continued to play at outside-centre. After suffering a heavy defeat in our first test, we were very competitive a week later in Auckland. However, the All Black back three of Christian Cullen, Tana Umaga and Jonah Lomu proved the difference. They were a class apart and seemed to be able to conjure breaks from nothing. A pattern had begun to emerge where our pack was starting to play very well and at times we dominated the possession stats, but any time we lost the ball the opposition would run in scores from anything up to eighty metres. It was a lot of work for no reward, and was really a combination of two things: not having the same quality of attacking players was undeniable, but we also tended to go to ground too easily. This meant that although we were able to recycle possession, we never really looked like getting in behind the opposition defence.

International players in the UK and Ireland had only one thing on their minds – the 2001 Lions tour to Australia. Just to be on one Lions tour in a career is incredible – to prove that you were once up there with the best in the game. However, having experienced such a wonderful time with the Lions in 1997, I was totally focused on doing everything in my power to make it onto the trip to Australia.

The appointment of New Zealander Graham Henry as Lions coach had been criticized initially as being inappropriate because he was the first person to be in charge who wasn't from Britain or Ireland. This wasn't that much of a problem to the Scottish players at the time – it was the possibility of favouritism in selection towards his Welsh team that worried us. My brother had bought me Henry's autobiography for Christmas and he hoped, like me, that Henry would become my coach five months later. From a purely selfish point of view, I wasn't that upset when Henry had been announced as the first foreign coach of the Lions. A few years before, Keith Barwell, the Northampton owner, had informed me that Henry, who was the Auckland Blues coach at the time, had contacted the club regarding my availability to play for his side in the Super 12. Reading Henry's book gave me even more reason to believe that I was his type of player:

> *A player who's got everything is Scotland's Gregor Townsend. He's a gifted attacker who has benefited from playing with Brive in the French competition. It's obviously been good for him. He's always been classy but the players around him have not always understood what he is doing. He built a telling association with John Leslie in 1999 and they both played superbly.*

I knew that his views of me as a player would be less relevant if I was to repeat the season I had endured in 2000. I was determined to get back to top form, reclaim my place at stand-off in the Scotland side and show Henry that the previous season had just been a blip.

Prior to the 2000/01 season, I had discussed with Ian McGeechan the options I was considering with regard to where I was going to play my club rugby. I knew that if I'd stayed at Brive and repeated the season that I'd just experienced, there would be no way I'd make the Lions squad. London Irish, Harlequins, Toulon and Castres were my four options, with my preference being Castres who had qualified for the Heineken Cup and whose coach, Alain Gaillard, wanted me to play in the number 10 jersey. I was also keen to stay in France. Nevertheless, my fears were that I would be out of sight and thus out of mind in relation to the Lions selectors.

It made my decision on where to play a more difficult one, but I was reassured by Geech that the selectors were bound to check thoroughly on every player that was under consideration, no matter where they played. He said the selection process for 1997 was very exhaustive and they had even picked Irish prop Peter Clohessy who was playing for Queensland at the time. So, with the knowledge that I would have the opportunity to be watched in the French championship as well as in the European Cup and hopefully for Scotland, I signed for Castres. I knew it would have to be a season where my play was of a consistently high standard, especially after Christmas.

Castres, a town of 43,000 inhabitants, lay three hours south-east of Brive. I now found myself in the Midi – the heart of French rugby. The famous rugby strongholds of Toulouse, Beziers and Albi encircled this former weaving town situated on the banks of the river Tarn. The pace of life was even more sedate than in Brive and I settled in quickly to my new surroundings. My French was now at a reasonably good standard – chatting away with friends was pretty much error-free, but the odd live TV interview and speaking to those lacking patience could still prove troublesome. In Castres I also had to get used to the strong southern accent. On top of that, my team-mates confused me now and again by throwing in the odd word from Occitan (known as the *Langue d'oc*). But the biggest change was that the local twang seemed to add the letter g to most of their words. Thus, *paing*, *copaing* and *fing* became bread, friend and end.

Castres didn't make that much of an impression in the Heineken Cup, mainly because we had been severely handicapped by being docked two points for fielding an ineligible player. However, our form in the championship was very good and by the turn of the year, we were leading our section. (The French league was split into two pools of eight at the time.) This had included an impressive 29–0 home win over Stade Français and an away win against Perpignan that had contained three drop-goals from me – definitely something I wasn't going to repeat ever again in my career! Our experiences in Europe, where we had been very competitive against Munster and Bath, were of real benefit, and we were now regarded as outside contenders for the French championship.

My own form was certainly better than the year before and I was soon beginning to take real pleasure in my performances once again. Scotland had three autumn internationals and I was very pleased to discover that I had been selected at stand-off. I responded by playing well in our opening game against the USA. There were also signs that John Leslie was back on form. We won 53–6 and, having been given the goal-kicking duties after some success at Castres, I scored thirty-three points (which set an individual points record at Murrayfield).

Our next match, against Australia, was a much sterner challenge and had significance in that our opponents would also be playing the Lions the following summer. I'm sure there were a few of us thinking that a good performance against the Wallabies would make the Lions selectors take notice. Australia, the world champions, had a really physical side – each one of their backs (apart from the scrum-half) was listed as weighing in at over 100 kg (fifteen and a half stone). In contrast, we had no one in our backline that was even close to 100 kg. It wasn't the most enterprising of Wallaby teams, but they had an aggressive and organized defence allied to a game plan that was all about keeping the ball for phase after phase. We lost 30–9 after being level 9–9 at half-time, a couple of defensive lapses costing us dearly. I was happy with my game – I'd played with control and even managed one or two line breaks. The following week against Samoa, we cruised to a 31–8 win. All in all, it had been a satisfactory three matches and I felt on track.

Our first match in the Six Nations was away to France and we were determined to pull out a shock result that might go a long way to erasing the memory of our opening defeat in Rome the previous season. We started firing on all cylinders, very much like we had done in the same stadium in 1999. Up against my former team-mate and rival, Christophe Lamaison, I was feeling very sharp and made a break that put Cammie Murray in the clear and helped set up a lineout ten yards from the French line. We dummied a drive from the lineout and I surged onto off-the-top ball. I was tackled agonizingly close to the try-line – agonizing in more ways than one, as I was trapped between two French forwards. I became twisted back and felt the pressure of the two men holding me bearing down on my knee. As a result, I could do nothing as my medial ligaments were torn apart.

I was out of action for six weeks and missed the games against England and Wales. (Scotland had lost against France and at Twickenham but salvaged a draw at home to the Welsh.) My comeback game was against Mont-de-Marsan and it was here that I saw the game I fell in love with. It had colour, history, personality and romance. I'd got out on the field early and went out and stretched on my own. There was already a big crowd in the surrounding terracing. This was real rugby country – I could easily have been in Limerick, Gloucester or Taranaki. Half an hour earlier I'd been chatting with André Boniface, a legend of French rugby and an absolute gentleman. The stadium at Mont-de-Marsan was named in honour of his brother Guy, who was killed in a car crash at the age of thirty-one, after having partnered André in the centres for France throughout the Sixties. It felt like a special arena in which to play rugby.

There are times when the game shares its essential character with you – that night I looked past the game plan, the expectations, the pressures and the disappointments and took everything in. Maybe the reason I felt so exhilarated was because I was fit again. No matter, it brought home what rugby really meant to me and I treasured the moment. I ran, kicked and tackled with aplomb, and we came away with a hard-fought victory.

The following week I was recalled for Scotland against Italy, this time at outside-centre. We went on to win 23–19, although we hadn't played that well. I was relieved to have come through the game unscathed, but my hopes of getting another taste of Test match rugby that season – and the possibility of playing at stand-off – were dashed, as our final match against Ireland was called off because of the foot-and-mouth epidemic. I had just over a month to get back to the form I was in before my injury and prove to the Lions selectors that I deserved to be in the final touring party. And I was soon back into my stride, helping Castres back to the top of the pool, equal on points with Stade Français.

The Lions selectors announced an initial squad of sixty-seven in March and, from a Scottish perspective, there was a hugely disappointing level of representation. Of the sixty-seven players, twenty-two were from England, eighteen were from Wales, fifteen from Ireland and only twelve from Scotland. After all, this was a team that had won the Five Nations Championship less than two years before. There were four stand-offs listed – Jonny Wilkinson, Neil Jenkins, Ronan O'Gara and myself. The following month, a week before the touring party was due to be announced, I received a call from Lions manager Donal Lenihan.

'Hi Gregor. I thought I'd warn you that Graham Henry and I are coming out to watch you in Paris this weekend. We're looking at both yourself as well as Jeremy [Davidson].'

'Oh, great. You've picked an easy match – away to the champions!'

'Yes, I know, but we're trying to see as many players as we can before we sit down to pick the final squad. As you know, we're going to take three stand-offs on tour and you are one of the four that are in contention.'

'Just out of interest – has someone watched me in France before?' I asked.

'No – but you were seen when you played over here in the European Cup.'

Excellent – the first time that I was to be seen in France and it was up against a Stade Français side hell-bent on revenge and looking for a win that would decide who qualified as top seeds for the knock-out stages of the French championship. It was the most nervous I'd felt before a game in years – a different feeling to a Test match, more like a trial game in which you are the only player under observation.

As it turned out, the game couldn't have gone any better for me. I played well and late on I broke through the Stade Français defence to score the match-winning try. We had won 37–34, which was very unusual for a French side away from home, especially against such quality opposition. I didn't see Lenihan or Henry afterwards and had no feedback on my performance, but French journalists were saying to me that I must now be a certainty to tour. The reasoning seemed logical: I had performed as well as I could in the only club match that I'd been watched in. I, on the other hand, still had my doubts. With Wilkinson a deserved shoe-in, I knew Neil Jenkins would be well regarded by Henry (he'd had an excellent match for Wales that season in their defeat of France). My club colleague (and Irish second-row) Jeremy Davidson also told me that Ronan O'Gara had close ties to Lenihan, as they were both from the same club, Cork Constitution. I felt distinctly out of the loop.

My fears were compounded on 25 April, the day before my twenty-eighth birthday. I knew it was the day the squad was going to be announced and, as I hadn't heard anything, I thought I might have to wait right until the press conference.

That morning, rays of sunlight edged through the shutters of my bedroom window. It looked like it was going to be another warm day in Castres. I looked over at the bedside clock – it was 8 a.m. I'd been awake for ten minutes or so, but I was still lying in bed when the phone rang. I picked up the receiver. It was Donal Lenihan on the other line. When I first heard his voice, for some strange reason I thought he must have been calling me to tell me the good news. This was no doubt because Ian McGeechan had told me on the morning of the announcement in 1997 that I'd made the touring party. What he said was, 'It was a tight call, but we've gone with three recognized goal-kickers as the stand-offs for the squad in Ronan, Neil and Jonny. Sorry, but you just missed out.'

There was so much I wanted to say, but I knew it was already too late. I could never pretend that I was anywhere in the class of Jenks or Jonny as a goal-kicker, but I had kicked that season for Castres and could be an option for the Lions. I was going to say that two world-class goal-kickers should be more than enough or what about having goal-kickers in other positions, as had been the case in 1997? The coaches must have been aware that scrum-half Matt Dawson had already kicked well in the lead-up to the tour. However, it wasn't a long conversation and I decided to keep my thoughts on the matter to myself.

Immediately afterwards, I called Jeremy to find out whether he'd heard anything. A week before, he had been told that it was going to come to a decision between Ian Gough, Stuart Grimes and himself for the last second-row place on tour. He hadn't played that well in Paris and all week he'd been down, resigned to the fact that the selectors were going to choose one of the other two. However, he had been given good news that morning – he was going to Australia. I was delighted for him, as he was a totally committed player, a great tourist and had been a revelation in South Africa in 1997.

From my own perspective all I could think of was the fact that I wouldn't be a part of the Lions of 2001 and, having set it as my main goal of the season, I was devastated. My non-selection was without doubt the biggest disappointment of my career.

From the amazing highs of winning the last ever Five Nations Championship in 1999, Scottish rugby had suddenly been dismissed as an insignificant force. Only three Scotland players – Tom Smith, Scott Murray and Simon Taylor – were chosen for the tour, even though the touring party had increased from thirty-five to thirty-seven players since the 1997 campaign in South Africa, when five Scots had been selected. Wales this time contributed ten players. We had won the last ever Five Nations in 1999 and, although we had finished second last in 2000, we ended up third in that season's Six Nations, one place above Wales. Despite this, no Scottish backline player was deemed good enough to be selected.

It seemed obvious why this had been the case: the management team for 2001 comprised Welsh head coach Graham Henry and England coaches Andy Robinson, Dave Alred, Steve Black and Phil Larder. The manager, Donal Lenihan, was Irish. From having the two main coaches on the 1997 tour, no Scot was involved in the management structure. It is no coincidence that we had been overlooked.

That's the way Jim Telfer saw it anyway, and he revealed his anger to the media after the tour had ended. This was someone who knew what he was talking about – he'd coached on two Lions tours, and in 1997 had resisted the temptation to call up more of his fellow Scots:

> *It is a crime in a way that Gregor Townsend was not there. He is a quality player whereas Neil Jenkins and Ronan O'Gara were never in contention for Test selection come the end of the series. The coach and the manager went for players they knew. There was something a bit nationalistic in selection this time.*

Lions captain Martin Johnson also believed that Graham Henry had made a mistake. This is from his book about the tour, *Agony and Ecstasy*:

> *I would have taken Gregor Townsend instead [of Neil Jenkins]. In fact I would have taken Gregor as one of the fly-halves ahead of Ronan O'Gara. My argument is that he has that class that very few people possess. He can open teams up, which is always needed. He is also adaptable, having the ability to play centre as well as No.10, not that that is a prerequisite with a squad of 37.*

It was heartening reading Jim and Jonno's remarks – they didn't have to comment on my omission – but in truth it probably cemented the grievance I felt at not being included. It felt so unfair at the time as I was playing much better than I had been in 1997. In April, just a few weeks after recovering from my knee injury, I had been voted player of the month by the French rugby paper *Midi Olympique*. However, it was clear that my performance against Stade Français had counted for nothing. I began to think that I was watched that day in Paris in the hope that I wouldn't have played well and that the game could be used as a convienent excuse.

A few weeks into the tour, while reluctantly watching the Lions take on New South Wales, I noticed that Rob Henderson had gone down injured. I felt another stab of disappointment. This was a scenario I had once pictured in my head – coming off the bench to play at stand-off with a dream centre partnership outside me of Jonny Wilkinson and Brian O'Driscoll. Instead, I had to look away as Ronan O'Gara ran on to play at fly-half.

A week after the NSW game I received a call from Dublin of all places – it was from the secretary of the Lions. She told me that both Neil Jenkins and Will Greenwood were carrying injuries and it looked like I would be needed out in Australia as soon as possible. She said that I had been booked on a flight from Toulouse to Paris the following morning in order to get the connecting flight from there out to Sydney. There was still an outside chance of both of them recovering, but this seemed very unlikely. I was to wait for her to call first thing in the morning for final confirmation before heading from Castres to Toulouse airport.

After a sleepless night of packing bags and trying to contain my excitement, I was on the phone to Dublin first thing in the morning. I was informed that no decision had yet been made and that I had to wait for further information to come through from the management in Australia. Time ticked by, so much so that it was now going to be impossible for me to make the Toulouse flight. Eventually, a few hours later, I was told that both Will and Jenks were going to be allowed to stay on to see if their conditions improved. I never heard from the Lions again. Getting hit with a second major disappointment in the same month was a real body blow. Martin Johnson recalled the incident in *Agony and Ecstasy*:

*It had been abundantly apparent, since before we left the UK, that
Jenks' knee was dodgy. By the time of the New South Wales
Cockatoos game during the week of the first Test, he was, to all
intents and purposes, unable to continue on tour. Graham Henry,
almost in passing, said: 'Shall we send for Gregor Townsend?' I felt
this was the right option. Gregor has great class and would have
added a lot but I never heard the issue raised again, unfortunately.
Henry should have taken the difficult decision and Gregor should
have been on a plane on the evening of that Cockatoos game, June
26. But it didn't happen.*

Just to add to my frustration some more, for the first Test, there
wasn't even a recognized stand-off on the bench – Austin Healy
had been promoted ahead of Jenkins and O'Gara. It made a
mockery of the previous insistence on a goal-kicking number
10 as cover for Jonny Wilkinson. Scrum-half Matt Dawson,
who was also a replacement, had been kicking ahead of O'Gara
in the midweek games. Still, I felt no pleasure at the Lions failure to win the Test series, or the many reports that it had been
a wretched time for many of the players.

It looked like the management had drawn some lessons
from 1997 but not the crucial elements that made it work –
that is, keeping the squad as one. From what I could gather,
the cohesion of the party was damaged by a concentration on
the Test side that left others feeling isolated. The tour was crit-
ically undermined by splits, jealousies and factionalism as a
result. On the Monday before the first Test, the midweek
team were left largely to their own devices as the coaches
worked with the Test side. In 2005 in New Zealand, having a
different coaching staff for the midweek side further exacerbated this. At some stage you are going to rely on people from
the midweek side, so they need to feel they are getting a fair
chance of making the Saturday team. With all we have
learned from tours past, it was infuriating to watch another
Lions tour crumble because of rifts within the squad.

In 2001, just as in 1997, the squad went through some punishing training sessions. Tom Smith told me it was even harder than in 1997. I think this missed the point – in 1997 the game had gone professional and we needed to do a vast amount of work, particularly in defence, to catch up with the level at which the Springbok players were competing. Four years later, the game in the northern hemisphere was at a much higher level, and the Heineken Cup was similar in its quality and intensity to the Super 12. The last thing the players needed was a 'beasting' after a punishing season. The reasons given at the time were that players from other nations had a lot of work to do to get up to speed with the defensive systems used by the English players under the tutelage of Phil Larder.

From a Scottish point of view, the neglect of so many quality players was a disgrace. It was bad enough in 2001, but things got ridiculous in 2005. With a hugely inflated touring squad of forty-five, only three Scots were selected. It wasn't as if there weren't plenty of talented individuals – Jason White, Ally Hogg, Mike Blair, Chris Paterson, Sean Lamont and others had all performed well that year. On any Lions tour, selection is the key. History shows that it had been right in 1997 but not in 2001 or 2005.

I tried to console myself the best I could with the fact that I still had a few games remaining of the French season while the cream of British and Irish rugby were preparing to leave for Australia. Castres had topped the section and we had gone on to beat Colomiers in the quarter-final of the French championship. It was the first time in six years that the club had made it to the semi-finals and the town was buzzing with anticipation that we could make it through to the final at the Stade de France. Standing in our way was the best known, and best-funded, side in France – Toulouse. Worse still was the fact that the semi-final was due to be played in Toulouse, a stroke of luck for our opponents as the venues had been decided some months before.

If ever there was a game that reminds me about the best elements of French rugby, then this was it. The atmosphere was amazing – 40,000 passionate supporters made more noise than any international match I'd played in. Unfortunately, more than 30,000 of them were cheering for Toulouse. The colour, banners, and racket from the stands created a fantastic backdrop on a blisteringly hot afternoon. Toulouse had just hit some form late in the season and started the match on fire – racing to an early ten-point lead. In their side that day were two eighteen-year-olds, centre Clément Poitrenaud and scrum-half Frédéric Michalak. They performed exceptionally well and, despite matching Toulouse on the try count, we were never able to claw back their lead.

Although we lost, we vied with Toulouse for the majority of the game, and in our minds we contented ourselves with the fact that we were probably the second best team in France, as Toulouse went on to record an easy win in the final over Montferrand. It was the only compensation I could think of for what had been a thoroughly disappointing few weeks. To paraphrase the legendary Buddy Guy, 'Damn right, I'd had the blues.'

CHAPTER 12

Full Circle

*If you really want something in this life, you have to
work hard for it. Now quiet, they're about to
announce the lottery numbers.*

Homer Simpson

'Geech, do you realize what the reaction is going to be?'

'Let me worry about the press.'

'We're not just talking about the media – this is going to make a lot of people involved in Scottish rugby very angry.'

With that, I think the penny dropped for Geech. His decision to select Brendan Laney, a New Zealander, for a Test match against Argentina just four days after he'd arrived in the country, was more significant than he had at first thought. It had already caused a great deal of consternation within the Scotland squad. This was why we had called an unprecedented crisis meeting with him in the hope that we could persuade him to change his mind.

The international season had started early for us that year, as we had to play our rearranged Six Nations fixture against Ireland in September. The Irish were being tipped for a Grand Slam, as they were unbeaten with three games remaining. We had a strong team out and were keen to make a statement to the Lions selectors that they had been wrong in only picking three Scots for the tour to Australia. I was back at stand-off with Bryan Redpath partnering me at scrum-half while John Leslie and Jim McLaren formed a new centre combination.

After a shaky start with the boot, I carried on my good form of the previous season and was involved in all four of our tries. Chris Paterson took over the goal-kicking duties from me and we played some great rugby to record a resounding 32–10 win. The renowned rugby writer, Norman Mair, described it as 'Scotland's best post-war defensive performance'. We had kept Brian O'Driscoll quiet and the Irish only came into the game when David Humphreys replaced Ronan O'Gara in the last quarter. Their solitary try had come in injury time. It had been pleasing to banish some of the pain we'd experienced in Dublin the previous year, but our performance probably increased the injustice many of us felt at being overlooked by the Lions.

Two months later I missed out on our win at home to Tonga through injury, but I was passed fit for our following game against Argentina. The Thursday before the match, while we sat together for lunch, we discussed whom the coaches might bring in to play full-back. Glenn Metcalfe had picked up an injury that morning at training and would definitely miss the game. With Chris Paterson also injured, the options seemed to be either the uncapped Stuart Moffat, who had been at full-back for Scotland A against Argentina earlier in the week, or the more experienced Derrick Lee. The management would have to make a decision fairly quickly, as we only had two more team sessions planned before the match.

By the time the coaches arrived after their daily press conference, there were only a handful of us left in the hotel restaurant. I asked Geech if he had decided on a replacement for Chris yet. He smiled, 'It's not who you might think. We've gone for the best player available – someone that's already played Super 12 rugby this year.'

Geech's bold announcement didn't get the enthusiastic reaction he had been hoping for. I noticed one player shaking his head in disbelief. The coaches had decided that Brendan Laney was going to be brought into the squad later that afternoon and would start at full-back on Saturday. A few of the squad had met him already, as he had also been at the Scotland A match. I remember him saying that he was struggling with jetlag – he'd just arrived from New Zealand that day. Little did he know that he'd just flown into the middle of a media storm.

Whenever I am asked my opinions on foreign players representing Scotland, I struggle to give a definitive answer as I have mixed feelings on the subject. Some of my good friends – Shaun Longstaff, Glenn Metcalfe and Budge Pountney – have had distinguished Scotland careers without having an earlier attachment to the country. They have all been valuable assets to the national team, just like the Leslie brothers were in 1999 and Nathan Hines is today. I also believe that signing quality non-Scottish qualified players is necessary in raising the standards of our professional sides. Nevertheless, I always feel uneasy whenever we select someone that has had no previous connection with Scottish rugby.

In my last involvement with Scotland at the 2003 World Cup, we had players born in Sittingbourne and Chatham in Kent; St Helens in Lancashire; London; Newcastle-upon-Tyne; Wagga Wagga, Sydney, Brisbane and Melbourne in Australia; and Wellington and Auckland in New Zealand. All were eligible under various rules – and this makes it difficult to argue that the policy is wrong. If other countries are allowed to do it, why can't we? The All Blacks, the best rugby side on the planet, import many of their key players from Fiji, Tonga and Samoa after all.

There's no doubt that the New Zealand rugby union has been happy to grab any talent available down the years. Players such as Bryan Williams, Frank Bunce and Michael Jones were all born in Samoa, and of the current squad, Rodney So'oialo, Joe Rokocoko, Mils Muliaina, Sitiveni Sivivatu and

Jerry Collins were born outside New Zealand. We must not forget, however, that these days, most All Black players with Polynesian blood are New Zealanders. Everyone in the squad learnt their rugby in New Zealand.

Also, overseas players representing Scotland is not just a modern-day phenomenon. Scotland's record try-scorer, Ian Smith, was born in New Zealand and went to school in England. Indeed, of the famous Scotland three-quarter line that helped win the Grand Slam in 1925, only G. P. S. Macpherson had been born and learned his rugby in Scotland. There have also been a huge number of 'Anglo Scots' who have worn the navy blue jersey – well over 100 internationalists have come from London Scottish. No other club can match that record, not even Hawick. It is only very rarely in our rugby history that have we been able to field a team of players born in Scotland.

However, what worried me about the selection of Brendan Laney was that a trend of importing players to plug gaps in the national team as a short-term measure was now becoming an established policy. This, unquestionably, had the potential to stifle home-grown talent. Quick fixes have been undermining Scottish rugby ever since the game went professional. And the sight of players picking up a cap after a very short time in the country was in danger of devaluing the national jersey. John Leslie played for Glasgow Caledonians against the touring Springboks within days of arriving in Scotland and then, eleven days later, made his Scotland debut against South Africa at Murrayfield. I think the coaches believed that because John's early introduction to the team had been a success they were going to get Brendan involved as soon as possible. A precedent had been set even if this time things were being taken to the extreme.

After chatting to several of the squad and a few Edinburgh players we'd met that day, it was obvious that if Brendan played that weekend against Argentina the coaches would be sending out a message that could have been very damaging to Scottish rugby. I can only imagine how disappointing it must be for a young player who has followed his dream and worked extremely hard to get so close to winning a cap only for some guy from New Zealand to suddenly come over and jump the queue. To be fair to Brendan, he never proclaimed any right to be picked for Scotland and only did what was being asked of him. He had given an interview when he arrived in Scotland saying that his goal was 'to win his place in the Edinburgh team and try to play well enough to have an outside chance of playing in the Six Nations'. Andy Nicol, Scott Murray and myself explained our concerns to the captain, Tom Smith, and it was decided that we should all meet with Ian McGeechan as soon as possible.

Our meeting went smoothly and I think we all felt we managed to get the point across to Geech – that rushing Brendan into the team was going to create an unwelcome story in the press as well as sending the wrong message to players in Scotland. Geech at first didn't appreciate that this had troubled us: 'What I am doing is, I believe, going to improve the team. Surely you must all be happy with that?' He genuinely cared for the national team, even at the expense of upsetting fringe players. We also wanted what was best for the team – but in this case it was wiser for whoever was deemed the best player to win his place in the side. Brendan could do this in the weeks ahead. When we adjourned, Geech hadn't appeared to have changed his mind, but we had given him some food for thought and he was no doubt going to discuss things with his fellow selectors and SRU Director of Rugby, Jim Telfer. Later that evening he informed us that Derrick Lee had also been called up to the squad and a decision on who would start at full-back would be made the following day. Derrick got the nod and had to quickly acquaint himself with his new team-mates, the game plan and our backline plays. We believed we had achieved a minor victory for Scottish rugby.

We outscored the Pumas by two tries to one but didn't handle the wet conditions as well as our opponents and lost 25–16. Derrick Lee scored a try and was voted man of the match by the media – some achievement considering he was only brought into the squad two days earlier. However, the coaches decided that his performance hadn't been good enough to warrant another outing at full-back the following week against New Zealand. Chris Paterson had recovered from injury but he only came into the side on the wing. Not surprisingly, Brendan Laney was chosen in the number 15 jersey.

The reason that it wasn't surprising was that earlier in the week, Brendan was selected to play for Scotland A against New Zealand, pushing Stuart Moffat to the bench. He was replaced midway through the second half and from then on it seemed inevitable that he would gain promotion to the senior side. So, the man from New Zealand was about to play against his countrymen twice in the space of a week. The irony seemed lost on our coaches. They obviously thought that now Brendan had played a game in his adopted country, it would no longer be an issue in Scotland.

The opposite was the case and Brendan had to face a hostile press and fierce criticism from former Test players. He didn't deserve this and neither did the likes of Derrick Lee and Stuart Moffat who had been ignored along the way. The pattern of quick fixes by the SRU had continued and another blow was made to the incentive for young Scottish players striving to reach international status. As for the game itself, Brendan and the rest of the team didn't let the week's controversy affect what was a very competitive Test match.

In my experience, every time Scotland played the All Blacks we always started the game by giving them too much respect. It's not until the match is well under way that you realize that they are very good rugby players but not supermen. Time and again we have improved for the second Test matches on tours to the country (in 1990, 1996 and 2000). Two years earlier, at the World Cup, we had come back to win the second half 15–5. This time around, right from the start of the match we showed them no respect and targeted them with aggressive defence. It was incredibly tiring but at last we were in the same league as them for most of the game.

It wasn't until the seventy-second minute that New Zealand scored their first try. At that point we were trailing 18–6. However, our defensive work had sapped most of our energy, and we were picked off in the closing stages of the match, the All Blacks scoring two tries in the final three minutes. I was exhausted by this stage and gave up possession while trying to forlornly pass out of the tackle. The All Blacks exploited my mistake by scoring at the other end of the field. It is one of those games I would love to watch again, but with the last ten minutes of the tape conveniently erased at the end. I don't think I'd ever put in as many tackles in a match before and I also managed a few half-breaks. If only I could have kept it going to the end.

Tana Umaga, Jonah Lomu and Richie McCaw were outstanding on the night. The performance of McCaw – in only his second cap – reminded me that New Zealand number 7s have invariably been the best in the world. McCaw had an extra string to his bow in addition to his superb athleticism, commitment and aggression. He was taller than normal open-sides – his extra reach in defence and in securing turnovers meant that running anywhere near his defensive channel was a no-go area.

Chris Paterson, uncharacteristically, missed with a couple of very kickable penalties that would have put the All Blacks under real pressure. Chris has gone on to become perhaps the best ever goal-kicker Scotland has produced, but that night saw him officially enrolled in a group we had formed called 'Kick Club'. The rules of kick club were:

1. You do not talk about kick club.
2. You DO NOT talk about kick club.
3. You must have missed a kick at goal while playing for Scotland, either by missing in front of the posts or by kicking the ball along the ground.
4. You must have a sense of humour.

Kenny Logan, Rowan Shepherd and myself had already fulfilled membership obligations – I suppose it was a form of gallows humour to deal with the trials and tribulations we all faced in our time as Scotland's goal-kickers. We decided Gavin Hastings should be named honorary president after his crucial penalty miss in front of the posts against England in the World Cup semi-final in 1991.

Tom Smith made it a night to remember by trying his best Frank Sinatra impersonation, which took everyone (especially the All Blacks) by surprise. It all came about because the week before, Omar Hasan (a 120-kg Argentine prop who could give Pavarotti a run for his money) had sung a couple of songs at the end of the official dinner. His deep baritone voice was amazing – it's no wonder he plans to be an opera singer after he retires from rugby. Scott Murray then made a bet with Tom Smith that he wouldn't have the balls to sing at the after-match dinner the following weekend.

All Black skipper, Anton Oliver, was the first of the captains to make a speech. He spoke in a hushed tone about how his squad had spent Remembrance Day on the battlefields of the Somme before visiting the graves of the many New Zealanders that had fallen in World War One. It was a sombre and emotional address and by the earnest look on their faces you could tell that the rest of the squad had also been moved by the event. Oliver returned to his seat with a subdued ripple of applause. Next up was the Scotland captain, Tom Smith.

The air of poignancy was immediately shattered as Tom took one look at Scott Murray and began to sing – 'Start spreading the news ...' None of us had known about the bet but were already laughing by the time Tom said, 'That'll be £10 Scott, thank you.' However, the All Blacks didn't seem to get it. As we were trying hard to hold back our laughter they looked on nonplussed. The contrast couldn't have been any more pronounced.

Earlier in the season, while I was away playing for Scotland against Ireland, Castres lost at home to Bourgoin – their first home defeat in the championship in over three years. When I arrived back there was a feeling of unrest among some of my team-mates. We then went on to lose away at Bordeaux-Bègles. The following Monday our coach, Alain Gaillard, was sacked. This seemed incomprehensible to me, as the previous year he had led us to the semi-finals of the French championship – the best the club had achieved since 1995. We were only into the second month of the season and about to embark on a series of important matches in the Heineken Cup. Incomprehensible but not surprising – player power and the whim of the president drove decision-making in French club rugby.

Nonetheless, it was evident that French rugby was changing – Bernard Laporte had transformed the national side by continually stressing the importance of discipline and consistency. Things were becoming much more professional at club level, too. During my first year at Brive we had started off with two weights sessions a week, but then the players had got together and called a vote to ditch one of them. They said the coaches were working them too hard. Three years on, this romantic idea of rugby just being a weekend showcase of your skills and emotions was gradually fading throughout the leading French clubs. It was translated in fewer penalties being given away and better performances in away matches.

In our first Heineken Cup game of the year, we came within a whisker of beating Munster at Thomond Park and went on to record pool wins away to Harlequins and Bridgend. Despite the change of coach, we carried on our good European form at home, winning all three matches. This included a 21–13 victory over Munster, which meant we finished top of the pool to guarantee a home quarter-final.

The Heineken Cup is a magnificent model of all that is good in professional rugby – travelling across Europe, playing against the best clubs in the northern hemisphere could be as special as playing for your country. I had been made captain for the European campaign – mainly because of the fact that I would be speaking the same language as the referee. Our new coach, Remy Tremulet, must have thought it had worked well, as he kept me in the role for our championship matches throughout the spring. I leaned heavily on French skipper Raphael Ibanez who was one of the guiding lights of our tremendous run in the Heineken Cup.

Raphael was a reassuring presence in the dressing room and was a consistent performer on the field. We played open, attractive rugby – mainly because we had a quick and skilful back-row and some very talented backs. Ismail Lassissi at blind-side flanker was one of the best forwards I've ever played with. He was quick, had a low centre of gravity and was a devastating tackler. Bernard Laporte had tried to pick him for France, but was unsuccessful – Ismail had already played international rugby for the Ivory Coast. He would have been a revelation in the Six Nations. I used to love attacking the line with Ismail on my shoulder – more often than not one of us would get through a gap.

Outside me I had the awesome Norm Berryman. Big Norm had played once for the All Blacks and had brilliant passing range, awareness of space and a wicked side-step. He was a dream to play alongside. Former Scottish winger Shaun Longstaff showed how a change of scene could sometimes give your career a boost. From being on the bench for Glasgow he quickly established himself as a key player at one of the leading sides in France. However, even though he ended up as second top try scorer in the French championship, he continued to be ignored by the Scottish selectors.

We won our quarter-final 22–21 against Montferrand to become the only French team left in the tournament. We were drawn to play Munster – the fifth time we had faced them in two seasons. The four previous matches had all been close affairs and there was no love lost between the two teams. Allegations of biting and racism earlier in the season had clouded what had been pulsating encounters. Munster were up in arms that the semi-final was due to be played at Beziers – only 100 km from Castres.

They needn't have worried – Munster's legions of fans were used to travelling all over Europe to watch their beloved team. At the Stade de la Méditerranée some 10,000 supporters from Ireland had travelled to the south-west of France and they certainly made their presence felt. The resulting atmosphere and intensity was equal to a Test match.

Munster used all their cunning to prevent us from building any real continuity in our play. Scrums were twisted and dropped, much to the irritation of our pack. Referee Chris White told me later that it was the hardest game he'd ever officiated. We led 9–6 at half-time but it was obvious from the expressions of my team-mates that we were all bitterly disappointed – we had dominated proceedings and had been 9–0 up at one stage. With the inspirational Ibanez off injured, we were acutely aware that we might not be able to repeat another ferocious forty minutes of play. Our fear was that Munster seemed to have a lot left in the tank.

Munster's experience and discipline led them to take control of the second half. Their eventual 25–17 win was thoroughly deserved. Only the hand of Leicester's Neil Back, who illegally knocked the ball out of Peter Stringer's grasp in the dying minutes of the final at the Millennium Stadium, prevented them from being crowned European champions. Our props said that they had got a taste of their own medicine, but even if we had been allowed to scrum properly, I don't think we would have won that semi-final. We didn't possess enough players that had been in similar situations before – we lacked composure at times and didn't have the stability and professionalism of a club like Munster. Two days after our defeat, the players presented a petition to the president asking for the removal of the coach, Remy Tremulet. Our president duly obliged.

On the international front, three defeats in the Six Nations – at home to England and France, and away to Ireland – generated the standard criticism of the team from the Scottish media. It is always hard losing a Test match, and more so in front of your own supporters at Murrayfield, but sometimes I do think we are unrealistic in our expectations. We had won two away games against teams at a similar level to ourselves, which was a decent achievement. There was no escaping the fact that Ireland, England and France were better than us at the time and losing shouldn't always have the automatic reaction that something is drastically wrong with the national side.

With John Leslie out injured I had been moved to inside-centre for our opening match against England. Following the subsequent 29–3 defeat – which saw Hodgey become the latest member of 'kick club' after a couple of woeful penalty attempts – the selectors brought in Andy Henderson to wear the number 12 jersey for our trip to Rome and I was moved back to stand-off. With memories of our shock defeat against Italy in 2000 still fresh in the mind, we were under tremendous pressure to win what was being described in the media as the wooden spoon decider. We played some ambitious rugby throughout the match, but it was the goal-kicking of Brendan Laney that kept us out in front. Brendan had taken over from Chris Paterson, who was still struggling to find any consistency in the kicking department, and we went on to win 29–12.

After losses to both France and Ireland, we went to Cardiff for a match to decide the fourth and fifth places in the table. It was a significant game for the rugby-viewing public, as it was to be Bill McLaren's final Six Nations match broadcast. Bill had been a magnificent servant to the game for a number of decades and he made the Borders and Scotland very proud, not just in his wonderfully objective commentary style, but also in the manner he conducted himself. He was always at the ground the day before a game to get himself acquainted with the players and if you were lucky he stopped to chat to you and handed out some of his favourite sweets – Hawick balls. He has left a legacy that will be extremely difficult to equal.

It was a shame that the game itself was probably one of the worst Bill has commentated on. Handling errors from both sides meant that there wasn't much free-flowing rugby on show. We won 27–22 after two tries from Gordon Bulloch, both emanating from driven lineouts. The match saw me win my sixty-sixth cap, beating the Scottish record set by Scott Hastings. It hadn't been my finest hour, but at least we had won. My thoughts now turned to the possibility of coming home for good.

Throughout the Six Nations I spent a long time thinking about my future. My contract was coming to an end at Castres and, although I'd begun discussions with the club, the removal of two coaches during the season had made me question the wisdom of signing on again. Also, the SRU had announced that they were establishing a third professional team, scheduled to play in the Borders. This had been some-thing I'd been arguing in favour of for a while – my hope was also to see a fourth team based in Caledonia. During the Six Nations, Jim Telfer had approached me to check on my avail-ability. It had been seven years since I'd left the Borders and it was exciting watching the likes of Gary Armstrong and Doddie Weir signing up, but it was the club that I had left the

Borders to play for that initially seemed to be a more attractive proposition.

Northampton coach Wayne Smith had been in contact with me several times and met me in Edinburgh following a Scotland match. Smith, the ex-All Black coach, had an impressive résumé – Tabai Matson, who played under him at the Crusaders had told me on many occasions that he was the best prepared coach in the world. After spending less than five minutes in his company I knew he would be great to work with. Highly analytical and a former number 10 himself, he had the makings of being the perfect coach for me. And he wanted me to play at stand-off.

There were issues to mull over about returning to a former club – my experiences at Warringah suggested it could be a good thing, but I had only gone to Australia in the off-season and hadn't quit the club as such. My last year at Northampton hadn't been particularly enjoyable and with Paul Grayson still on the books I knew there would be people there that might resent the fact that I'd come back. On the other hand, I felt I had some unfinished business and I was sure the supporters would now see a much better player. What fascinated me was the chance to play in the new-look Franklin's Gardens, a majestic stadium that was full for every home game.

As well as talking to Wayne Smith, I was in constant contact with Rob Moffat who had just been named as assistant coach to the new Borders side. Rob had been a major influence on my developing career, as he had been in charge of the Gala Academy 1st XV as well as the Scottish Schools team. More than any other coach I'd worked with, he had taken time to help me with my own game and fundamental skills like passing and kicking. You couldn't meet a nicer man and his enthusiasm and devotion to helping others knows no bounds. With Rob on board, I had an even more difficult decision to make between Northampton and the Borders.

Of course, you have to consider all the details – the pros and cons. It was important to me what other players would be in the new Borders team, and with Claire expecting our first child in the summer, other factors had to be taken into account. With the World Cup coming up the following year I wanted to feel fresher than I had done in the previous two seasons. Being based in Scotland would undoubtedly help my body.

It had been a long season and it was probably just as well I hadn't made the Lions tour, as my body was only just managing to cope with the demands of French club rugby and all the travelling I had to do for matches and training sessions with Scotland. It was anything between six to ten hours for each trip to Scotland – journeying back to France the day after an international was definitely not the best way to recover from a game. There was also an increasing number of squad sessions at Murrayfield during the season, and I was starting to feel the strain. With our extended run in the Heineken Cup, I turned out a few times that year carrying injuries – on one occasion I couldn't even take part in our warm-up before we played Munster. I knew this couldn't continue.

It probably sounds a bit trite, but when I was agonizing over what I would do, and the contracts that were being offered, there was one night where I started to think about what it would be like to run out at Netherdale once again. After speaking to Tony Gilbert (the former Otago coach who had been appointed head coach of the Borders), the excitement just grew. When I used to play at Gala it would be hard to sleep some nights before a game as I would be thinking of moves that could help us win. I've never had that strength of feeling at the other clubs I have played for. You miss the thrill and pride of representing your home area. The buzz of the Borders team getting put together and the thought of returning home had made me feel the same sensations all over again.

Considering I had improved more when playing outside Scotland and all the risks involved with a team that were building a club, a squad and an identity from scratch, I still felt I'd made the right decision in signing a three-year deal with the Borders. I didn't intend to move ever again and I was happy in the knowledge that I'd be finishing my career in Scotland. Talking with the coaches, we knew it could take a couple of years to get up to the level of Edinburgh and Glasgow, never mind the best in Europe, but as we approached pre-season, the players were determined to be at that level as quickly as possible.

Although the coaches missed out on a number of players they had wanted to sign, our squad wasn't lacking in experience. With overseas guys like Paul Thompson, Semo Sititi, Campbell Feather and Tanner Vili added to local players such as Doddie Weir, Cammie Murray, Steve Scott and Kev Utterson, we had the makings of a team that would be competitive at least. At scrum-half and captain we were blessed to have the presence of the inspirational Gary Armstrong.

I am sometimes asked who is the best scrum-half I have played with in my career and it is a very difficult question to answer. I have been lucky enough to be partnered at half-back by a number of world-class players, many of whom have different strengths to their game. For example, Bryan Redpath had the best pass I've seen in the game – his strong wrists and wide stance meant that he got the ball away fast, wide and accurately. Gary's toughness and commitment were what people talked about whenever they've played with or against him but, for me, his kicking game and ability to break tackles were just as impressive.

Scotland has been very fortunate over the last twenty years to have produced so many quality number 9s. Along with Gary and Bryan, both Roy Laidlaw and Andy Nicol were respected throughout the game. Incredibly, we still have two players capable of greatness. Chris Cusiter, my

half-back partner in my final season back at the Borders, has
already made it on a Lions tour, and is almost as competitive
as Gary. He is very quick off the mark and is the best cover
tackler in world rugby at the moment. I hope his recent
injury problems are now a thing of the past. Mike Blair, Scotland's other regular scrum-half, is a different player to Chris,
but very effective nonetheless. He reminds me of a French
number 9, as he is very good around the fringes of rucks and
has a great awareness of how and when to put others into
space. His creativity has led me to believe that Scotland could
play him further out in the backline – I hope that before his
career is over he has taken on the twin challenges of playing
at stand-off and playing club rugby in France. I'm convinced
he would thrive in both endeavours.

At Brive, I had the pleasure of playing alongside Philippe
Carbonneau – one of the all-time great French scrum-halves.
His timing of the pass was exquisite, no doubt because he had
played a lot of rugby as a centre earlier in his career at
Toulouse. There was no better man you wanted at number 9
when you had quick ball.

Before I went to France I played with Matt Dawson at
Northampton, although not nearly as much as I would have
liked. On the days that I was moved from outside-centre to
stand-off, I loved running off Matt's wide passes. There didn't
seem to be a weakness to his game – he was strong in the
tackle, quick on his feet and an excellent tactical kicker. He
also preferred to get the play moving quickly and ran tap
penalties at any opportunity.

But even Matt's all-round game couldn't match that of Rob
Howley, my Lions half-back partner in 1997 until he picked
up a shoulder injury. Rob had the pace of Chris Cusiter, the
centre of gravity of Gary Armstrong and, although not in
Bryan Redpath's league, was still one of the best passing
number 9s I've played with. He was a tremendous professional and set himself very high standards. If I was pushed on

who was the best scrum-half I've played with I'd have to plump for Rob – although the others have all made my life much easier as a stand-off.

I missed the first day of Borders training, as our son, Christian, entered the world on the same day. Having children has proved to be as good as anything I've achieved in my rugby career and the love, the enjoyment and different perspective of a seeing a child grow has sometimes made playing in front of 80,000 people pale into insignificance. Christian's timing couldn't have been any better, as the opening day of training at the Borders was apparently incredibly punishing. It was a theme that our coach, Tony Gilbert, continued throughout our pre-season.

Tony was an engaging and vastly experienced coach who worked us very hard and this made us quickly form a strong bond as a group. He had researched the history of the Borders and held regular team meetings at the William Wallace monument (just outside of St Boswells), explaining how Borders people throughout history had fought many battles against the English and also had excelled at a warrior sport – rugby. It made such an impression on our number 8, Semo Sititi, that he christened his son Wallace Sititi. I'm sure young Wallace won't find anyone else with the same name as him back in Samoa!

For all that Tony was a great motivator and hard taskmaster, we didn't play to our potential in our opening games. We lost our first four matches, albeit three of them by less than two points. I believe that if we had concentrated more of our efforts on technical areas and getting to know each other as rugby players, we would have had a much better start to the season. We looked rusty – which was somewhat inevitable given that we had just come together in the summer – but if only we had spent less time doing fitness work and concentrated more on rugby training we could have conquered our shortcomings.

Still, we improved the more we played together and our first game at Netherdale – as the pitch at Gala had just been re-laid – saw us record a 23–18 win over Leinster. A 4,000-strong crowd warmed to our performance. It's funny now to think that we had actually been disappointed with 4,000 – with crowds under 2,000 at all three Scottish pro-sides a few years later, we would quite happily turn the clock back. As the Celtic League split into two pools of eight, we had only seven competitive fixtures before playing a domestic tournament against Edinburgh and Glasgow to see who would qualify for the Heineken Cup. The momentum we had started to build up was cut short, as there wasn't much rugby after Christmas.

After having been below par in my first three matches, I started to play much better thereafter. I was feeling fresher back playing in Scotland, finally clear of the niggling injuries I'd carried with me from a long season in France. This was vitally important, as I was determined to go to the World Cup in Australia firing on all cylinders.

CHAPTER 13

Spirits Lifted:
Rugby World Cup 2003 Diary Part 1

*Everyone wants to live on the peak of the mountain, without
knowing that the real happiness is in how it is scaled.*

Gabriel Garcia Marquez

Wearing only shorts, socks, earmuffs, a pair of clogs and a face
mask, we shuffled along an empty corridor, led onwards by
an unsmiling Eastern Europe giant. He announced that our
scant clothing would protect us from acute frostbite. What
looked like steam – but was in fact liquid nitrogen – poured
out as he opened the door to a room adjacent to us. We were
told to enter the freezing chamber. The temperature inside
was -140°c, something so cold as beyond comprehension. The
thick door was slammed shut hurriedly behind us. For three
and a half minutes we huddled together to avoid the onset of
hypothermia, nervously trying to repel the overwhelming
feeling of claustrophobia and impending death. Finally,
once we were returned back to the real world, our bodies
slowly began to thaw. We were in Spala, Poland, two months
before the 2003 World Cup undergoing 'cryotherapy' treatment – the latest attempt to raise fitness levels in the Scotland
rugby squad.

Ten years on from my first cap for Scotland, there had been
some dramatic changes to the way rugby players trained and
prepared. Fitness and conditioning has become a mantra for
those involved in the professional game. Weight training was

virtually non-existent before 1996, and training seldom stretched to more than a twice-weekly runabout under the floodlights. Now players are on controlled diets, spend half their life in the gym and attend yoga and pilates classes to strengthen and tone their bodies. That year had even seen us train in the greenhouses at Edinburgh's Botanic Gardens to simulate the heat and humidity we might face in our opening World Cup match in Townsville. Our ten-day camp in Poland at an elite Olympic preparation centre was ostensibly to squeeze as much training as possible into a short period of time through the use of a cryogenic chamber.

The idea was that we could train hard and then spend three and a half minutes in a chamber, reducing the build-up of lactic acid in our muscles. It sounded easy in theory. What worried the players was that the staff at Spala had mentioned that after six minutes inside no one would come out alive. There was some anxiety at times – one or two players banged on the door wanting to be let out before the allocated time. Mostly our team spirit made it fun – we sang songs and played a naming game (which we called 'freeze while you think') to make the time pass quicker.

The chamber certainly helped with our aching muscles, although two players did pull their hamstrings near the end of the camp. This was mainly because we trained as hard as I've ever experienced. Our day started at 7 a.m. with twenty lengths of the 25-m swimming pool. Then, after breakfast, we had a heavy weights session, which was followed by the first of our two visits to the chamber. After this we hopped on a bike for twenty minutes to help with recovery. In the afternoon we had a demanding rugby session and finally some lung-bursting fitness drills. By the time we had been frozen for a second time we were doing well to stay awake for dinner.

The trip to Poland was intense and exhausting but because there were no distractions, and we all had a good fitness base, it was not as tough as we had feared. It might seem hard to believe, but I actually enjoyed the ten days of training. We took pleasure in each other's company and we all realized that the hard work had to be done if we were to make an impact in the World Cup, which was less than two months away.

Our preparations on the field that season had fluctuated wildly between a handful of impressive performances and some shocking defeats. Although I had made a poor start playing with the Borders, I had rediscovered my form and was looking forward to being involved in Scotland's autumn internationals. On the Monday before we played our first match against Romania, Ian McGeechan chatted to me about what plays I felt we should incorporate into our build-up to that weekend. It was like any normal conversation I had with Geech – he was great to talk to about rugby and wasn't afraid of input from players in deciding the best strategy. At the end of our chat he told me he was thinking about experimenting with the team selection: 'I think this is a great occasion to allow Gordon Ross an opportunity to play Test rugby. You are still our preferred number 10 and you'll be starting against South Africa.'

'Whatever you think is best. It seems to make perfect sense to me,' I replied.

'Good. I just wanted to run it by you before we announced the side.'

Scotland began their autumn Test series with a comfortable if unspectacular victory over Romania, winning 37–10. As we sat down for the team meeting prior to the next Test, against South Africa, I had no inkling of the shock that was in store for me. I had come on at stand-off for the last ten minutes of the Romania match and felt sharp and so I had convinced myself that I would play, especially as I had heard nothing to the contrary. Geech read out the team and my name was missing. I was numb.

Competition for key places like stand-off is vital, especially ahead of a World Cup, but I was deeply disappointed as I believed I was playing well. I also thought the disjointed and ill-disciplined Springbok side were there for the taking. Although I was very angry at being left out, I didn't mention to Geech about his previous plan for me to play against the Springboks. After speaking to Claire, my folks and Borders coach Rob Moffat, I managed to get things off my chest. I resolved to do the best I could to help Gordon and the rest of the team prepare for the match. The coaches had outlined a very limited game plan, which involved a lot of kicking in an attempt to negate the aggressive Springbok defence. I thought such a lack of ambition had no chance of being successful.

I was proved spectacularly wrong as we recorded an historic 21–6 victory. I managed to replace Gordon for the last twenty minutes, which was actually a bit unfair on him as he'd been playing well. While we might count ourselves very lucky that we scored two tries – neither Nikki Walker nor Budge Pountney seemed to have grounded the ball over the try-line – the victory was thoroughly deserved.

Our forwards dominated the Springbok pack. There was an arrogance to the approach of the South Africans that suggested they thought we were a pushover. The heavy rain helped our kicking strategy a great deal. The coaches had been right to use such a tactic. Unlike the opposition, we played the conditions perfectly and our commitment and defence was on a par with the Calcutta Cup win in 2000. Bryan Redpath was outstanding, but even his contribution was overshadowed by the performance of Budge Pountney. Unquestionably, Budge played his best game in a Scottish jersey. Within two months, however, he had retired from the international game.

Budge's retirement created much controversy at the time and even took the players by surprise. Like Roy Keane had done with the Irish football squad at the 2002 World Cup,

Budge branded the set-up of the national team as shambolic and unprofessional. He said that every week before an international was like a fight – a constant battle to get simple things like water after training, food, kit or whatever else. The culmination of seemingly minor incidents had driven him to the end of his tether. As a result, he walked out on the Scotland team, which put an end to his chances of playing in the World Cup in Australia.

I knew where Budge was coming from – the Scottish team wasn't nearly as professionally run as an English or French club side – but this had always been the case and we had got on with it. There is a tremendous pride playing for Scotland and the negatives in the way we prepared were a small price to pay for the honour of representing the nation. Still, rugby had been transformed in the previous few seasons into a brutally physical sport, with many demands now being asked of players. Budge, as an open-side flanker, played in the most punishing position on the rugby field and had himself suffered some horrendous injuries playing for his country and his club team, Northampton.

I'm sure that these injuries were a factor in his decision to concentrate solely on playing for Northampton who had treated him well during his long tenure at the club. Cracked cheekbones, knee surgery and the loss of a testicle would have been enough to force many people to have jacked in the game altogether. Budge was one of the most honest, unassuming and hard-working players I've ever played with and I believe his attack on the SRU was a genuine attempt to improve the situation for the team-mates he now left behind.

Looking back, the only time I can recall Budge being unhappy was during the week after the Springbok match. The forwards had been hammered at training – it was Jim Telfer's way of reminding the players not to take anything for granted. However, the pack didn't perform well a week later against Fiji, despite us winning the match 36–22. As captain,

Budge no doubt had tried to get the coaches to rest the players as much as possible after their monumental efforts against South Africa. I remember Budge having a stand-up row with Jim at the debrief of the Fiji game after the latter had questioned the commitment of the forward pack following their failure to repeat the intensity they had shown against the Springboks. Budge took umbrage at this, responding that thay had been 'knackered' after a very hard week of training.

Maybe Budge wouldn't have felt so strongly if he hadn't been involved in dealing so much with the management in his role as captain – who knows? What is certain was that during his short reign as skipper he led the side to two magnificent performances at Murrayfield – the 32–10 victory over Grand Slam chasing Ireland in 2001 and the 21–6 defeat of South Africa. His retirement did help improve things as dialogue between senior players and management became a regular occurrence. Also, immediately after his walk-out, the SRU provided each player with two pairs of recovery leggings (known as 'skins') – the week before we had been asked to send them a cheque for £120.

So, without Budge, we started our Six Nations campaign against Ireland. The win over the Springboks had glossed over our ineffective attacking threat, but our game plan remained the same. I believe that against certain international sides, we need to score at least twenty points to have any chance of winning – an ever-improving Ireland were one such team. By aiming to put the ball behind the Irish and thus kicking away so much possession, it seemed our only way to score points would be through penalties or capitalizing on the opposition's mistakes. What worried me even more was the acquiescence of the players by not demanding a more positive playing strategy.

Ireland were at a different level from us in terms of skill and ambition – they went on to notch up a 30–9 victory, which was a record win for them at Murrayfield and the first

time they had won in Scotland in eighteen years. The following week we were equally inept, losing 36–3 away to the
French. The two defeats resulted in a change of personnel and
a new game plan that, although some way from attacking
wide with ball in hand, was a step in the right direction. Brendan Laney, who had replaced Gordon Ross at stand-off for the
French match, was dropped after performing poorly in our
two opening games. I had come on at inside-centre for the
last twenty minutes of the Irish match and had started at
outside-centre against France. For our next game, at home to
Wales, I was brought back in to wear the number 10 jersey.
Just like my first three appearances for Scotland some ten
years before, I had once again been selected to play in three
different positions in as many games.

The selectors also included Glenn Metcalfe, Kenny Logan,
Jim McLaren, and Kevin Utterson in the backline. These players hadn't started the match against South Africa, which was
only three months hence. I had said to Bryan Redpath in
1999 after he had missed out on our Five Nations win that his
peers knew he was good enough to be in the team and that
he would soon be back. I was repeating this to Glenn and
Kenny after they had been dropped for the autumn internationals. Moments move on very quickly in international
rugby – especially for the Scottish team.

There was huge pressure on us, because of the criticism
over the first two games, and the fact that we were playing at
home. The favourite question from the media going into the
match seemed to be: 'How are you going to cope with the
pressure this Saturday?' At least it was a change from the
usual, 'Do you still feel you have something to prove in a
Scotland jersey?'

Michael Johnson once said that pressure is just the shadow
of great accomplishment and like a shadow, there is no
substance to it. I've always felt that it is how you respond
when you are put under pressure on the pitch that determines

how good you are. I was acutely aware that I had a to make a statement of intent in the match. Being dropped had sharpened my resolve and not affected my confidence. I knew that pressure in Test match rugby was being able to make the right decisions in the face of an aggressive defence.

The game went well for me and I crossed for a try after only five minutes. Unfortunately, Argentine referee Pablo Deluca disallowed the score. As television replays would later confirm, Martyn Williams had let go of my legs, meaning my second surge to the try-line was perfectly legal. Despite missing out on seven points, we played some direct, accurate rugby. When I was replaced late in the match we were on our way to posting a record score in the fixture, as we led 30–10. Even two injury-time tries by Wales couldn't take the shine off our morale-boosting victory.

It was obvious to the players that Ian McGeechan wanted us to play a more attacking game plan, in contrast to what seemed to be Jim Telfer's view that we should play to our strengths – the forward pack. Geech gradually got the upper hand over his experienced assistant coach and by the end of the Six Nations we had begun to show signs that we could play wide, attacking rugby, even during a heavy defeat at Twickenham against a brilliant English side. In our 33–25 win over Italy, our back three of Glenn Metcalfe, Chris Paterson and man-of-the-match Kenny Logan were becoming much more involved in the play. I felt I contributed a fair bit to this added width to the game, although against the Italians my kicking was far too loose. It was an area I knew I had to work further on as we approached the World Cup.

We headed to South Africa before our summer cryotherapy sessions in Poland, aware that this would be a precious opportunity to develop our new attacking threat. We proceeded to play the best rugby by a Scottish team since 1999. Despite losing 29–25, we had dominated the home side for the majority of the match. Outscoring the Springboks three tries to two was tremendously encouraging and it was great to see our much-maligned backline producing some fantastic individual performances. Chris, Kenny and Andy Craig all had their best games for Scotland. Also, our back-row of Jason White, Simon Taylor and Andrew Mower had been outstanding, constantly knocking back the bigger South African forwards. In fact, almost all of the side were in sublime form and at last it seemed we had discovered a game plan and a starting fifteen that could mount a credible challenge in the forthcoming World Cup.

However, given our dominance, we should never have lost the match. Going into the final quarter we led 25–12, but mistakes at crucial areas on the field and indiscipline saw our lead disappear. The Springboks also benefited from a stroke of luck as Louis Koen's attempted penalty struck an upright and South Africa recovered the ball to score a vital try. Despite this, and the fact we went into the final minute of the match trailing 29–25, we still had a fantastic opportunity to win.

Having worked our way up the field, we started to pound the South African line. Under intense pressure the Springboks gave away a succession of penalties and eventually their captain Joost van der Westhuizen was sent to the sin bin. As we launched yet another attack it looked like we would be awarded another penalty or even a penalty try. But just then second-row Nathan Hines picked up from a ruck close to the try-line. Despite having two hands on the ball, one of his arms was pulled back by a defender as he stretched over the line. The ball broke free just inches from the ground and bounced harmlessly away – with it went our hopes for a first ever Scottish win in South Africa.

'If only' seemed to be on everyone's lips after the game. If only we hadn't been penalized at a five-metre scrum early in the match as Simon Taylor had already picked up from number 8 to crash over for a score … if only Louis Koen's kick had not rebounded back from the left-hand post … if only

Kenny had caught Bryan Redpath's pass in our 22, as the turnover resulted in a try for South Africa ... if only Nathan hadn't had the ball knocked out of his grasp in the act of scoring a try ... if only referee Joel Jutge had returned to the penalty he was going to award us after the final knock-on.

Ultimately, our defeat showed that we couldn't yet be regarded as equal to any of the top five sides in the world, but there had been indisputable progress since we had reached our nadir after losing our two opening Six Nations games. We lost the second Test 28–19 at Ellis Park as South Africa responded to criticism of their performance in Durban by showing much more passion and intensity in their play. Nevertheless, we competed well, and at one try apiece only better fitness and finishing prevented us from matching our efforts of the previous weekend.

While I was delighted that we had opened up our game plan, which led to an improved overall performance, I knew that my own game hadn't been error free. In the first Test I was controlling and varying the play as well as I'd done in a while, but I had two or three poor kicks, which was disappointing. Together with wanting to improve my fitness level, my main aim in the build-up to the World Cup in Australia was to have a stronger kicking game. Regarding the fitness side of things, I worked hard during a two-week holiday to Corsica. Fortunately I had a training partner in Glenn Metcalfe, whose family shared a villa with us. It was very hot but we pushed each other on and we both felt comfortable in the training camp in Poland.

With a month to go before we left for Australia, Scotland played three warm-up matches. I was selected in the second of our friendly games, away to Wales. I was a little disappointed not to play in the opening match at Murrayfield against Italy, as the side that was selected was very strong on paper. Gordon Ross was at stand-off and he played well as Scotland won 44–12 against a disappointing Italian team.

Although we had dispatched Wales earlier that year, this occasion would be much more difficult. Having been whitewashed in the Six Nations, the pressure was now on Wales to produce a winning performance. On the eve of the match we heard that Welsh coach Steve Hansen would be sacked if we were to win in Cardiff. Our team was not exactly a 2nd XV, but there were only a handful of frontline players. As it was the first game for the squad, we were very rusty at times but we still dominated the second half in terms of territory and possession. Unfortunately, we were unable turn this pressure into points. The rugby truism that 'the team that wants it the most will win' summed up the day, as Wales defended courageously to win 23–9.

I hated the fact that we had lost but I took some satisfaction from my kicking game, which was a huge improvement from the end of the previous season. Worryingly though, there had been a clicking noise coming from my left knee whenever I started to run. There wasn't too much pain but I went straight back to the hotel after the game to be treated by our medical team. After some rigorous testing, it seemed that I hadn't done any serious damage to my knee. As the rest of the squad finally came back from the Millennium Stadium to join me at the hotel, I was told by our media officer that the Scottish press were going to go for me 'big time' in the next day's papers. Being criticized by certain journalists was not a new phenomenon to me but I was taken aback somewhat as I believed my own game hadn't been too bad. I suppose there were many people who thought I had been in the team for long enough and playing in a losing side would give them plenty of reason to have a go at me in print.

Although I didn't buy a newspaper that week, I had a number of phone calls and emails explaining some of the negative comments that were directed at me. The majority of the media had seemingly concentrated on the fact that Glenn and I had worn white boots in the match. This seemed to be an act of heresy for a few journalists. Reebok, my kit sponsor, would have been pleased with the amount of press coverage their white boots received, but I thought it was ridiculous.

I was also perturbed by some of the ill-informed comments about my performance – one scribe suggested that, following the defeat, I should now be omitted from the thirty-man World Cup squad, another that I was 'past it' at international level. I know that I'm never as good or bad as any single performance, and I've tried very hard to ignore both criticism and praise, but I found this short sightedness was incredible given that it was my first game of the season. My role in our previous two Test matches, where we had played some outstanding rugby against South Africa, had obviously been forgotten.

I watched the tape of the game again and still felt happy with how I had performed even though I always look closely at areas I can make better and whether I made the right decisions or not. My kicking game was much improved, and I had taken most of my passes on the run, an area I'd also wanted to work on. I had tried very hard to get others into the game, but for whatever reason we hadn't been able to break down the Welsh defence. There were certain actions that were by no means perfect, but for my first game of the season I was content with how things were progressing. On the other hand, I was disappointed with the result and I knew that the players who had been involved in the Italian game would be favoured over those who played in the defeat by Wales.

There is only one way to respond to criticism and that is to get back playing as soon as possible and play well. However, I had the growing suspicion that the coaches were beginning to share the media view that I should no longer be stand-off for Scotland. I wasn't included in the twenty-two-man squad for our last preparation match at home to Ireland and I felt I was getting the cold shoulder from Ian McGeechan and Jim Telfer.

Right It was a joy playing at Franklin's Gardens. Coming up against class players such as Harlequins' Will Carling made it feel close to Test match level.

Left Scoring a crucial try in the closing minutes at Cardiff Arms Park in 1996. The win set up a second Grand Slam game with England in successive seasons.

Below The biggest night of my rugby career – 1st Test against the Springboks, Cape Town.

Two of my best ever Scotland games came against the Irish, in 1996 and 1999. I'm pictured here during our emphatic win at Murrayfield in 1999.

Above Trying to find a hole between David Wallace and Ronan O'Gara playing for Castres in the 2001 Heineken Cup semi-final at the Stade de la Méditerranée, Beziers.

Left This time I'm in opposition to Castres, and their stand-off Yann Delaigue, while playing for Montpellier in 2004.

Right Cycling to training during the World Cup in 2003. It looks like Nikki Walker and I are feeling much more enthusiastic about it than Glenn Metcalfe.

Above Claire and I on our wedding day, July 1998.

Above At Buckingham Palace to collect my MBE in 1999.

Above I'm already enjoying retirement and spending more time with my family. Me and my boys, Christian and Luke, on holiday in July 2007.

or fish depended on what cutlery there was on the table. You can imagine the scramble that ensued as the players tried to swap fish knives for steak knives. Only half the squad ended up happy. When complaints were made, the staff ominously replied that they hadn't been told what food to prepare for us.

Still, the squad saw the funny side of things – we joked that we were in a similar position to Ally MacLeod's notorious Scottish football team who went to Argentina for the 1978 World Cup in Argentina. 'Ally's army' left Scotland with high hopes but their ill-fated campaign ended in disaster. I hope things don't turn out anything like that for our squad. Inspired by the more recent football World Cup of 2002, we also started guessing who would do 'a Roy Keane' – having the nerve to tell the coaching staff it wasn't good enough and catching the next flight home.

1 October
Day Two

The management have told us what they had in mind when deciding our accommodation for the World Cup. Apparently, the reason that our base in Coloundra was chosen was to give us some space and the ability to make our own decisions on what we want to do. This means that if we aren't happy with the food we can cook something else in our apartments. Likewise, if the laundry isn't getting done in time for training we can do it ourselves. The players are still moaning to each other but it's more like banter than real worries that our World Cup chances are being hampered. If anything it fills the quiet times. To be honest, things like this can help forge team spirit. And, as an added bonus, the food improved today.

We have all been given bikes to 'give us the freedom' to make our own way to training, which is a mile up the road. Less than a couple of hours after picking them up, though, the police had already reported back to our manager Dougie

Morgan that players were spotted riding without helmets and riding on footpaths – all against the law in Queensland.

Actually, there is quite a heavy police presence around us – we had three officers guarding our team Portakabin today. The officer in charge is just like Chief Wiggum from *The Simpsons*. In another development, our team Portakabin has been re-named 'Camp Scotland' by Ian McGeechan. The players are already calling it 'Camp X-Ray'.

The medics, who are usually a good bunch of jokers, have now really started taking the piss. Literally. Yes, we now have to provide a daily urine sample in order that our team doctor can ascertain whether we are hydrating enough during the day. A score is given at the end of the day on how dehydrated we are. The older guys in the squad have a sneaking suspicion that the test is really to uncover if anybody has been out drinking the night before. We joke that our teetotal winger Chris Paterson will have a queue of players outside his door at breakfast looking for an untainted sample.

2 October
Day Three
Food update: We are now allowed $40 each to buy our own food and cook it in the apartments if we want. The only downside is that you have to decide early in the day in order to warn the hotel – so no sneaking a look at what's on offer and *then* deciding to visit the local supermarket.

It still doesn't feel like the World Cup is only a week away. This was reinforced later in the day when I looked across at my team-mates during a strategy meeting before training. I struggled to take things seriously as we were all sitting with our bike helmets still fastened on, listening to the coaches discuss tactics for our opening game against Japan.

Training has picked up in intensity, though, and my knee is beginning to feel better with every session. It's still agony in between times however. Ice baths (or wheelie bins filled to the brim with ice and cold water to be exact) now follow training. Fortunately, there is a jacuzzi at the hotel, which is the perfect tonic to a hard day's training (and a good alternative to an ice bath!).

A third consecutive day of rain has helped us acclimatize much easier than we thought. Dougie Morgan joked at a civic reception we attended in the evening that they should rename the area the Sunless Coast. We all laughed, but it looked like his joke had gone down like a lead balloon with the Mayor of Coloundra. These receptions can be a bit of a drag for the players but are sometimes made fun by the person you end up speaking to. Or, more importantly, what you end up telling them. Winger Kenny Logan told everyone he met that he was a donkey farmer, which had the local MP wound up at least. An awesome electrical storm outside the reception provided a good excuse for most of the squad to sneak out early.

3 October
Day Four
The weather was wonderful this morning and I'm glad I was training in the first group for speed and weights at 8:30 a.m., as the guys who were out after us were badly sunburned. You can't help but laugh though as they were all wearing singlets – with their pale Scottish bodies it now looks as if they are still wearing white vests with very red arms and shoulders.

There has been more media interest in the team today and even the legendary Wallaby winger David Campese has talked about us. He called us 'weird' and 'big drinkers' with not much chance of winning. We'll hopefully prove him wrong on at least one of the three points he made.

In fact some of the press cuttings that are being sent from back home (which are left in Camp Scotland) are providing a source of chat within the squad. Ian McGeechan has been quoted in one paper as saying 'it was a very bad decision' not to have accepted the English coaching job. It's probably not the best timing to have just mentioned this to the media, but I'm sure Geech has been misquoted. Our hooker, Gordon Bulloch, has said in his weekly newspaper column that the English will wilt under the pressure and not win the World Cup. Why would you say something like that? Tempt fate too much and they might go and win.

Our hardest day of training yet in unbearable heat and it went well: a good sign. I think the journey is now finally leaving our systems.

As I went into Camp Scotland late last night I was invited to join a few boys in playing a relatively unknown sport called 'Red Ass'. This involves everyone having to do the same number of 'keepy-uppies' with a football as the person who passes you the ball. If you fail to do this three times you are the loser. Unfortunately I was to be the loser in my first game. I then discovered why the game is called Red Ass. The forfeit of losing is that you must bend over as each of the other players kick the ball as hard as they can towards the exposed area above the hamstrings and just below the lower back. Who said professional rugby players don't have fun anymore?

4 October
Day Five
Despite the presence of four Coloundra police officers guarding our team room there have been reports of a missing training jersey and a computer (worth £10,000). Chief Wiggum is going to have to deploy more resources to Camp Scotland. (I can't imagine they have these security problems at Camp X-Ray.)

Today was a good day. Training (a full-on heavy contact session) went well and my knee now feels much closer to 100 per cent. I have felt some pain at every session so far, and I know Jim Telfer has been watching me closely, checking to see if I am fully fit or not. Nonetheless, today my knee was given a real test and I feel that I can now train with much less pain and apprehension. Also this morning's session was the last until Monday – granting us an unprecedented one and a half days of free time, give or take another civic reception or two.

5 October
Day Six

Police Update: I walked into Camp Scotland this morning after breakfast and counted five police officers sitting watching our newly installed TV. There have been unconfirmed reports that there were in fact eight officers lounging in our chairs at another time later in the day. We must be the crime capital of Queensland. (Still no sign of the computer or the training jersey though.)

There are a few sore heads this morning as we got the first chance to unwind last night by sampling the nightlife of nearby Mooloollaba. It didn't feel too different to being back in Scotland as some of us watched the Rangers–Celtic game live at the local Surf Club. Also, in each of the three pubs that we visited, The Proclaimers' 'Five Hundred Miles' was being played live by different bands. Apparently they are massive out here. There will be no more sarcastic comments from me about the local police as the boys in blue took six of us back to Coloundra in two patrol cars which was handy as the queue for taxis stretched for miles.

An afternoon of sunbathing by the pool was followed by our second civic reception of the week. Scott Murray and I escaped out of a side exit after half an hour, as the Australian Rugby League Grand Final was about to kick off. I'm glad we rebelled because the final was one of the best games in league history – an intensely physical battle in the rain that saw Penrith Panthers defeat the reigning champions, the Sydney Roosters, 18–6. The best player on the pitch was Britain's Adrian Morley.

6 October
Day Seven

Today we started with a weights session in the morning, which was followed by rugby training in the 'avo' (as they say over here). Our focus was intensified somewhat by the announcement of the team to play Japan in our first match on Sunday night. I'm on the bench, which is disappointing, but not surprising. Hopefully I'll get some game time and be given the chance to start in our second match against the USA. Having been at a senior players meeting with the coaches, the feeling is that there will have to be changes for our two opening matches. This is to first give players a chance to recover adequately for the French match and also to allow competition for places.

Unfortunately this afternoon's session was very poor. It was basically a semi-opposed training run for Sunday's team to go through their plays for the first three phases. On many occasions the ball never got to the third phase, as there was a lot of poor handling. Captain Bryan Redpath had to twice get the boys in a huddle and lay it on the line that this wasn't good enough. The coaching staff thought that the team announcement together with not having trained for two days meant that some of the squad had temporarily lost their focus. I have another theory.

Before the session Geech had laid out a new game plan that involves playing differently in certain zones of the pitch. This apparently comes from Australian Matt Williams who has recently been announced as Scotland coach (he takes up the post after the World Cup). The zones are as follows:

White Zone   –   Up to our 22 m
Blue Zone   –   22 m to halfway
Purple Zone –   Halfway to opposition 22 m
Green Zone   –   Opposition 22 m to try-line

It seems Blue stands for 'Build' and Purple for 'Penetrate'. We've yet to be told about the relevance of White and Green. Anyway, it's not rocket science but it is pretty much new to the players. It seems strange that these changes are being introduced less than a week before our opening match and it may take a while for the squad to get on top of this latest set of instructions. But they will – hopefully in time for this weekend.

7 October
Day Eight
We awoke this morning to monsoon weather and I thought (or, rather, hoped) that training would be cancelled. This wasn't to be the case, which was unfortunate for me as I had a bit of a mishap during the session. Defending our try-line, I shuffled quickly to my left, colliding with some force into one of the goal posts. It was a whiplash injury that had me on the ground for a few seconds. Luckily there doesn't seem to be any long-term damage. It has been a law for a few years now that rugby posts must have padded protectors on them. I was too embarrassed to point out lack of said protectors to the coaches.

We had our first floodlit session tonight, which is useful as we play three out of our four pool matches at night. Confusion still reigns as to what we should be doing in the Green zone. As the Japanese are perceived (wrongly in my opinion) as being less physical than other teams, the plan now seems to be for the forwards to try and overpower the opposition at close quarters. At tonight's session, the coaches had the forwards driving all the lineouts in the Green zone. This was done against somewhat passive opposition and resulted in tries being scored after thirty metres of mauling the ball to the line. This was unrealistic to say the least – I have never before seen a Scottish side score a try from that range in a game. Driving lineouts at every opportunity is a very low-risk strategy but I fear it's one that won't succeed.

8 October
Day Nine
Geech showed the squad video clips from our recent match against South Africa to illustrate what has recently worked for us in the Purple and Green zones. Interestingly, in the first Test in Durban we scored two tries by moving the ball wide in the Green zone. Training was a bit flat today as a lot of the players complained of feeling heavy and stiff – probably a reaction to yesterday's double session on a muddy pitch. Nevertheless, training continued at a fair pace and by the end, centre Jim McLaren and Kenny Logan had both hobbled off with muscle strains.

My spirits were lifted later in the afternoon. I phoned home and managed to time it just as my one-year-old son, Christian, was waking up. Although it was heartbreaking not being there, I felt I wasn't too far away. He was showing off as I could hear him in the background saying 'duck' – a new word he has recently learned.

9 October
Day Ten
Training was short and sharp this morning, which was just as well as it was our hottest day yet. It was an unopposed team run led by the captain, Basil (Bryan Redpath). With no outside influence or distractions, it's amazing how smooth a session can be. We now have the opportunity to rest until Saturday. By then we will be in Townsville, only a day away from our first World Cup match against Japan.

We have had a look at the Japanese side in their recent games against England and Queensland. They are a quick, busy and committed team. Pace is probably their major asset. Basil was possibly thinking the same when he was asked at a press conference what he thought about the Japanese team. Unfortunately, and with much accompanying laughter, he called them 'nippy'.

10 October
Day Eleven: Townsville, North Queensland

We arrived in Townsville in the middle of a hot afternoon – luckily we are playing at night – and were greeted with an enthusiastic reception. Pipe bands, school kids and a lot of Scotland supporters made us feel very welcome. I think we might have the 'home' advantage against the Japanese.

This evening we were presented with World Cup caps along with the Japanese squad at an official welcoming ceremony. And, at long last, the World Cup finally began with Australia defeating Argentina 24–8 in a pretty mediocre match at Stadium Australia in Sydney.

11 October
Day Twelve

Today was a long day. The day before a match is usually drawn out and today was even more so as we were advised not to venture out into the sun. The physios perform their 'rubathon' on the eve of a match, which means a twenty-minute massage for each member of the squad (or forty minutes if you've got a 'gold card' and are one of the older players like me). Watching three episodes of *The Sopranos* and setting a new world record of sixty-nine for heading tennis with centre Andy Craig filled the rest of my day. There's a rumour that this figure was beaten later on in the day but we have demanded video evidence to prove it.

There were World Cup games on TV as well but the matches were rather one-sided and not very appealing. Even a crucial match in our pool – France against Fiji – ended up being an easy win for the French. To make the games a bit more interesting, Gordon Ross managed to get in touch with his UK bookmaker to put some bets on for a few of us; we had no success whatsoever.

This evening saw our 'Captain's Run' at the wonderfully named Dairy Farmers Stadium in Townsville. The pitch is in excellent condition and the high-sided grass bank should create a cracking atmosphere tomorrow night more akin to Thomond Park in Limerick. Despite the predictions that the temperature and humidity in Townsville would be unbearable, the weather was nice and mild and we hardly broke into a sweat during our thirty-minute run-through. There is a tremendous sense of anticipation and excitement as we drive back to our hotel. We are all acutely aware that the next time we board the team bus, it will be with one goal in mind – to start Scotland's World Cup campaign with a win.

CHAPTER 14

Breaking Point:
Rugby World Cup 2003 Diary Part 2

The real glory is being knocked to your knees and then coming back. That's real glory. That's the essence of it.

Vince Lombardi

12 October
Day Thirteen: Dairy Farmers Stadium, Townsville
Scotland 31–11 Japan

Well, we got our campaign off to a winning start at least. For a while, though, it seemed to have gone pear-shaped. We were only 15–11 ahead going into the last quarter of the match and were looking ragged in defence and lacking confidence and ambition as well as sufficient depth in attack. With the introduction of two or three subs (including yours truly) and – more crucially – Japan spilling some ball in their own half, we fortunately increased our lead. Another try from a Japanese handling error in the final minute made the scoreline somewhat flattering to our scratchy performance. I was glad to get a run and obviously delighted that we scored three tries near the end of the match, but I made a couple of errors that disappointed me. My impact could have been much more telling and I hope I get a chance to prove myself next week against the USA.

The atmosphere at the ground was excellent, and our hard work in the greenhouses of Edinburgh proved to be unnecessary – the weather was a mild 23°C with little humidity.

13 October
Day Fourteen: Coloundra
Six hours of travel back to Coloundra didn't help with the aches from yesterday's match, but it would appear that we have no injured players. The press cuttings from back home have made their way into Camp Scotland. Unsurprisingly, we have been pilloried for playing terribly – the standard over-reaction from the Scottish media. It's true that we didn't play anywhere near our best but Japan were very competitive and a five-try-to-one scoreline represents, to me, an acceptable start to our World Cup. Both Ireland and Wales had similar results against comparable opposition, but I'm sure they won't be hitting the proverbial panic button just yet.

14 October
Day Fifteen
If only I'd had a tape recorder … The team was announced today to play our next match against the USA on Monday night. There are a few changes – the good news is I'm starting at 10. Four of the squad have now been left out of the twenty-two for our first two games. Anyway, the team announcement didn't prove to be the talking point of this afternoon's meeting. Instead a speech from assistant coach, Jim Telfer, rattled a few feathers.

Basically he said that our game plan was predictable and that we should not have played a tight game against Japan (even though that was mainly what we had practised leading up to the game). Later it got back to the players that Geech was raging about what was said but hadn't argued with Jim at the meeting, which was probably for the best. Luckily Basil did an excellent captain's job and called a players meeting immediately afterwards. He said we had to disregard what had just been said and that we have a game plan that can do very well in the tournament. I spoke up in agreement and added that the group must get tighter and more proactive as we are the ones that will be making the decisions on the field.

Training was low-key and not of great quality. Jim had only one more comment to add – that the first Test against South Africa in June (which was unquestionably the best game we've played since 1999) had to be forgotten. South Africa, he said, were terrible that day and no team would let us get away with the breaks we had made during the game. Undoubtedly Jim is trying to motivate us and wants to see us show some sort of reaction to our uninspiring performance against the Japanese. Let's hope it works.

15 October
Day Sixteen
Pat Lam (the assistant forwards coach), who has had little input out here so far, was in charge of a session today regarding our play in contact. He demonstrated to us that the best option at ruck-time was to block opposition players by standing firm at either side of the breakdown. This might sound a minor technical detail, but for many years Jim Telfer has urged supporting players to drive low directly over the ball, not to branch out to either side of a ruck.

So, in not so many words, Lammy has now refuted one of Jim's core beliefs and the main style of rucking used by the team. Perhaps Jim's speech yesterday has shaken things up for the management. It seemed to have got the desired response as training was much better than yesterday. However, there was some bad news as Andrew Mower (the only genuine open-side flanker in the squad) broke down injured and will now have to be replaced.

Off the field we were front-page news in the local papers here and on tonight's TV news for something unrelated to rugby. The management decided (after advice from Chief Wiggum) that we should leave Coloundra three days earlier than planned. The reason for this is that on Friday a notorious crew of Australian bikers called the 'Bandidos' are staying in our resort for their annual few days of partying and, by all accounts, general mayhem. Over 150 of them will be here and they have apparently all paid $1,000 each in advance for damages that might be caused.

Tonight saw USA play Fiji – two teams in our section. USA were very unfortunate to lose 19–18 and will be tricky opposition for us on Monday night in Brisbane. On their current form Fiji will struggle to beat Japan and hopefully will be as disjointed as they were tonight when they play us.

16 October
Day Seventeen
Training was again reasonably hard today; defence work in the morning followed by team attack in the afternoon. It was hot for the second day running. It brought home to us that we have been lucky with the weather, as we would have struggled to train in this heat on a daily basis. The coaches also informed us today that one set of lineout ploys that we have used for the last year have now been changed for new moves. They were removed because they weren't effective against Japan (even though they had previously worked well). This impulsive change happens quite a lot with Scottish teams I've been involved with and is something we have had to cope with.

17 October
Day Eighteen: Hilton Hotel, Brisbane
The 'Bandidos' just began arriving at our resort in Coloundra while we were preparing to leave. They seem to be nice enough folk underneath all their tattoos, body piercing and long hair – one of them kissed my head as we had our photo taken – but it was probably a wise choice by our management to leave for Brisbane today. Their welcoming reception is scheduled to start at midnight tonight!

Our afternoon training had gone well and the players' spirits were genuinely lifted as we checked in to a five-star hotel in the city. Our stay in Coloundra was pleasant enough but there will be less chance of boredom affecting us in a place that has much more to offer. Tonight, for example, we got out of the hotel and watched rugby in a sports bar. Flanker John Petrie and myself then emptied our wallets in the city's casino. The 'Dirt Trackers' (that's those who are not involved in the upcoming match) had an even livelier evening.

19 October
Day Twenty

Cammy Mather has now joined our squad, replacing Andrew Mower. We had a light run this morning at Ballymore (home ground of the Queensland Reds). The Dirt Trackers were just finishing a hard workout when we arrived – covered in sweat that had an aroma of rum and coke. A few of us re-enacted previous moments from Scotland games at Ballymore. Second-row Stuart Grimes relived his 40-m 'breenge' against the Wallabies five years previously. Grimesy reminded us that Jim Telfer had berated him at half-time for not chipping full-back Matt Burke and going on to score a try. Kenny Logan took us even further back, to eleven years earlier when he had won his first cap at the ground. He had to relive an agonizing moment as we set up an Australian score that involved Michael Lynagh chipping over his head. We also replayed David Sole's score in that match – the last ever four-point try in international rugby.

Tonight our captain's run was at Suncorp Stadium, a very impressive arena. Apparently, tomorrow night's match against USA could be a 50,000 sell-out. This is slightly more than the 9,000 or so that turned up at Murrayfield for our game against Uruguay in the 1999 World Cup. Unfortunately, I have picked up a bug, which meant that I was feeling pretty rough tonight. There is a virus still lingering within the squad – hopefully it will be gone by tomorrow evening.

20 October
Day Twenty-One: Suncorp Stadium, Brisbane
Scotland 39–15 USA

There were 47,000 at tonight's game, and probably 46,000 of them were supporting Scotland. The atmosphere was great despite the fact that it was a Monday night and a mediocre match. There were far too many stoppages, injuries and handling errors. The referee penalized us seventeen times including a yellow card. Also, it had rained most of the day so the ball was difficult to handle, but both sides were guilty of mistakes. I'm sure that if we had held onto the ball for more phases we would have easily extended the try count, which was still not too bad at 5–0 in our favour.

Despite still feeling below 100 per cent before the match, my own game went really well and I managed to sneak over for a try late on. We played better than last week and the mood amongst the squad was very upbeat after the match. Even during the game there were some incidents that we smiled at, and the try celebrations showed that we were clearly enjoying ourselves.

We watched the game on TV when we got back to our hotel. The commentary provided us with some entertainment as I was described, 'as playing well for a thirty-five-year-old'. For the record, I am not yet thirty and a half.

21 October
Day Twenty-Two: Cronulla, Sydney

As last night's match was only my second full eighty minutes of the season, my body was fairly tender today and I felt more like a fifty-five-year-old. Also, I woke up to find my head had been partly scalped – a clash in the game has left me with even less hair than usual. All the bruises and lack of comfort travelling the day after a game were worth it tonight though: Claire and Christian arrived for their two-week stay in Sydney. Despite Christian looking like he has aged two years in the last three weeks, he made my day by smiling at me as I met him at the airport.

22 October
Day Twenty-Three
The focus of our attention has already moved from last Monday's game to our next match on Saturday against France – now only three days away. The team was announced today (I'm still in at 10), and we have two players unavailable. Unfortunately they were the only ones in the squad who have played open-side flanker at international level. John Petrie has an injury and Martin Leslie has been suspended for twelve weeks for kneeing an opponent in the USA game. This sentence is exceedingly harsh given that he didn't actually injure anyone. So, Cammy Mather has gone from playing for Glasgow at Hughenden ten days ago to being selected as open-side flanker against France at Stadium Australia this Saturday.

On a rugby show on TV tonight we were highlighted for our recent exuberant try celebrations. Chris Paterson scored our final try against the USA and as he was lying down, having dived over the try-line, Basil came up behind him and patted his backside. On camera it looks hilarious and was tonight described by an Aussie comedian as the 'Scottish handshake'. The French no doubt would have found it perfectly normal behaviour and probably thrown in a couple of kisses for good measure.

23 October
Day Twenty-Four
Today was our day off, and I had a relaxing time with Claire and Christian at their apartment and on the beach. Cronulla,

where we are now based, is a relatively quiet Sydney suburb with a great surfing reputation. For some reason I was up early this morning, and even at 7 a.m. there were at least twenty surfers out on the water. The only real negative is that we are forty minutes (by train) from the centre of Sydney. Most of the squad ventured into the city this afternoon – hopefully I'll get up to Manly and the northern beaches some time next week.

This afternoon I was the only player allowed to attend the traditional pre-match press conference. The management had made a decision that media access to the players was now to be severely restricted. This was in response to a series of negative articles that had caused consternation within the squad and had visibly stressed out Geech. It was a bold move that turned out to be counter-productive, as it made one or two members of the Scottish press even more antagonistic. I was sent to the press conference because I could speak French, as many of those present were from France. Given a choice, the press conference was the last place I wanted to be – there were a couple of journalists present who I felt had stabbed me in the back in the last few months. Although I could tell the Scottish media were angry – and there were rumblings that our management had broken IRB regulations – I tried to be as upbeat as possible and spoke to as many people as I could.

24 October
Day Twenty-Five
Training this morning was a bit different as Princess Anne was in attendance. We actually trained well and she later mingled with the players at lunch – she's very easy to speak to and knows her rugby. She will be supporting us against France tomorrow night.

25 October
Day Twenty-Six: Stadium Australia, Sydney
Scotland 9–51 France

So, we've arrived at our first defeat of the tournament and it was a whopper. The match was very similar to our defeat this season to England. We were very competitive in the first half, and, despite not creating much, France rarely had us under real pressure (in fact they only had one set piece in our 22 throughout the whole match). However, our scrum was beginning to creak and it was from a twisted scrum (and a missed tackle) that France scored the only try of the first half. At the break we were 19–6 down, which wasn't a real reflection of the play and our confidence was certainly dented.

France got more impressive in the second half, especially up front. I kicked a lot (which isn't usually like me) as most of the ball we won was in our own half. Mostly, the kicking went well but it was frustrating not to have options to attack the French. I managed a couple of line breaks and put in a lot of tackles, but I was tiring going into the last few minutes of the game. Maybe this was down to the fact that I hadn't played much rugby this season or that the match was at a level of physical intensity that we weren't ready for.

Sitting in the changing rooms after the game, I was physically and mentally drained – international rugby has become such a collision sport nowadays. I winced as I remembered defending a short lineout and sprinting up in the line to tackle French flanker Serge Betsen. I hit him with everything I had. Likewise he did not shirk the impact. I managed to stop him on the gainline but I didn't seem to have achieved a great deal, as the French proceeded to set up another phase. They played a power game that sapped our energies. I had to ask myself, if this is now the direction the sport is taking, can my body continue to allow me to play at the highest level for much longer?

To get no reward for the huge effort we had put in is incredibly disappointing, but I hope not demoralizing. France scored a couple of late tries (from our possession) to make the scoreline look like it had been a stroll in the park. It was a major let-down in front of a crowd of 78,000, but we will have learned a lot from the game. If our confidence suffers a real setback, next week's match against Fiji will be a struggle. The losing team will be on a flight home.

On a lighter note, the highlight of the evening (and possibly of the World Cup so far) was our *cri de coeur* during the national anthem. Martin Leslie (who is still suspended for twelve weeks) has a nervous twitch when he plays rugby and we decided just before the match to show our support for him and to protest at the severity of his ban. When the camera moved along the line of players, over half of the squad twitched to show we were behind him in appealing his suspension (it was also his birthday on Saturday).

My own twitch was a poor effort as I was finding it hard to sing and twitch at the same time. I was also focused on not being disrespectful to our anthem 'Flower of Scotland'. After the first couple of twitches the crowd caught on and cheered every effort. I know we will be criticized by the media for our actions, especially as we went on to be heavily defeated, but to me it was a sign of our strength as a team and didn't affect our commitment as we actually started the game very well.

26 October
Day Twenty-Seven

For the second week running I am sore and ill the day after the match – this time it is a cold/flu brought over from Scotland by Claire and Christian. We had a barbeque today with over fifty Scottish supporters (including my mum and dad) at our hotel. Most of them were very upbeat, just like the supporters we met in Townsville and Brisbane, despite last night's hammering by France and the negative press coverage since our first game against Japan.

27 October
Day Twenty-Eight

My symptoms got worse during the night and I have now been quarantined in a room of my own. Hopefully, antibiotics should get me back to normal by the end of the week. I woke this morning to see the TV news and all the Monday papers talking about the Scotland team – not about our rugby (thankfully) but the twitching 'Flower of Scotland'. They were universal in their opinion that we had shown great team spirit and solidarity in our gesture. On TV tonight a rugby show called it the most memorable event of the World Cup, and the presenter said, 'everyone will remember where they were the day the Scots twitched their way through their anthem'.

This is how *Planet Rugby* described it:

> ### Moment of the match
> *As the TV camera went down the line of Scottish players during the anthems, each man offered a slight shake of the head in protest of flanker Martin Leslie's 12-week ban. It was a dignified, silent gesture – and showed that the soul of rugby is still anchored in the notion of fraternity.*

28 October
Day Twenty-Nine

The team for our crucial game against Fiji was announced and the coaches have sprung a surprise on us (and me). Together with three changes in our pack, Chris Paterson has been selected at stand-off (which will be the first time he's played there at Test level) and I have been moved to outside-centre (where I have only played on two occasions at any level in the last three years). Geech actually spoke to me before the team meeting and said that the reasoning behind the decision was that the team needed a point of attack further out in the backline. He also said that I have been playing really well at 10. I hope this is true as I feel my game has been good in the last two matches, but it could be argued he only said that to keep me happy.

Chris was worried that I would be upset at being moved from 10. I have a lot of time for Chris, not just because we were both brought up in Gala but also because he has an infectious enthusiasm that is a positive influence within the squad. I reassured him that I was looking forward to our new-look midfield, which includes Andy Henderson at inside-centre. All three of us have similar senses of humour so I imagine we'll be having a few laughs at training and during the game. In fact, playing outside Chris might turn out to be an exciting move. For some strange reason I feel much less annoyed than if I had been shifted to centre after playing badly. The only regret for me is that the way Fiji defend in the backs should mean there will be a lot of space for the stand-off to attack.

However, looking at the decision objectively, it must be said that the coaches have taken a huge gamble: Scotland's biggest game in four years and they play someone in the most crucial position in the team who has never played there in an international match. Chris will handle the pressure fine – he is very self-disciplined and will approach the game with confidence – and here's hoping the backline can click into gear outside him.

I didn't train today as my cold/flu still lingers on. Basil also missed training as he injured his foot jumping off his bed last night. He was taken to hospital this morning for some stitches to a deep gash. He's got too much energy for a thirty-two-year-old! He's probably the only person in the squad that could have suffered such an injury so close to a game and still make the coaches laugh. What a start to a big week for Scottish rugby.

29 October
Day Thirty
The training session this morning seemed to be our worst of
the World Cup so far. Players argued with each other and
coaches shouted at players as the tension mounted. At times I
was glad to be at outside-centre as those closer to the action
were having a rough day. The quality of the training wasn't
really that bad, but I think we are all beginning to realize how
important Saturday's game is. If we lose we will be the first
ever Scottish side not to qualify for the quarter-finals of a
World Cup – and we'll all be back home playing club rugby
the following weekend.

   Martin Leslie had his ban reduced from twelve weeks to
eight weeks today. This makes no difference to Martin, or us,
as he is set to retire at the end of the World Cup. They again
showed the incident on TV tonight, and it still seems fairly
innocuous. The suspension looks even harsher than normal,
as two Argentine players were today found guilty of the
much more dangerous and repugnant act of eye gouging.
Their bans were just six weeks and nine weeks respectively.

30 October
Day Thirty-One: Darling Harbour, Sydney
We have moved into the city in preparation for Saturday's
match. This wasn't originally the intention but a combination
of our hotel (they struggled handling the demands of a rugby
team) and our location (forty-five minutes from the city) has
persuaded the management to change their plans. It is definitely a positive move and together with having today off, the
mood in the camp has improved greatly from yesterday's low
point. I am now confident of us winning on Saturday.

31 October
Day Thirty-Two
A good captain's run today and the squad seem to believe that not only can we win the match but we will win it. Highlights of the day included Tom Smith having to sing a song on the bus (it's his birthday and he wins his fiftieth cap tomorrow), his choice being Kylie Minogue's 'I should be so lucky'. The locals would have described his rendition as being 'very ordinary'.

My room-mate, Simon Danielli, was looking a bit nervous later at night. He confided in me that he was trying not to think about tomorrow's game as he hates playing against small, explosive wingers. His opposite number tomorrow, Rupeni Caucaunibuca, is explosive, extremely fast and not very tall. I didn't tell him that I'd read an amazing statistic about Caucaunibuca in the paper earlier today: on top of his sensational performances in the Super 12 for the Auckland Blues, he has scored six tries so far in his three Test matches for Fiji. An average of two tries a game makes him a phenomenon.

1 November
Day Thirty-Three: Aussie Stadium, Sydney
Scotland 22–20 Fiji
Well we made it … just. The score was 15–20 with less than five minutes to go but the result was never in doubt – honest!! Tom Smith scored the try that sealed the win, which was appropriate. Good things come in threes apparently.

Fiji scored both their tries through the best winger in the world right now: Rupeni Caucaunibuca. Despite showing some violent tendencies – he broke Simon Danielli's nose with a forearm smash – he was awesome; just like Jonah Lomu in his prime. Fiji didn't just rely on one player, though, and they really attacked us in the first half. We played some good rugby at times but finishing and handling errors let us down. I have to take a fair bit of responsibility for some poor passing, as I struggled to get to grips with playing centre again for the first hour of the match. My pace on to the ball and angles belatedly improved – if I get a chance to play next week I am confident my decisions will be much sharper having now had a full eighty minutes at centre under my belt.

Chris did exceptionally well at stand-off given the circumstances. The Fijians, as expected, defended well in the wide channels and left holes for Chris and our forwards to exploit. That they did. Chris should now be given the chance to play there after the World Cup and I said this to the media after the game. I don't know where that would leave me (playing centre, on the bench, out of the squad, or retirement are the options) but Chris can only progress by playing in the number 10 jersey more often.

After the match we watched Ireland outplay Australia but lose 18–17 in their pool decider. However, their performance gives us some hope when we take on the Wallabies in the quarter-final next week.

2 November
Day Thirty-Four: Brisbane
Today was yet another travel and recovery day. This was my last day with Claire and Christian for three weeks (or a week, if we don't make it past the quarter-finals).

We watched the game of the tournament so far on TV tonight. Wales (with what before the match was claimed as being far from their strongest team) had a real go at the mighty All Blacks and came very close to pulling off the shock result of any World Cup. There was some great attacking play by both sides, but the All Blacks were just that bit stronger at the end of the match, holding on to win 51–37. This was another dose of inspiration for us before Saturday night's match.

4 November
Day Thirty-Six

We were back into full training today, and it was pretty tough in very warm conditions. The pitch we were training on, though, was like a village road in Fiji and a couple of the boys fell over randomly during the session. We started to wonder if maybe the Aussies had sent a sniper to our training.

Slightly worrying for me was that I pulled up with a thigh injury. I probably can't blame the pitch entirely, as since my knee operation I've not been able to fully stretch my quadriceps. The medics reckon that I have split my fascia and not torn my quads, which is welcoming news. Also good news is the team, where I am still in at 13 – I feel mightily relieved as I feared my poor passing last week would cost me my place.

Kenny Logan and I treated our bodies to a well-earned pamper this afternoon. We booked a two-hour massage and reflexology session that will hopefully keep two of the older squad members going for another week at least.

Today was also Melbourne Cup Day, which is a huge event in Australia (much bigger than our Grand National). The squad held a $5 and a $10 sweepstake and some of the boys went to a racecourse in Brisbane to savour the atmosphere. As luck may have it, my horse, Makybe Diva, won the race. This was in the $5 sweep, which meant I had an extra $60 to put towards my afternoon massage. Unluckily for my new room-mate, Jim McLaren, he only just missed out on the 'Trifecta' as his horses came in first, second and fourth. If the fourth had managed to hold onto third place for five seconds longer he would have won $20,000. Ouch!!

5 November
Day Thirty-Seven

It certainly didn't feel like a normal Guy Fawkes Night as the temperature reached 30°C today. We had another fairly intense session in the heat this morning followed by a golf day in the afternoon. I missed the golf due to my thigh injury. Happily, it feels less painful than yesterday and I managed to do over half of the session. There will be plenty time for golf after the World Cup.

6 November
Day Thirty-Eight
Our last session (of the World Cup?) today – the captain's run – at Suncorp Stadium went well in the heat. We usually would do it the day before the game but, for some reason, the stadium cannot be used tomorrow. Even though the press have focused on Australia rather then ourselves so far this week, today we heard some comments on our chances in Saturday's match. Bookmakers have the Wallabies at odds of 1-100 to win the match. Bob Dwyer (the former Wallaby coach) said that Australia could win the match blindfolded. Cheers Bob, that's given us some extra motivation. The Wallaby coaching staff have also been fairly condescending towards us in their pre-match comments, saying that they have to win the match by a big margin or they'll be disappointed. Eddie Jones (the Australian coach) came out with a classic line in a press conference declaring that Scotland would probably resort to starting a fight to try to win the match. If only!

8 November
Day Forty: Suncorp Stadium, Brisbane
Scotland 16–33 Australia
And so our World Cup adventure ends. We gave it a good go, though, in our attempt to reach the last four. In terms of effort we performed as we had in the first half against the French but continued to match the Wallabies for the majority of the game. Our forwards also had their best performance of the tournament by a long way. However, our skill level and accuracy weren't good enough to win a World Cup

quarter-final. Nevertheless, for long periods of the game it didn't seem that this deficiency was too much of a problem, as Australia made numerous handling errors themselves. We shaded the first half in terms of territory and possession and probably deserved better than the 9–9 half-time scoreline.

The second half continued in the same vein until the fifty-first minute when a breakaway try for Australia (we were in their half attacking with ball in hand) gave the Wallabies bags of confidence and knocked us for six. For the next fifteen minutes they played their best rugby of the World Cup and won the contest. We again finished strongly and did ourselves proud. Despite not being the best team, if a couple of decisions had gone our way the game could have easily swung in our favour. One incident in the first half should have led to seven points for us. Kenny Logan was racing to score after I had kicked into space, but the referee, Steve Walsh, unaware of Kenny's run, brought the play back for a penalty to us. Also, Phil Waugh was so far offside for Australia's crucial first try that I thought he was playing for us.

My own game was much better than last week although there was more defending than attacking to do. However, my thigh is now completely torn and I also went over on my ankle. It was an emotional time after the match as we walked (or limped) around the pitch to salute our supporters. The completion of a World Cup always coincides with the retirement of certain players and two of the squad have now hung up their boots. Both Basil and Kenny had already announced this would be their final appearance for Scotland and I was sad knowing that in the future I would now be seeing much less of my two friends. It did seem as if we were entering a new era – Geech and Jim would also have no more involvement with the team.

As I waved to the Scottish supporters I chatted with Chris Paterson and Andy Henderson and realized that with players like them and Simon Taylor, Jason White, Bruce Douglas and

Mike Blair, the long-term future of the national team is in good hands. Despite the sacrifices and exertions of this World Cup year, I still want to be involved in the short term. I have a wild dream that, if my body holds up, I'll make it to the next World Cup in France at the age of thirty-four.

Our quarter-final against the Wallabies provided yet another memorable off-the-field incident. Fifteen minutes before the kick-off, a stray punt from our replacement, Ben Hinshelwood (who can really kick a ball), struck Chris Paterson on the side of his head. As he lay spreadeagled on the ground I, like most of the crowd, thought that it was part of an act and couldn't help laughing. After a short while I was worried that Chris was going to get in trouble for fooling around before such a crucial match as he was still lying there. When I eventually got alongside him it was suddenly obvious that he had been knocked out cold. My pathetic attempts at trying to get him on his feet and give him water were useless; fortunately our doctor, James Robson, arrived on the scene and told me to step aside. It wasn't looking good though.

The scene in the changing rooms was one of pandemonium. One of the Dirt Trackers was now going to have to find some kit and be prepared to sit on the bench. I was trying to remember the team calls as it looked as if Chris was out and I would be playing stand-off. Miraculously, two minutes before we were due to line up for the anthems, Chris reappeared looking very groggy, but available to play. He actually played very well again and even put over a 45-m drop-goal for good measure. Unbelievable. Maybe David Campese was right in saying before the World Cup that the Scots were a weird bunch.

9 November
Day Forty-One
Less than twelve hours after our exit at the hands of Australia, the squad were on a flight from Brisbane at 10 a.m.

on the first part of the long journey back to Scotland. To fly for over twenty-four hours the day after a match is not something any player would relish. To do it the following morning after such an exhausting Test match made it look like the squad's well-being was no longer a priority.

Luckily for me and a few selected others (the antipodeans in the squad and some senior players) our manager Dougie Morgan had managed to postpone our departure date for as long as we liked. Stuart Grimes and myself had put back our flight home for another day. It gave us a chance to recover from the Australia match and watch the two remaining quarter-finals – and, of course, drink as much beer as we could.

We had tickets to watch the England–Wales match at Suncorp Stadium, but a vote was taken and it was decided that we would spend the day in a pub. The first match on TV was France–Ireland, and even though I wasn't concentrating fully, I thought France produced the best rugby of the tournament so far in winning 43–21. In the first hour they were untouchable – at one stage they were leading 37–0 before they took their foot of the gas near the end of the game. This was against a side that before the game was ranked third in the world.

The England–Wales match was a classic, even more exciting than the Wales–New Zealand game earlier in the competition. Through a drunken haze we saw some tremendous attacking rugby from the Welsh as they outscored the English by three tries to one. They were desperately unlucky not to have won, and outplayed England for large parts of the match – all this from a side who hadn't won a game in this season's Six Nations. It's amazing what a bit of self-belief and some momentum can do for a team.

England's experience and the second-half introduction of an impressive Mike Catt steered the World Cup favourites to a 28–17 victory. In the early hours of the morning we met up with the Welsh players in a bar near our hotel. We bought them drinks for their fantastic effort, but it didn't seem like they were running short of alcohol.

We had a great night, letting off two months of steam. I spent a lot of time with Basil and Kenny, who were both staying out for a few extra days. They tried hard to get me to announce my retirement like they had just done, but I told them I was going to see how I felt once I was back home. Kenny was particularly emotional. He revealed to me that he had gone through a life-changing experience that year. Despite his confident exterior, for many years he had hidden the fact that he was dyslexic. He told me of the knot in his stomach he'd experienced ever since his school days.

I can only imagine the frustrations, anguish and challenges he had to overcome being an elite sportsman with dyslexia. Earlier in the season his wife Gabby had encouraged him to admit he was dyslexic and enrol on a DDAT course. This was to be a turning point in his life and his rugby career – for it was in his final season with Scotland that he played his best rugby. It was no coincidence that this came after succeeding in admitting to, and triumphing over, dyslexia.

10 November
Day Forty-Two
I woke up this morning with a thumping headache to find there was a skateboard in the corner of the room. I thought I was dreaming, but when I opened my eyes again it was still there. Somewhat surprised I looked at the attached message – 'Please could you bring this skateboard back to Scotland, which is a present for my Grandson. Thanks, Jim Telfer.' This request was in keeping with the many bizarre happenings of my first overseas World Cup.

By the time Grimesy and I arrived at the airport in Brisbane, it seemed that the global rugby community were all queuing up to check in for flights to Sydney in preparation for the following weekend's semi-final matches. Unfortunately for us, our own travel arrangements had not been registered and we had to miss the flight. We then had to wait a few hours before we could at last get on a plane back to the UK.

It was during this wait that the English squad came through the airport and I talked to Will Greenwood about the previous night's epic game against Wales. It was obvious that the game had given the English squad an almighty fright. Although the squad looked somewhat dejected, Will assured me that the fact they had survived the Welsh match had made them even more determined to go the whole way. Will was bemused to see me holding a skateboard – he didn't believe my story that it belonged to Jim Telfer.

I also bumped into Matt Williams, who was probably now the de facto Scottish coach. Although he had been in the same hotel as the team over the past few weeks, it was the first time he had spoken to me about the future. He was very upbeat and said he was going to phone me in the next couple of weeks regarding planning for the Six Nations.

Just as we were about to board the plane, I found an intriguing text message on my mobile from my agent, Bart Campbell. All it said was – 'How would you like to play Super 12 rugby next year?' Hurriedly I phoned Bart, who told me that the Durban-based Natal Sharks, were keen to sign me. Although I was flattered by their interest, I thought it wasn't a feasible option. Even so, my mind started thinking that at last I could fulfil my dream of playing in the Super 12. As I stretched out to sleep on the flight home, I pictured myself running out at Kings Park for the Sharks in front of 40,000 supporters.

23 November
England 18–15 Australia
So, England did it. Thanks to a drop-goal in extra-time by the most famous rugby player in the world, Jonny Wilkinson, the best team of the previous eighteen months were crowned

world champions. If his kick hadn't sailed between the posts there would have been the bizarre prospect of a penalty shoot-out to decide the winner. Fortunately such a scenario was avoided and the better team on the day deservedly won the match. England had saved their best performances for their last two games, their ageing pack having dominated both France and the Wallabies. Although Wilkinson is now guaranteed an iconic status to rank alongside David Beckham, he had a quiet tournament, which was hardly surprising given the suffocating attention he had received over the previous two months.

The key member of the English side – and the stand out performer of the World Cup – was captain Martin Johnson. He will be irreplaceable as a captain and a player. Despite England's large playing numbers, they will not be the same force without Johnson and other stalwarts such as Lawrence Dallaglio, Neil Back and Will Greenwood. The England World Cup squad had fourteen players aged thirty or older and at some time in the near future there will need to be a huge amount of rebuilding work done to replace these players.

This World Cup, just like the Sydney Olympics of 2000, is already being described as being the best we've ever seen. The Aussies certainly know how to organize a sporting event. I thought it was a fantastic tournament with some memorable games. More important was the involvement of the Australians themselves. The stadiums were nearly always full, even for matches involving the competition's minnows. Also, the travelling supporters made their presence felt and there was a real buzz in the streets of Brisbane and Sydney. Finally, although I'll have to whisper it in Scotland, it was great to see a northern hemisphere side at last winning the World Cup.

From a Scottish perspective, losing to the runners-up in the quarter-final was probably as well as most people would have expected us to do. However, we didn't play as well as we had on our tour to South Africa and were pretty lucky to beat Fiji.

I had the impression leading up to the World Cup and while we were in Australia that there hadn't been a concrete long-term plan for how we would attack the tournament; or, if there had been a plan, it changed whenever we lost a game.

This had been in evidence after our defeats against Wales and Ireland before the World Cup when we reverted back to playing a risk-free game. Also, despite Geech stating at the time that he had planned all along to play Chris at stand-off at some time during the World Cup, this didn't seem evident to the players (including Chris), as he had never ran Chris at number 10 in training while we were in Australia. Our heavy defeat against France was the reason for the change in personnel and we went on to play our most important fixture of the tournament with an untried backline combination.

When I finally got back home to Scotland, there seemed to be universal media condemnation of our World Cup campaign. Much of the content of these articles, it must be said, was not a criticism of our on-field performances but rather reflected the deteriorating relationship between the media and the squad. There was a fair amount of antagonism at times during the six weeks, probably because we often used the same accommodation as the press. No player likes to read what they consider to be unjustified criticism and seeing members of the media on a daily basis perhaps reminded players of that criticism. After our game against Japan, our dealings with the media turned sour very quickly.

It would have undoubtedly been a better idea for there not to have been press cuttings placed in our team room, as the last thing a squad that is preparing for some huge challenges needs is negativity. Some players began to refuse to speak to certain journalists, which only caused more friction. Unfortunately, the Scottish media proved to be as stubborn as the players and felt that we were getting what we deserved. The criticism continued unabated. There were even articles suggesting that players' wives were distracting our focus and things came to a head when one journalist wrote an article about an alleged altercation he had in a pub with a few of our Dirt Trackers.

The players were definitely not blameless for the escalating problems and I'm sure things would have been sorted out amicably if there had been a social event organized for the media and the squad. The management's decision to ban the press from speaking to the players before the French game seemed a natural response at the time, but only ended up exacerbating the situation.

The role of the media in rugby has changed dramatically over the past 15 years. I clearly remember that Bill McLaren – when he combined TV commentary work with writing for the *Herald* – analysed games objectively and I found him to be spot-on in his summations. I used to cut out and keep his match reports, as they gave me pointers to what I should be working on in my game. Since rugby has gone professional, this factual style of reporting has been replaced with a more comment-based approach.

Moreover, with the rise of talk radio and internet blogs, sports journalism is looking increasingly like an extension of fandom. Sometimes the sports pages read more like a group of supporters discussing their views in a pub. The emotional range is stretched to the limits – anger after defeats, ecstasy after victories. This change in reporting hasn't been restricted to the world of sport. As Tony Blair stated in his last days as prime minister, 'It is rare today to find balance in the media. Things, people, issues, stories, are all black-and-white. Life's usual grey is almost entirely absent ... these are concepts alien to today's reporting.'

Andy Murray, after winning his first ATP title in San Jose, commented that the absence of the Scottish press had taken the pressure off him. I know exactly what he meant. Early in my career I got caught up in the media's expectations when I should have been focusing more on the process of trying to improve each time I played. There were even times during some matches when I was actually wondering how my game might be reported in the papers the following day. One piece of advice I would give to any aspiring rugby player – do not read your own press. If you are confident in your own ability you don't need the ego boost from good press, and reading the press after a loss or a bad game can only be harmful, unless of course you are of a masochistic disposition.

Like any international sportsman, I have had to deal with criticism that I considered to have been unjustified. Generally, though, I feel that I have been given a reasonably fair deal over the years and there have been many journalists who have been really supportive. Although there are one or two reporters who have never appreciated my style of play, I can think of only one person who has continually made personal attacks on me throughout my career. It seemed his sole purpose in life was to mention me negatively at any opportunity and it had got to such a laughable stage that at one time I thought he must have some crazy obsession with me. Although his colleagues have told me many times that they are embarrassed by him, I know his comments did upset those close to me on a number of occasions.

Even though I would like to think that I am a good friend to most of the rugby journalists I have met throughout my career, it is undeniable that an uneasy relationship exists between the players and the press these days. I hope lessons have been learned from our time in Australia in order to make sure such volatile resentment never resurfaces in the future.

Setting aside our problems dealing with the media, my overall impression of the World Cup was extremely positive. Considering that I nearly missed the competition with injury, I felt blessed to have been involved in such a tremendous sporting occasion. It was a hard road at times, and our flirtations with disaster placed strains on players and management that I'd seen before only rarely, but our sense of humour was kept intact and for me it had been a hugely enjoyable time. I loved being part of the squad and still found playing international rugby massively addictive. I was as determined as ever to wear the Scottish jersey for as long as was physically possible.

CHAPTER 15

Farewell to All That

After all is said and done, more is said than done.

Aesop

Coming back to my Borders home in St Boswells, I was looking forward to being settled again and spending much more time with my family. My focus over the previous year had been firmly fixed on the World Cup in Australia. In addition to the six weeks we spent down under, the South African tour, our training camp in Poland and many other squad sessions, I had spent a great deal of time away from home.

But there was still one burning issue to resolve: whether or not I would accept the tempting offer to play Super 12 rugby for the Natal Sharks, one of the biggest clubs in world rugby. The Super 12 had always excited me since its inception in 1996 and I believed it showed not just rugby but sport in general at its most breathtaking. Up until a few seasons earlier, the quality of play witnessed in the competition was far beyond the capabilities of domestic rugby in the northern hemisphere. Although that had changed with the increasing improvement of the Heineken Cup and England adopting a fifteen-man approach to the game, if visitors from outer space landed on earth and wanted to know what rugby was, I'd have sent them to watch a Super 12 game.

I had a clause in my contract with the Borders that allowed me to leave for six months to play in the Super 12 if the situation ever arose. I never once thought that it would be a possibility and the main reason I had this opt-out was that I had been worried that the SRU might change their view of funding a third professional team. In 1998, and without warning, the SRU cut the number of professional sides from four to two, leaving many players forced to look elsewhere for employment. I feared this might happen to the Borders, and already it seemed that we were unwanted by the SRU after only one year of existence. Our budget had been cut despite the fact that we had qualified for the Heineken Cup, and rumours circulated that the team might be axed at the end of only our second season. It was a sorry state of affairs – we actually needed to add to our squad, which had been assembled hastily the year before.

The Sharks coach, Kevin Putt, had spoken to me a few times about the reasons why Super 12 rugby in Durban would be a great option for me. I knew it would be a once-in-a-lifetime opportunity and that my game would hopefully be suited to the Super 12 style of play – fast, dynamic, ball-in-the-hand rugby. Kevin said that the Sharks needed experience in the key decision-making position of stand-off and had negotiated an agreement with the South African Rugby Union to allow an overseas player to play for the Sharks. The normal rules in both Australia and South Africa were that the Super 12 was open only to players available for their national teams. I was aware that if I turned down the Sharks offer, I would never again have the chance to play in the Super 12.

It was a significant dilemma as deep down I'd always planned to finish my career with the Borders – back where it all began. As a family we felt at home and the group of players at the Borders was among the best in terms of team spirit that I'd ever been involved with. While we didn't have the resources to make a real impact in the Celtic League, and we were probably going to struggle in the Heineken Cup, I was relishing playing once more for the team. I had come back from Australia with playing ideas, kicking strategies and new moves that I gave to the Borders backs coach, Rob Moffat. However, my leg injury was exasperating as it kept me from training and playing with the side. It also meant I had more time to agonize over my immediate rugby future.

The only people I had told about the Sharks offer were my family. I didn't want to mention it to anyone at the Borders, as it would be a distraction for them that would probably come to nothing anyway. Nevertheless, I felt I needed to speak to someone in the rugby community for some advice. I turned to Ian McGeechan to whom I'd listened in the past for guidance. He had recently been installed as Director of Rugby at the SRU.

Geech and I had chatted many times before on rugby matters and I outlined to him the predicament I now found myself in as well as the confidential nature of the approach from the Sharks. I said that this was a wonderful opportunity to improve as a rugby player but I was worried about leaving the Borders and being unavailable for the upcoming Six Nations. He realized that it was a tough decision but he thought that my departure would be difficult for the Borders given their meagre playing resources.

I agreed with Geech that I would be leaving the Borders in the lurch, and this ultimately tipped the balance – I would stay in Scotland. I'd dreamed of playing in the Super 12, but I was determined not to dwell on the fact that my last chance had now gone.

It was very hard telling Kevin Putt that I wouldn't be joining his squad in Durban – part of me couldn't believe what I was saying – but I also felt happy to be staying at the Borders. I was also really looking forward to working with the new coaches in the Scottish international set-up. Having had the same coaches for most of my international career I was keen to hear a different voice. Also, from my experiences at Warringah, I thought I would enjoy an Australian coach – I hoped he would focus on improving our handling skills and move Scotland towards a more expansive, running game. After the prolonged nature of the build-up to the World Cup and the tournament itself, I was looking for something to re-ignite my career – I thought staying in Scotland would give me this 'second wind'. Also, I just couldn't bring myself to retire from international rugby – attempting to be selected for Scotland was still the driving force behind trying to improve my game.

I had said during the World Cup that Chris Paterson – our winger at the time, but a former Gala number 10 – deserved to be given a run at stand-off but that didn't mean that I wouldn't fight for my place in the team. The French have a saying – *La verité du terrain* – that translates as 'the truth of the pitch'; in other words, that only your performances on the pitch can prove if you deserve to play. Captains and coaches in French rugby used it a lot to tell their players that there was no hiding place in the professional game. I accepted the French philosophy – if I wasn't playing well enough, I wouldn't deserve to be selected. But I still believed I had a lot of good rugby in me.

There were a few different scenarios in my head that I hoped could develop over the season. The first was that I could take on a David Humphreys-type role (the veteran Irish stand-off), acting as an experienced number 10 in the squad to help and challenge Chris in his new position. I also thought I might be able to play at number 12 outside Chris, a role that former stand-offs Mike Catt of England and Elton Flatley of Australia had performed so effectively during the recent World Cup. Moreover, the midfield combination of Chris at stand-off, Andy Henderson at inside-centre and myself at number 13 had played well in the quarter-final against Australia – our last match – and I felt that maybe we would have the chance to develop further. On top of that, my dad, who had watched my rugby career closer than anyone, told me that he thought I could thrive if moved to full-back – although I still had to be convinced on that one!

I knew that there would be some 'down time' after the intensity of the World Cup, but the fact that I injured my thigh against Australia allowed me to slowly get back into my day job. The Borders had qualified for the Heineken Cup and I was keen to be fully fit for these matches. Unfortunately, I wasn't deemed ready for our first match away to Agen, which we lost, but I was determined to be available for selection for our home game against Llanelli, due to be played a week before Christmas.

Although there had been no contact from new Scotland coach Matt Williams, I had heard that there would be a squad session at the end of December. Chris Cusiter (the Borders scrum-half) told me that he had recently trained at Murrayfield under the guidance of Williams. Other players involved were scrum-half Mike Blair, Chris Paterson and Brendan Laney. Chris was in just his first professional season with the Borders but already looked like an international player. It was great that he seemed to be figuring in Williams' plans. The fact that I hadn't been invited to Murrayfield was disappointing – I was now back to full fitness – but I didn't read too much into it. I was sure that once I got back playing again I would be able to show that I was still capable of performing at the highest level.

Matt Williams finally phoned me at home some four weeks after our meeting at Brisbane Airport. I moved into my study for some privacy so I could digest fully what he was about to propose. He wanted to know my intentions for the forthcoming Six Nations. I told him that I was available and was due to be back playing for the Borders against Llanelli the following weekend. I could tell from Matt's voice that this may not have been what he wanted to hear.

'Well Gregor, in an ideal world, I'd have you and Glenn [Metcalfe, our full-back, who was thirty-three at the time] in my team, but you have to appreciate – I've got to think about the future. I had a conversation with Glenn about this yesterday. He's decided to retire.' I didn't say anything. Matt took note of the pause and continued quickly: 'Mate, I've had a good look at Scottish rugby and it's clear there's a real shortage of midfielders with international experience.' I agreed with him – for that reason alone, I was thinking Williams would be in need of someone like me.

'The thing is mate, the only way I can fill this hole is to bring on the young guys, straight away. That's what I'm going to do. How does that affect your plans?' I said that I would still be available, and if I wasn't selected in the team, then that was his choice but not a problem. He then said, 'Well look, I'm going to announce the [squad of] forty-four in the next few days, and you're not part of it.'

Obviously I was bitterly disappointed – and I can't deny that it came as something of a shock – but once again I told him that this wouldn't change my decision to remain available for selection. Williams continued, 'That's going to put me in a difficult situation. It's too big a news story, you know? The first thing I do as national coach is drop Scotland's most capped player from the squad? The press will be all over it. I can't have that dominating the announcement of my first training squad. Surely you wouldn't want that?' Gritting my teeth, I told him that I had decided a while ago that I still wanted to play for Scotland and would probably review the situation at the end of the season, but for now I was still available regardless of whether I was selected or not. What came next almost floored me: 'Ok then, you leave me no option. I can't have "Williams Axes Scotland's Most Capped Player" as my first headlines. If you're adamant that you still want to be selected, then I'll put your name on the squad list, but you're not to come to the sessions.'

Knuckles white against the phone, I told him that I would have to get back to him. He had hit me with a sucker-punch.

He announced coolly that we would have to meet in the next day or two as he intended to announce the training squad on the following Monday.

As our conversation was winding up I felt a growing incredulity at what I was hearing. I hung up the phone and told Claire what had happened. And then it began to sink in – my international career was over, and what's more, someone who had never done anything for Scottish rugby had ended it. I was outraged. I thought of the sacrifices I had made over my eleven-year involvement with the Scottish team and I was being denied even the chance to prove myself to the new coach. It sickened me. I felt there was nothing else I could do but retire.

Having decided at the end of the World Cup that I would continue to try to be selected for Scotland, Williams' bombshell put all my plans in disarray. The only person I told about it – apart from my family – was Glenn Metcalfe. I tried to switch my focus to playing for the Borders in my comeback game against Llanelli. Perhaps I was too embarrassed to tell people how I had been treated but I also didn't want Williams' extinguishing of my career to be a talking point throughout Scottish rugby. I resolved to try to save some dignity from the situation and let the announcement of my retirement be as low-key as possible – there would be no mention of what Williams had done. In fact I tried to talk up the new coaching regime and I made a rule for myself that I wouldn't comment on the team's performances for at least a year.

My immediate response to any setback is to look for the positives. I had many great memories from my time with Scotland and I told myself that I had been unbelievably lucky to be involved for so long. I knew that I had been fortunate in other ways, as rugby had given me the chance to see the world. Also, the timing of the game going professional had allowed me to live out my passion on a daily basis and get paid for the pleasure. However, at other times I was over-whelmed by sadness. A group of friends would now drift away from me and no longer would I experience the pound-ing emotion and adrenalin that surged through me whenever I played for Scotland. It's difficult to put into words the feeling of loss that this entails.

When I finally met up with Williams at his office in Murrayfield, I decided to tell him early on in our discussion that I would retire from international rugby. He looked me straight in the eye, held my gaze and said, 'Mate, I think you've made a very courageous decision.'

Although I felt this was incredibly patronizing, all of a sudden he was very relaxed and began to ask my opinion on various issues, including who should be the next Scotland captain. I suggested Jason White but he seemed to have settled on either Scott Murray or Chris Paterson. He went on to reveal that there would be openings for me if I wanted to go into coaching. A full-time coach of Scotland Under-21 might be appointed some time in the near future.

Offering me a job that didn't exist is quite an easy thing to do, but he then asked if I was interested in sevens rugby. Player-coach perhaps? (Glenn told me later in the day that he had offered him the exact same thing.) We soon ended our chat. However, I was astonished once more by what he still had to say. After I wished him good luck he revealed to me that he was going to pull out all the stops to bring back flanker and former captain Budge Pountney. This left me feel-ing further resentment towards Williams – Budge at thirty years old was the same age as me.

I switched on Teletext three days later to read through the names of the forty-four-man training squad – so much for the talk of developing young players. In the squad there were two forwards at thirty-two and thirty-four years old. Also, in the backs there were two players at thirty years old. Utility back Derrick Lee and I had played together in the same Scottish

Schools team and New Zealander Brendan Laney covered the same midfield positions as myself. Derrick's a very underrated player and I was pleased to see him recalled, but the selections clearly showed that Williams hadn't been that concerned with having backline players in their thirties.

Laney, who is only six months younger than me, had been omitted from the Scottish World Cup squad. He is a very talented player who had certainly been in good form for Edinburgh while the rest of us were away at the World Cup, but the fact was that he had rarely reproduced his club form at international level. Yet he was now clearly in Williams' plans despite the apparent need for younger players to be promoted in the midfield.

Later that night I was in my kitchen moping around and trying to help Claire prepare dinner when I heard Williams interviewed on the radio. He said that he would have loved to work with me if only I had been younger. Perhaps he had forgotten to check my date of birth? Apart from forcing my retirement, both Glenn and centre Jim McLaren had also been encouraged to end their international careers.

Williams has since said about his actions: 'If I'd kept even one or two of them, it would have created a problem further down the line. We would have found ourselves asking very inexperienced guys to come into key positions when the rest of the team had matured.' A nice sound bite maybe, but it made little sense when you thought about it. The best time to bring in inexperienced players – in any position – is when the rest of the team has matured and is winning matches.

I tried to work out why he had come to his decision, which was similar in a way to what John Mitchell had done with the All Blacks. He had left out world-renowned players like Christian Cullen, Anton Oliver and Taine Randell, all guys with a wealth of experience. After failing to reach the 2003 World Cup Final, Mitchell was replaced by Graham Henry who immediately brought back older players like Oliver and made the thirty-year-old Tana Umaga the All Black captain. Also, England's World Cup winning side had six players over the age of thirty. Obviously Scottish rugby has only a fraction of the playing resources of New Zealand or England and that made it even more puzzling that Williams would not want to have as many experienced players as possible.

I thought of other reasons why he excluded me – did he think, for example, that I would be against the different methods of a new coach? In fact the opposite was true, and I was looking forward to fresh ideas and training methods. Only Williams would know why I had been singled out as someone not to be included in his future plans, but something he said during our meeting kept coming back. He stressed that having a positive relationship with the media is one of the most important factors in coaching in the professional era. He said that he hadn't realized this when coach of New South Wales in Australia and that was why he had lost his job there. Maybe this explains his determination to see me retire from playing for Scotland? He would certainly have noticed that a section of the Scottish press corps felt that I had outstayed my welcome in the Scottish team. Was winning over a journalist the real reason for excluding me? I'll never know, but in his first week in office Williams seemed to conduct a charm offensive on the Scottish media.

Williams had also said to me during our meeting that he had heard about the approach to play Super 12 – I don't know how – and thought it would be a great idea for me to pursue. He said that he would make sure the Borders would not stand in my way and even though I said that I had already turned down the Sharks, he encouraged me to see whether the opportunity still existed.

Bart Campbell, my agent, told me that the Sharks had not signed anyone since I had declined their offer of ten days before. I was so angry about how I had been treated that, despite the financial implications of leaving behind a good contract with the Borders (which still had eighteen months to run), and, more importantly, the fact that I would be letting down my team-mates, I knew I would feel like a spare part if I stayed in Scotland. South Africa seemed as good a place as any to get away from it all.

CHAPTER 16

Swimming with Sharks

You miss 100 per cent of the shots you never take.

Wayne Gretzky

'Guys, you know the drill – swim out past the pier and back to the shore. Remember on the way out the current takes you into the pier – on the way back it's the opposite.'

I looked at the Indian Ocean ahead of me – the pier seemed to stretch out for at least 100 yards. Huge waves rolled serenely by on their way to the shore.

'What on earth I am doing here?' I asked myself. My expression must have been one of extreme apprehension as the team's fitness coach came over to try and make me feel more at ease.

'Don't worry Gregor, there's a lifeguard here that you can swim alongside if you want.'

'That sounds like a good idea. Thanks.'

We were nearing the end of our pre-season training and the players had been given the choice of a weights session or a swim – both of which began at 7 a.m. After some encouragement from my team-mates, I decided that I'd join in with the outdoor session. What was I thinking? I'm really not that good a swimmer, and at the best of times struggle to do two lengths of front crawl in a 25-m pool without having to stop to take a breather. Why this had not occurred to me earlier, I cannot say. I suppose the idea of swimming out round a pier and back sounded easy enough – relaxing even – but when you factor in 10-ft waves, a long pier, a demanding current to negotiate and an inability to swim in open water, my venture out to sea was very quickly transformed into a nerve-racking experience.

Without the lifeguard to help usher me around the pier and back to dry land, my South African adventure could have been very short lived. After less then a minute of swimming, the other players were but dots in the distance. They managed to do three laps around the pier – I gave up after only one lap, exhausted and coughing up mouthful after mouthful of salt water. I felt like I'd swallowed half of the Indian Ocean.

As I sat down on the sand, trying to clear my head, it struck me how fundamentally my world had been turned upside down over the previous few weeks. Less than a month before, during my final training session with the Borders, we had to move to an artificial pitch normally used for hockey because of the freezing weather conditions, as the temperature had plummeted to -10°C. My first few days in South Africa could not have been more of a contrast. People had warned me that January in Durban could be unbearably hot and humid. With temperatures consistently over 30°C, I struggled to adjust to the tropical climate – my body had been dragged from one extreme to another. I hoped it would be worth it.

Even though playing in the Super 12 had always been an ambition of mine, I knew I was taking a huge risk after making the decision to leave Scotland for a playing stint in South Africa. Signing such a short-term contract of six months wasn't the most financially sound option in a sport as physical as rugby. Also, with Claire just discovering she was pregnant for the second time, taking both her and Christian so far from our family home had started to weigh heavily.

In the days leading up to my departure for South Africa, I was looking for signs to show me whether or not I was making the right decision. In the back of my mind, I wondered if there would be a backlash or an inquiry as to why I was suddenly no longer deemed good enough for the Scotland squad at the age of thirty. *The Scotsman* newspaper did a fantastic piece about my career, and ex-Scotland manager Dougie Morgan wrote me a considerate letter, but it seemed that everyone else involved with Scottish rugby carried on as normal. I was beginning to realize that there was little room for sentimentality in the chiselled-down sport of professional rugby.

I first spoke about the possibility of playing in the Super 12 with the Borders coach Tony Gilbert on Christmas Eve – nine days later, Kevin Putt, head coach of the Natal Sharks, was shaking my hand at Durban airport. It was immediately obvious that I had joined a very professional set-up. The Sharks' two training pitches and Medical Centre (which was located inside a Virgin Health Club) were situated either side of ABSA Stadium, the 50,000-capacity arena formerly known as Kings Park. I also soon found out that I'd arrived in one of the few places in the world where rugby dominated a section of society as football does in cities like Glasgow or Liverpool. In the first week of arriving in Durban, a number of supporters had already welcomed me to South Africa, coming up to me even when I was on the beach with Claire and Christian (and there was me quietly assuming there would be no chance I'd ever get recognized).

I was pleasantly surprised by how easy it was to feel comfortable in my new surroundings. This was mainly due to the friendliness of the players. I seemed to get on well with every player and my time in Durban will be remembered with real affection as a direct result of the relationships I struck up, as well as the rugby experience. We had a squad that was a microcosm of South Africa's 'rainbow nation' – Xhosa Africans, 'coloureds', Afrikaners and English-speaking Whites. This latter group were jokingly referred to as *Saut*

Peels or *Sauties* for short. *Saut* means salt in English and *peel* is the Afrikaans word for penis. Apparently the English-speaking South Africans have one leg in South Africa, one leg still in Britain and their *peel* is in the sea. A nickname carried over from colonial times, I imagine. I became known simply as 'Scotsman'.

Kevin Putt had told the South African media that I had been signed mainly as a back-up to Butch James, but his actions in private showed me that I had a good chance of making the Sharks starting line-up for the Super 12. At training I was running at stand-off with Butch filling in at inside-centre. Moving Butch to centre probably wasn't going to go down well with Trevor Halstead or Adrian Jacobs, two Sharks players who had turned out in the centres for the Springboks that season. Nevertheless, I was hoping that Butch would be chosen at inside-centre for the Super 12 as it would mean that I would probably start at stand-off, the only other recognized number 10 in the Sharks squad – Herkie Kruger – having just been banned for two years after failing a doping test.

Butch James was a cult figure in South Africa – he combined a laid-back attitude with a ferocious tackling style, and had been a regular visitor to the sin bin for both the Sharks and the Springboks. This had merely enhanced his reputation with Sharks fans – I was told that in a few games the previous season, despite the fact that he hadn't played because of injury, supporters had still voted him man of the match. It was going to be very difficult, especially as a foreign player, to be picked ahead of Butch who was one of the most naturally gifted players in South Africa. However, if the views of two supporters I met one night after training were anything to go by, I had an excellent chance of being selected.

I bumped into them on my way back to the changing rooms at the end of an evening training session. They were two large Afrikaners down from Pretoria on holiday and they had approached me for an autograph. The English-speaking South Africans would have called these two 'Dutchmen', and they pretty much conformed to the stereotype of being gruff, opinionated and drunk.

'We just want to say it's an honour to meet you, man. You are one of the best kickers in the world.'

'Thanks very much – I don't think I've ever been described like that before.'

'No, it's true – we know our rugby in South Africa. You are world class.'

I knew South African beer was strong but I started to get suspicious, as not even my mum would praise my kicking to such a level. We continued to chat after I had a photograph taken with them. They carried on talking about how great it was to have such a good player like me at the Sharks. Then, one of them said: 'We love your anthem, too. It must be really special to sing it before a game, no?'

'Yes, I agree. It's one of the best anthems in the world,' I replied.

'Ja, but it's not as good as "Flower of Scotland" – that's our all-time favourite.'

Now I was confused. It wasn't until we made it to the car park and I said my goodbyes that I worked out what was going on. They smiled as they patted me on the back: 'Good luck for the season. Thank you for the photo, Neil.' I had to put them out of their misery – I turned back and told them I wasn't Neil Jenkins. From that day on my nickname of 'Scotsman' was changed to 'Jenks'.

Before the Sharks had played any matches we had to endure some gruelling pre-season training work – a second time in six months for me. On my first day in South Africa I had to undergo strength and fitness tests in the morning, followed by an intense skills and fitness session later in the day. Speed tests showed that we had some terrific athletes with full-back Brent Russell and winger Henno Mentz recording the quickest times seen in South African rugby. Even two of our forwards managed to break five seconds for the 40-m test, which is remarkable. I quickly made a resolution never again to stand outside Brent Russell when doing a passing drill. His breathtaking speed off the mark meant I was left stranded so deep behind him that I wasn't able to reach his pass.

South African rugby has always been blessed not just with speed but also size. We were no exception as our pack was huge. The likes of A. J. Venter, John Smit and Johann Ackerman just don't exist in Scotland. In fact I began to get the impression that everyone in South Africa was enormous. I had my suspicions that anyone less than six feet tall has been shipped out to somewhere else in Africa – perhaps apartheid had been replaced by some size-prejudiced policy. I was told that the real reason for the abundance of huge South African men is that they zealously consume the creatine-filled strands of dried meat known as biltong. My son, Christian, and I were soon hooked on chewing this local delicacy.

After a month with the squad, we were at last approaching the final stage of our build-up to the Super 12, which was to include three games. The rugby sessions couldn't have progressed any better for me – I had trained well and was at last beginning to get familiar with the set plays and style of rugby the management wanted us to play. I was also constantly encouraged by Kevin to point out to him and the players what I felt needed to be changed in order to become a successful team.

My experience of coaches that I'd had at club level had been very different up to then. I'd found in France that coaches were loath to share responsibility, despite the fact that they had no direct control over players during a match. Even at the Borders, Tony Gilbert was at times unwilling to hear players' views on what we could change to make ourselves a better side. This approach can lead to coaches surrounding themselves with 'yes' men and viewing differing opinions as a threat to their own position. I was pleasantly surprised that things were different at the Sharks.

After only a week in the country, Kevin asked me to join Butch James, captain John Smit and himself for a meeting to decide team moves and principles of play. It was great to get to that level of responsibility so early and I was impressed by Kevin's openness to input from others. The following week we had a backs meeting and I surprised myself by ending up doing most of the talking.

Most of the new moves that the team adopted were the ones I had given the coach earlier in the week. I hoped that the players didn't view this negatively. The coach seemed pleased and the rest of the backs were fairly supportive. It would have been even better if they had contributed some more, but I found out that this was not the South African way of doing things. One of the backs told me later that Afrikaner players tend to follow instructions and traditionally weren't inclined to put forward their own opinions. As more than two-thirds of our thirty-man squad for the Super 12 were Afrikaners, our backline was a fairly quiet group.

Our first pre-season game was a strange experience as we flew to the UK to play against Harlequins. Due to the number of South Africans living in London, the Sharks had for a few seasons played Quins before the start of the Super 12, the game always being a sell-out. Swapping sunshine for snow and a long flight probably wasn't the best preparation for the Super 12, but I was glad to get a run-out with my new teammates. I was selected at stand-off with Butch James partnering Rudi Keil in the centres.

We started the game in great form. Playing with pace and width we scored three tries to go 19–0 up. However, our opening twenty minutes would be the only time we played well and poor defence and shocking lineout work allowed Quins to come back and almost win the match. Butch had picked up an injury and I had to kick a last-minute penalty to enable us to win 29–27.

A difference in our build-up to the match was that one of the players said a prayer while we linked arms in the changing room. I've seen this before in the NFL, although watching on television tends to make it feel less authentic. Given the nonsense that is sometimes said in the changing rooms before a game, it seemed the ideal moment for a prayer. After all, we were about to go out and put our bodies on the line for each other. It was some contrast to the pre-game activities I'd experienced at Brive where head butting had once been the preferred method of motivation. Our influential openside flanker, Luke Watson, led the prayer: 'Lord, we thank you for giving us the opportunity to play tonight's game. We ask for your blessing and that we can give our best out on the field. We pray for our loved ones back home and that both teams can be protected from injury.'

It was a great bonding moment and was genuinely heart-felt. The ideal attitude before a match is to be physically relaxed but mentally sharp. The mood in the changing rooms was calm and focused. The silence, though, was broken just as we ran out when one of the forwards shouted, 'Let's murder these English bastards!'

We followed our match in London by winning two more friendlies back in Natal. They were typical pre-season games with little structure and lots of errors that had our coaching staff visibly stressed. For them, our lacklustre form so far had made our opening match in the Super 12 a daunting prospect indeed. We were due to kick-off by playing the Blue Bulls in Pretoria. Less than three months earlier, the Sharks had been hammered 40–19 by the same side at the same venue in the previous season's Currie Cup Final. With the Bulls strengthening their squad by adding the ten Springboks who had missed the final because of their participation in the World Cup, no one in South Africa was giving us any hope of winning.

The coaches, to their credit, tried to keep the players as relaxed as possible and actually named our starting line-up ten days before the match. Such an early team announcement was perhaps unconventional, but it helped our preparations and our focus immeasurably. I couldn't wait to make my Super 12 debut and I was delighted to be selected at stand-off. However, a week before my Super 12 debut in Pretoria, my thoughts drifted to another match – Scotland were taking on Wales in the opening game of the Six Nations. It was the first time in twelve years that I hadn't been present for a Scotland game.

I missed the atmosphere surrounding the build-up to the Six Nations and yearned to be with the team as they prepared for their opening match in Cardiff. I left a message with new captain Chris Paterson and also managed to speak to Chris Cusiter who was making his debut at scrum-half. Scotland were well beaten by an adventurous Welsh side and the final scoreline of 23–10 could have been much greater for Wales. With two more away games to come it was going to be a tough season for coach Matt Williams. Watching the game itself with A. J. Venter and Butch James, my new team-mates at the Sharks, I felt a reasonable amount of closure. It was brought home to me as both sides lined up for the anthems that time stops for no one and I realized that I had to move on. My mind was firmly fixed on performing well in Pretoria.

Leading up to the game there was a positive vibe within the squad as our hooker, John Smit, had been announced as the new Springbok captain. Three days before our match we launched our Super 12 marketing campaign with a breakfast in a huge marquee on the hallowed turf at Kings Park. Over 200 supporters turned up before 7 a.m. In anticipation of this, our forwards had arrived at 6 a.m. to practise their lineouts. It was an unusual way to prepare for such a huge challenge, but it proved to be an inspired decision.

On a typical high veld afternoon, with the sun hot and oxygen scarce, we took on the Blue Bulls in the hostile environment of Loftus stadium. We showed great character and application to record a totally unexpected 23–18 win. Our season couldn't have started any better, although our game plan was more English Premiership than Super 12. This involved a lot of kicking from myself and Craig Davidson, our outstanding scrum-half. It proved to be very effective although it was obvious that the Bulls had underestimated us. Their Currie Cup victory had led to complacency and they didn't play anywhere near to their potential. On our part there was a lot of room for improvement if we were to carry on winning overseas.

The playing schedule for South African teams in the Super 12 was very tough, as we had to play all our away matches in a block before returning to Durban for our home games. It was an arduous fixture list – after Pretoria we left to play two matches in Australia, then two more in New Zealand. The first of these games was in Sydney against the Waratahs who always seemed to make a flying start to the competition.

On the eve of our match I watched one of the best games of rugby I have ever seen as the Blues took on the Brumbies, scoring fifteen tries between them. This was what I had always believed made the Super 12 the best rugby competition in the world by a long way. Unfortunately our performance the following day at Aussie Stadium was nowhere near the superlative standards set by the likes of Carlos Spencer, Rupeni Caucaunibuca, Stephen Larkham and Joe Roff.

From the highs of the previous week we slumped to a 47–14 defeat against a team that looked like they had been playing together for a while. We were destroyed in the line-out, which gave us almost no ball to work with and, in turn, had us defending for most of the first half. Things had started nicely for me, as I sneaked in for a close-range try in the opening minutes. However, it was to be a fleeting positive moment as I was replaced with about thirty minutes to go.

Our defeat led to a collective decision to open up our game plan and attack much more with the ball in hand. This was a heartening move as we were next due to play the best team in the competition, the ACT Brumbies. Unfortunately, I was dropped for the game in Canberra, which I felt was harsh although it didn't upset me too much as I was really enjoying my Super 12 experience. I had been aware that I would have to be in outstanding form to justify my place in the team as the only foreigner playing in South Africa. My disappointment at not being able to play against the best stand-off in the world, Stephen Larkham, was alleviated slightly as he had already called off the game with an injury. His absence, and the poor weather conditions, helped us greatly and we went close to beating a top-quality side. The losing bonus point we picked up did wonders for our confidence levels as we headed to New Zealand.

I was pleasantly surprised to see that the Sharks – players and management – worked hard at making sure we kept together as a group on tour, away from the daily rugby sessions and team meetings. Along with golf days and card schools, we had a tournament of carpet bowls up and running in the corridors of our hotel. Engendering team spirit has become less of a priority in the professional era and the atmosphere in many teams nowadays has changed greatly. In the past, you would have seen more players hanging around the team room, doing things together to alleviate boredom. It has now become much more individual. The most important thing is your selection of DVDs and the games you have for the PlayStation.

For the record, my 'Top 5' games on tour are table tennis; balderdash; indoor cricket; pool; and any card game from the following – poker, Yuka, '31' or 'Asshole' (a game played wherever there is a New Zealander in the squad, which means almost any rugby side on the planet). After I showed the boys at the Borders how to play '31', Chris Cusiter said it was the best thing I'd done for Borders rugby. This probably says as much about his enjoyment of the card game as it does about my performances!

In addition to the carpet bowls, my team-mates at the Sharks had some other interesting ways to amuse themselves on tour. One night I joined some of the boys on a trip to Starbucks. What made the trip more exciting than usual was that a couple of sleeping pills had been slipped into the coffee of our massive prop, Deon Carstens. The others thought this was hilarious, and I have to admit that I couldn't help laughing as Deon became increasingly lethargic before our eyes. Just before he crashed, Deon had been teaching me how to count in Afrikaans – a language I discovered was not too dissimilar to Lowland Scots. Numbers 1, 2 and 7 (*een, twee* and *sewe*) are pronounced like *yin, twai* and *seevin,* which is no different to how we would say them in the Borders.

If there's one game you want to win on tour it is the penultimate fixture, as it means your last week on the road is a much more enjoyable experience. Against seemingly insurmountable odds we produced a 36–35 win against the Highlanders in an incredible match. When I later watched the recording, there was no way we should have been even close to winning. The team played badly in the first half and had got a roasting from our coach at half-time. I got told to warmup as I was informed I'd be on very quickly – it seemed like I was going on at 15 as Brent Russell was having a bad day at the office.

After a brief comeback the team started to play even worse and it was 29–15 with twenty-five minutes to go when I eventually came on at 10. We then went further behind but the one positive thing I noticed was that there was no panic in the team and the players were still encouraging each other. Brent then scored an eighty-metre try to redeem himself and

Craig Davidson dived over from a quick tap penalty. I hadn't been directly involved in the tries but was making the right decisions and feeling sharp. Still, the Highlanders were back inside our 22, leading 35–29, with three minutes to go. After the home side knocked-on inches away from our try-line, we ran the ball back, forcing them into giving away a penalty. From the resulting lineout I made it over the gainline to set up a ruck from which Davidson scored the match-winning try.

It's funny how things can change very quickly in sport. At one stage I was convinced that we weren't going to hold onto our losing bonus point (which we probably didn't deserve anyway), but at the end of the game we were celebrating picking up the maximum five points and being the first ever Sharks side to win at Carisbrook – otherwise known as the 'House of Pain'.

Our next game was another one-point win, this time against the Hurricanes. I never made it onto the pitch on this occasion but watching the match I made an observation that must be true in many sports. That is, confidence is sometimes much more important than preparation. The Hurricanes certainly missed the injured Tana Umaga and had clear opportunities to win the game, but our players never once doubted themselves. Hardly any of the moves we had worked on at training were used and it was belief – not what we had practised – that won us our third away match from five games. We had equalled the best overseas performance by a South African team in Super 12 history, and the win moved us into the top four in the competition with six home games remaining.

It was great being back in Durban and seeing Claire and Christian after the four-week tour. We were given some time off so we spent a few days relaxing in the Drakensburg mountains. That same weekend Scotland played their last Six Nations match, away to Ireland. It was their fifth consecutive defeat in what had been a very disappointing campaign. However, I was more interested in the following week's European club fixtures – Brive were playing against Castres and Northampton were at home to the Borders. It was an uncanny coincidence, as these were the four professional clubs I had played for. It made me reflect on how sometimes things don't work out as you plan and you never know where you might end up, but I felt lucky to have had those opportunities and now to be able to experience the thrill of the Super 12.

In terms of leaving Durban with a standout memory, I thought it would be impossible to better the closing minutes of our win over the Highlanders in Dunedin. However, my first home game for the Sharks almost topped that.

I was once more on the bench for our match against fellow South African side, the Cats. We were losing 16–10 at half-time, which – despite our results – was no surprise given our erratic form. I was very happy to get on at stand-off with over half an hour to go and my kicking game again went well. I even managed a couple of breaks, one of which led to a try. We were much more direct in the second half and could easily have scored more tries in our eventual 42–28 win. Still, we managed to pick up another five points and were now tied for second place in the table at the halfway stage of the competition.

I was enjoying my time so much in Durban that I had never really stopped to think what the Sharks supporters really thought about my arrival at the club. As I prepared myself to come on as a replacement I listened carefully to the crowd's reaction. Usually I wouldn't have bothered with things like this. Away from home, I often revelled in a hostile atmosphere. Running out on to the Kings Park ground for the first time as a Sharks player the crowd gave me a rousing reception – I felt so buoyant that I broke through the Cats defence with my first touch of the ball.

I'm sure there were still a number of doubters, as I imagine there were many who believed that South African rugby didn't require the services of a former Scottish international. However, I received another boost when I was sent an article that rugby commentator Gavin Rich had written for the *Cape Argus* following our win over the Cats. He seemed convinced that the introduction of players from overseas was a step in the right direction:

Perhaps it is a little unfair on John Smit to keep harping on about the comment he made to the television interviewers following his side's fine second-half performance against the Cats in Durban last week. However, I cannot help picking on the new Springbok captain for saying that Gregor Townsend had shown in the match that 'experience cannot be bought'. We all know what Smit meant, and usually that is a saying that is commonplace when a long-serving stalwart helps his side to victory. Clearly though, the reality is that the Cats game showed us the exact opposite – experience can in fact be bought, as Sharks Kevin Putt did when he went over to the northern hemisphere in the off-season to sign up the Scot.

Experience was always going to be the big asset that Townsend brought with him to Durban. There were quite a few sceptics when the announcement was first made, yet as we go past the halfway stage of the Super 12, it is becoming clearer that Putt's move was in fact a masterstroke. While he has not made the starting line-up since the game against the Waratahs, Townsend has played a key role at some critical junctures of the games where he has come on. The first was in the match against the Highlanders in Dunedin. The Sharks were well behind on the scoreboard when Townsend came on in the last quarter. But he played no small part in the turn-around as his cool head kept those around him as cool and collected. Here Smit is 100%, this calmness and unflappability only comes through experience, and its presence rubs off positively on those around him.

Townsend's arrival was one of the factors that swung the game the Sharks way after a tricky start against the Cats. When Townsend came on 10 minutes into the second half he gave the players around him an object lesson on how the tactical kicking game should be executed. Cats coach Chester Williams was one of the first afterwards to admit the big role this had in changing the tide of the game. Quite apart from the different tactical option that the Sharks have available with him on the bench, what Townsend brings is tutorship to a side that up until this season has far too often played like 15 chickens with their heads chopped off. And yes, in answer to the inevitable question, a controlled influx of foreign players into the South African game may carry more benefits than negatives, as the northern hemisphere has shown through the way they have tapped into southern hemisphere resources during the last six years.

Despite being outplayed the following week for much of the game against the Crusaders – a side that hadn't lost to the Sharks since 1996 – we left the field having garnered another maximum five points. The Brumbies were now the only team above us in the table with four home games to play. However, we had been riding our luck for a while and could easily have lost all four of our previous matches. The coaches seemed to think everything was going well, though, and didn't want to change our game plan or the team itself.

Three of our four tries came from Crusaders mistakes and they must have been kicking themselves for being unable to build up a substantial lead going into the second half. With a 3 p.m. kick-off and the fact that they had only arrived in the country that week, they visibly tired as the second half progressed. We went on to win 29–25. I came on at stand-off once again, this time with just under twenty minutes left to play. The reception from the crowd was even louder than the previous week. It had an inspiring effect on me and I again started strongly, kicking well and making a break. However, I did have a couple of poor kicks later on, which was disappointing. Still, it was nice to leave the field shaking the hands of players like Andrew Mehrtens, Justin Marshall and Richie

McCaw, and being in the winning team. It had never happened before so I couldn't complain.

Our next match, against the Chiefs, was a turning point in the season as our inconsistent form finally caught up with us. The game was memorable for an event at the end of the match and it was the determining factor in our inability to register more than a solitary losing bonus point. Our winger, Henno Mentz, scored a try just after the full-time siren was sounded. As the referee arrived on the scene just after Henno's lunge, he could not see the ball grounded and referred the incident 'upstairs'.

The decision was hugely important as a converted try would have seen us draw the match 34–34, and would have included a further bonus point for scoring four tries. It took nine minutes for the video referee to come to a conclusion. Although it seemed impossible that Henno had failed to score, the try was disallowed, which was hugely disappointing for the 40,000 crowd. We again hadn't played that well but this time the opposition hadn't made any real mistakes for us to capitalize on. I got on the field with thirty minutes to go when we were losing 34–20. I probably tried too hard at times to create things and made a couple of mistakes, but we did manage to get back and nearly draw the game despite having little ball with to work with.

People were forever asking me how the Super 12 compared to rugby in the northern hemisphere. It wasn't that easy to give a definitive answer. In terms of spectacle, the Super 12 fitted somewhere between the Heineken Cup and the Six Nations, although the rise in popularity of the European Cup competition meant that there was increasingly more passion being shown by supporters in the northern hemisphere and the gap was narrowing.

As regards the standard of play between the two hemispheres, the Super 12 had the edge. Primarily, this was due to the weather conditions – a three-month season played during late summer and autumn was far more conducive to fast, skilled, attacking rugby than a long winter in the UK. It's always interesting to see the number of tries scored in matches at the end of the season in the Heineken Cup and the English Premiership compared to other times. It was no surprise last year to see London Irish score nine tries in a thrilling game against Wasps – the spring weather made it achievable.

The Super 12 also had a much higher concentration of quality players. Excluding Italy, there are thirty-seven professional sides competing at the highest level in the northern hemisphere, in comparison to just twelve (now fourteen) sides in the south. With the incredible depth of talent that exits in the southern hemisphere, the standard of play was much closer to international level than I'd experienced playing club rugby in France, England and Scotland. The Super 12 wasn't without its faults, however, and there were a few sides a long way off the quality of the likes of the Crusaders, Brumbies, Blues and the Waratahs. Another negative was the timing of the competition – it was the first rugby of the year for the players and with only eleven matches there were some rusty performances by some sides during the first half of the campaign. As we entered our final three games of the season, we were well into our stride and no longer had any excuses for unforced errors. However, our high expectations were about to come crashing down around us.

Despite the Reds being the Sharks' bogey team – the Queensland outfit having won every match between the sides since 1998 – we were confident before playing them, as they were lying eleventh in the table and had just travelled from Australia. However, we went out to play our worst rugby of the season. In fact the Reds played just as poorly and it must have been painful for those watching. At least they could claim to have seen a record-breaking game. Our eventual defeat by 6–5 was the lowest in the eight-year history of the

Super 12. It was also reported that the match had the highest ever error count in the competition.

I didn't escape the malaise – my appearance as a sub was the worst I'd played since I'd joined the Sharks. I didn't even see it out to the end of the game as I was on the receiving end of an accidental knee in the back from Reds full-back Chris Latham and went off with five minutes of the match remaining. It was probably the most painful injury I'd experienced, but the mental anguish of losing at home in such a pitiful manner was ultimately even more excruciating.

As my back was still extremely tender, the Sharks medical team were worried that I'd done some serious damage and I was referred for an x-ray. On the drive to the hospital it went through my mind that the match against the Reds could have been my last ever. It wouldn't have been a great memory and I was desperately hoping it wasn't to be my final playing contribution. Fortunately the x-ray didn't show any fracture to the spine or surrounding joints. However, I was informed that I had torn a muscle in the lumbar area – a hole the size of a 50p coin in my lower back confirmed this. There was now no chance of being fit for the remaining two matches of our season, which was doubly disappointing as I had been keen to play against Carlos Spencer of the Blues, our next opponents.

The defeat against the Reds had the paradoxical effect of liberating the team. They went on to play some great rugby against the Blues and in the final match at home to the Stormers. Although losing both matches meant that we finished just outside the top four, the season's efforts had been a big improvement from the previous year, when the Sharks had finished in last place. Not surprisingly, the final was between the Brumbies and the Crusaders, with the Australian team coming out on top after a terrific match.

Watching our last two games from the stands, I realized how lucky I was to have played in this environment. It also brought home to me the fact that rugby is the greatest sporting spectacle on earth. I was still in love with the game. Maybe one reason why some rugby players who retire from the sport avoid being involved in the game is that they probably miss it so much that watching it reminds them that they have lost something they treasure. I know I'll miss rugby but if watching it is as enthralling as supporting the Sharks was in the Super 12, I'll be arranging future holidays to coincide with their home matches. Being able to watch a night game in a T-shirt and then join in with thousands of other supporters having a barbeque (or *brai* in Afrikaans) on the surrounding fields of Kings Park until early in the morning really is a unique and richly rewarding sporting experience. If this sounds like a free advertising slot for the KwaZulu Natal Tourist Board then I apologize, but I can't help but sing the praises of the area – like many people, I found living in Africa to be very magical.

I'd been warned about the levels of crime in South Africa and how it was such a dangerous place to bring up a family. This was not my impression of life north of Durban. An abiding memory I will hold from my time there was of the overwhelming friendliness of the people, especially those at the Sharks. It seemed such a relaxed and contented place without cliques or gossip and I was forever being invited out for meals or rounds of golf with my team-mates.

Even though it was more than a decade since the formation of the rainbow nation, South Africa's bands of colour remained distinct and racial issues still bubbled under the surface. Race was a dominant political issue with the power to divide society. Obviously it was not going to be easy to erase three centuries of prejudice and social divisions. The actions and views of some supporters, players and coaches left me with the belief that not everyone in South African rugby was colour blind, but I considered these views to be in a minority.

The Sharks' playing and coaching staff were a mix of colours and languages and I never once felt any tension or lack of respect among peoples from differing backgrounds. Watching schools rugby on television gave me reason to believe that sport was playing an important role in shaping society. In such a rugby-mad country, there were regular rugby programmes on TV and at least one live school game a week. What struck me from watching this was that all the teams had an equal balance of white and black players. This suggests that South African rugby will be much stronger in the future as a previously untapped source is now being utilized to produce players who are taking up and excelling at the game. More importantly, the next generation of South Africans are growing up together, competing side-by-side and, with luck, consigning racial tensions to the dustbin of history.

I was very keen to extend my stay with the Sharks for at least another year and we started to get things organized so that Claire could give birth at a hospital in Umhlanga, where we lived. The club were also eager for me to sign a new contract, but the rules on foreign players had changed during my time in South Africa. When I was approached the previous December, the Springbok coach, Rudi Straeuli had proposed that there should be more overseas players allowed to play in South Africa. He believed that his team's poor showing at the World Cup had resulted from an isolationist policy in terms of players and coaches. Likewise, he noted that England had achieved success partly because of the influx of foreign players and coaches in the Premiership. SARFU initially concurred with Straeuli's wishes and allowed each Super 12 side to sign a maximum of two foreigners. The Sharks were the only team to act on this and I became the only overseas player in South Africa – in fact the only European to be playing in the Super 12.

However, a few weeks later, Jake White replaced Straeuli as Springbok coach and an all-South African policy on players was reintroduced. SARFU didn't have control over the Currie

Cup, which was played from July to October. The Sharks offered me a contract to play in this and expressed their desire for me to stay – if the laws were relaxed once more – for the following year's Super 12. I felt that being out of contract in October would have left me in limbo, what with the northern hemisphere season by then being well underway. It was disappointing as I would have loved to stay on with the Sharks, but instead I signed a two-year deal with Montpellier.

My rugby odyssey was now set to continue on the Mediterranean coast of France, but before I left South Africa there was one surprise in store for me. Nico Breedt, a talented back-rower at the Sharks with whom I had become good mates, had promised me for the previous few months that he would take me fishing for sharks before I returned home. Nico approached me after our last match against the Stormers: 'How do you fancy going fishing for sharks tomorrow night?'

'At night? Do you think that's wise?' I replied.

Nico tried to reassure me: 'Yeah – it's the best time. They feed from dusk 'til dawn so we should be able to catch one or two.'

I was worried about getting into a boat when it was dark – especially if there were sharks everywhere: 'What about we go at dawn? I'm not too keen to go in a boat at night.'

'Ag, man – we're not going in a boat. We'll catch the sharks from the beach!'

And so we did. Twenty minutes north from where we were staying I caught two juvenile sharks, each about a metre long – casting from the safety of the beach. In fact, I never got my feet wet the whole time we were fishing. The next day Nico took me fishing with a mate of his at 4 a.m. in the hope of hooking a great white. Unfortunately (or fortunately I think) we never trapped the big one but I again caught a couple of two-week-old sharks. Strange that no one mentioned how many sharks were around before my training swim around the pier. I experienced an involuntary shudder at the thought of a Great White chancing on fifteen or so bodies thrashing about in the ocean (with one obvious, vulnerable-looking straggler). Yet in the dawn sun, throwing the sharks back into the sea – and comfortable that I would think long and hard before ever dipping as much as a toe back in the water of that particular beach – I could be philosophical. It was another reminder that the most enjoyable moments in life can sometimes happen when you take a leap into the unknown. The Super 12 had proved to be a highlight of my career.

CHAPTER 17

State of the Union

Sport has the power to change the world.
It has the power to inspire in a way that little else does.

Nelson Mandela

Montpellier is the self-styled capital of the south of France, where the sun shines for most of the year. Its desirable location on the Mediterranean coast means that its inhabitants have the best of all worlds – a vibrant city life, glorious beaches and rolling countryside – right on their doorstep. We thought it would be an ideal place to unwind and once again appreciate the relaxed pace of life in *la France profonde*. However, as our second son, Luke, was born only three weeks after arriving, we were suddenly rushed off our feet looking after two young children in a foreign country.

Coming straight from South Africa, there wasn't that much time for rest anyway, as Montpellier faced a tough season. Almost every French rugby commentator was predicting that we were certainties for relegation. But Montpellier, in only their second year in the top flight, was a big-hearted club with ambition. They reminded me in many ways of Warringah – newcomers with no sense of snobbery or complacency. Everyone at the club knew they had to earn the right to belong. And, just as at Warringah, right from the President Thierry Perez down to the loyal supporters, they made me feel very welcome.

Things couldn't have started any better for us. Following a battling victory over Clermont Auvergne, we outperformed even our own expectations in recording a forty-point home win against Stade Français, the champions of the previous two seasons. Looking back, it was the best game I played for the club, and probably the highlight of my time there. Only two weeks later, during a narrow defeat to Toulouse, I suffered a neck injury that left me unable to tilt my head back as the muscles in my neck were in spasm.

After a few weeks of daily physio, which involved mobilization, massage and stretching of my neck and back, there hadn't been much progress. It was decided that I now required a series of cortisone injections into the nerves surrounding a disc in my neck.

For the injections to be accurately located I had to be placed inside an MRI scanner. Strapping my arms and legs together so I couldn't move, a needle was inserted in the left side of my neck. For the next five minutes I was moved in and out of the scanner while the surgeon checked the MRI pictures, and each time the needle was plunged deeper into my neck. It seemed to last an eternity and the longer it was taking the more I was thinking to myself – was all this pain worth it just to get back on a rugby pitch? I kept telling myself it was, and I hoped that the cortisone would have the desired effect and reduce the inflammation and the pain I felt.

Several weeks later, the pain in my neck and upper arm had improved sufficiently for me to play again, although I still experienced 'stingers' from time to time. This is not a nice sensation – you feel a sharp pain and then pins and needles all the way down to your fingertips. I'm sure it's a warning sign of further damage to the disc, but the nerve pain does tend to go away after a few minutes.

Less than a month after my return to action I managed to get a taste of international rugby once again, as I was selected for the French Barbarians against Australia. I was honoured to play at stand-off, especially as it was the final competitive outing for my half-back partner – former French captain Fabien Galthié. Despite a solid performance from our makeshift side we weren't able to hold out for an unexpected win. The match went reasonably well for me, although I still felt I was lacking adequate match fitness. At times though I was really enjoying myself – and the pace and intensity wasn't too much of a problem. That was until I got thumped in a tackle from flanker Radike Samo, giving me another 'stinger' that left me reeling on the floor. Like a boxer waiting for the referee to give him a count to ten, I lay prone until the pain subsided so that I could resume playing again.

After a promising start to the campaign, Montpellier failed to keep their place in the top half of *le championnat*. It was a pressure-filled season for a lot of French clubs, as the league was due to be reduced from sixteen to fourteen clubs. This meant that three sides were to be automatically relegated to ProD2 (as the second division is known) with the club finishing in 13th place facing a play-off against the second placed team from ProD2. We were generally dominant at our home ground of Stade Sabathé, but struggled to produce the goods on the road. A crucial win at Bayonne near the end of the season removed any worries that we might not stay up and our final standing of tenth place was a fair reflection of where we were: not far off qualifying for the Heineken Cup, but not too far away from relegation either.

Just a few weeks before the end of the season I received a call that would alter the path of my rugby career for the last time. Border Reivers coach Steve Bates contacted me in Montpellier, inquiring about my availability. The question he put to me was, 'Gregor, how would you like to come back and play in Scotland?'

I jumped at the chance – I had always wanted to finish my career back home and I also knew it would be great for Claire and the boys. The only problem was that I had a year left on my contract with Montpellier. Fortunately, I managed to work out an agreement with the club, as they could see how keen I was to finish my career back in the Borders. They announced to the media that I was returning home to move into coaching and would be playing much less the following season. However, my priority was definitely on the playing side.

I was back to my best form as the season got underway, scoring a try in a 9–7 loss to Munster at Thomond Park. A week later, at home to the Scarlets, I felt even sharper and started the match well. However, just minutes into the game, after making a line-break and heading for a try, I was tackled just inches short of the goal-line. My left foot twisted badly in the collision and I was left lying on the ground wincing with pain. I had broken my ankle, which forced me out of the game for three months.

My time spent at the Borders General Hospital coincided with that of Jonny Mitchell, another rugby player who had suffered an injury that weekend. Any prospect of feeling sorry for myself was soon over when I was told that Jonny's injuries – recieved during an accident when a scrum collapsed – would leave him in a wheelchair for the rest of his life. Unfortunately, these accidents are a part of the game. It is hard to imagine the daily struggles Jonny has to go through – I hope the rugby community never forgets his ongoing battle. Jonny, David Azhar, Struan Kerr-Liddell and the others that have suffered spinal injuries are rugby's real heroes.

During my time out injured I got an unexpected phone call from Frank Hadden, who had recently taken over as Scotland coach. The previous incumbent, Matt Williams, had been sacked following a run of record defeats during his time in charge and only three wins from seventeen matches (one of which was against the mighty Japan). In a strange turn of fate, Frank Hadden wanted to know whether he could include my name in the Scotland squad he was about to

announce to the media. After all, it had been one of Matt
Williams' first acts as Scotland coach to decide that he didn't
want me in his training squad some two years previously, and
I hadn't been asked about my availability since then.

I had actually missed playing for Scotland much more in
recent months than when I had first been forced to retire.
This was probably due to the fact that I no longer had the
fantastic thrill of playing Super 12 rugby. Also, earlier that
year I had managed to get to Murrayfield to attend two of
Scotland's matches in the Six Nations. Despite both games –
against Ireland and Wales – ending in record defeats for the
home side, I desperately wanted to be out there with my
mates back playing for Scotland again. Being at Murrayfield
for the first time as a former internationalist also brought
home to me the deep motivation and honour I had felt when
representing my country. I still missed it dearly.

While it was great to feel wanted once more, and I started
to think about the exciting possibility of playing for Scotland
again, I wasn't totally comfortable with Frank's request.
Being out of action meant that I wouldn't be able to train
with the squad and my injury would also keep me sidelined
for Scotland's three internationals in November. Frank
wanted me to state publicly that I was no longer 'retired' at
Test level. I obviously wanted to say 'Yes', but I knew a lot
depended on my form when I was due to resume playing at
the beginning of December. Coming back from injury to play
at the same level was becoming much more difficult as I got
older. I would have preferred that my intentions were known
only to the coach, and for my form after coming back from
injury to be the deciding factor.

Such is the way of things nowadays in a media-conscious
sporting world, I was persuaded to add my name to the list of
players that were unavailable due to injury (as opposed to
retired) released to the press with the view that this would be
a good news story for Scottish rugby. With the disastrous

performances from the national team in the previous two years and turmoil off the field (which had seen the SRU committee remove both the chairman and the chief executive), there hadn't been many positives to talk about.

After an exhausting run-around in the Dubai Sevens to prove my fitness, I was selected for the Borders in early December to play against Brive in the Challenge Cup, Europe's second-tier tournament. The match went well and I was relieved and delighted that my previous good form hadn't been affected by the enforced layoff. Unfortunately, only two games later I was injured once again, this time tearing a muscle in my thigh against Glasgow. Worse was to follow when, a few weeks after that, as I was trying to prove my fitness playing for Melrose, I tore ligaments in my shoulder. It was bad enough having to play for Gala's biggest rivals (for some reason professional players were only allowed to play for clubs that were in Premier One), but suffering a third serious injury scuppered any chance of being available for the Six Nations.

The disappointment of yet another injury persuaded me to announce that the following season would be my last and that my international career was now over. There would be no recall to the Scotland team. As Scotland, under the inspirational leadership of Jason White, had finally moved forward after two barren years, I thought it would be better to take myself out of the picture rather than having continued media speculation that I might yet make a comeback. (Following the team's heroics against England and France, it didn't look like the phone was going to ring anyway!)

Leaving myself with the goal of one last season with the Borders and no other distractions, I believed that this would liberate me to play the best rugby I was capable of. I was to be proved wrong.

My play was at a level below what I demanded from myself or had expected. There were a few occasions, like early in the season against the Ospreys, when my performances simply weren't good enough. Just as frustratingly, my time back in Scotland seemed to be as much caught up in dealing with off-the-field problems. These were not just debilitating for the Borders team, but for the future of Scottish rugby itself.

Ever since a third professional side had been re-established in Scotland in 2002, it appeared that some people running the game never bought into the idea of the Borders team as a viable entity. Jim Telfer had been at the forefront of setting up the Border Reivers (as the side had now became known), but since his retirement there weren't too many supporters of Borders rugby within the SRU hierarchy. Consequently, the team was never really supported financially.

I couldn't believe that the SRU had introduced a policy of different funding for their three teams. The three main teams in Ireland get equal funding and in Wales the WRU give their four professional sides £1.7 million each. The SRU's explanation of why Edinburgh were better funded than both the Borders and Glasgow was that they had been more successful in the past. I don't know about Glasgow, but as a new side, we had no past, so it seemed a convenient argument against us. I got the feeling that some people were worried that we might be successful and consequently more difficult to get rid of.

A lot of trust had been lost back in 1998 when the previous Borders set-up was merged with Edinburgh after the SRU had cut the number of professional teams from four to two. Our first season back in business had seen some hard work going in to regain that trust – encouraging crowd numbers of over 5,000 showed that we were having some success. However, despite qualifying for the Heineken Cup at the end of the season, we never got the funding to take things forward.

There then followed three years of under-investment not just on the playing side, but also in other areas such as facilities and marketing. This neglect had led to crowd numbers falling to below 2,000. By the time Steve Bates had contacted me in Montpellier, the Borders had the lowest budget, not just in Scotland but of any of the home nations, and were sitting at the foot of the Celtic league table.

Nevertheless, there did seem to be an air of optimism when I came back home – the budget had been increased and guarantees were being announced by the SRU that the team would be supported for a minimum of three years. This was heartening news and it was the first time that the rumours of closing the team were dispelled officially. Also, with one of Scotland's best-known players, Andy Irvine, recently installed as president of the SRU, things felt much more positive for everyone involved in Scottish rugby. One of Andy's first declarations was to state that the SRU were intent on finding a way to have four professional teams some time in the near future.

We surprised many people by being more than just competitive, finishing the Celtic League in ninth spot – two places above the previous year's standing. We were actually somewhat disappointed with this, as we had lost a number of games by the narrowest of margins. However, we had won back a lot of respect and home-grown players such as Chris Cusiter, Scott MacLeod, Nikki Walker and Kelly Brown could have walked into any team in the competition. We had beaten our Scottish rivals – Edinburgh and Glasgow – three times in our four matches and had secured the second Scottish qualifying place for the Heineken Cup. All this was achieved against an ever-increasing backdrop of uncertainty and suspicion.

Contrary to the SRU's previous announcements that four professional teams could be achievable, speculation was rife that they were planning to operate with only two sides, as they had done before between 1998 and 2002. Again, rumours resurfaced that we would be facing the axe, despite our improved position in the league and the fact that our average crowd numbers, while disappointingly still under 2,000, were above those recorded at Glasgow. In April 2006, the SRU made their intentions known to the wider public.

Two hours before we played Munster – who were on the road to winning the Heineken Cup that season – we were brought into the changing rooms at Netherdale for a crisis meeting. A few of the players knew exactly what we were about to be told by our coach Steve Bates. Unbelievably, before informing the players – their employees – the SRU had earlier chosen the afternoon of a crucial Celtic League match to call a press conference to announce that, without a seven-figure private investment for one of the three professional sides, one team would be disbanded in the summer.

SRU Chief Executive Gordon McKie revealed that he had only discovered in the previous two to three weeks that the loss made in his first year at the helm would be close to £3 million – ten times more than he expected a month earlier. It was hard to believe that a business with a turnover of nearly £30 million per annum could suddenly discover such an unpredicted set of circumstances, but McKie said it was due to nine accounting ledgers having been recently reduced down to one. Although this sounded like a red herring to me, there was no escaping the fact that the SRU were determined to further reduce the costs of the professional game. (Since 2004, over £2.5 million had been cut from the funding for international and professional rugby.)

There was no denying that the SRU had financial problems – their bank overdraft had risen to over £10 million and there was also an outstanding loan of £10 million plus interest still to pay. Gordon McKie was probably correct in his belief that the SRU had been overambitious in what it had taken on at the elite end of the sport since the game had turned profes-sional. Having said that, many English clubs had ploughed just as much money into the sport. The difference was that they had made professional rugby a vibrant, growing and now profitable business. Scottish rugby was unique among the leading rugby nations not to have made a success of pro rugby.

McKie's words stunned all those involved with professional rugby in Scotland: 'We can no longer fund three teams, it's as simple as that. I am very disappointed because I wanted to keep three fully-funded teams, especially in the lead-up to the World Cup in 2007, but we can only do what we can afford to do and we can't keep three teams.'

You can only imagine the mindset of the players as they prepared to play Munster, one of the finest teams in Europe. To be told that you could be made redundant minutes prior to warming-up for the match made our task much more difficult. We conceded two tries in the opening ten minutes and, despite coming back into the game, it wasn't nearly enough to see us win.

Rumours were flying around Scottish rugby that it would be the Borders who would be disbanded. When the Scottish Players Rugby Association called an emergency meeting of all contracted players in Scotland, the Glasgow players didn't turn up, as they had reportedly been assured that they would be safe from the axe. (This says as much about the solidarity of Scottish rugby as it does about the uncertainty.) Given the fact that the Borders had been axed once before, and that there was no longer anyone from the area in a position of power at the SRU, we were the overwhelming favourites to go. It appeared that the unexpected discovery of a £3 million loss was a timely justification for the SRU to do away with us. The only problem was that we were on our way to finishing two places above Glasgow and qualifying for the Heineken Cup.

The uncertainty lasted ten long weeks – right into the summer. It was enough to make some of our key players, like Scott MacLeod, Nikki Walker, Semo Sititi and Paul Thompson leave the club. And any chance of us signing quality replacements was greatly diminished. You can't blame those who left or didn't join – why would you sign a contract at a team that looked like being disbanded?

Given the challenges of producing a business plan, a strategy for the team's future and at least £1 million, it was probably a testament to the many people who still cared for Scottish rugby that twelve different potential investors approached the SRU. In July, it was announced that assent had been given to brothers Bob and Alex Carruthers to take over at Edinburgh. It was the first time that the SRU had given up control of running a pro team. The future of professional rugby in Scotland had been assured. For now ...

I found it interesting to note that in the SRU annual report, published a few weeks later, and contrary to previous warnings, the loss made for the financial year was not as bad as had been predicted – not the £3 million the SRU had said because of the 'nine ledger' problem, but the £0.4 million they had originally forecast. For all those that had been on the verge of being made redundant, it had seemingly been a lot of worrying over nothing. And with the franchising of Edinburgh, the likelihood was that the SRU would soon be making a profit once again.

The annual report also contained a declaration that substantiated what most people in Scottish rugby already believed to be true. That is, 'The success of the national team is closely linked to the success of the three professional teams.' It seemed the SRU understood that if there were any reduction in this number, Scotland would struggle at international level. This desire was confirmed by Andy Irvine, in an interview with *The Scotsman* in January, who said, 'It would be better to have three poorer-funded teams than two better-funded teams, and there is general consensus among the rest of the board that that is the way forward.'

However, actions were speaking louder than words for all of us at the Border Reivers. In the summer, necessary maintenance work on the pitch at Netherdale was ruled out because of the costs involved. (This would hurt us later, as our biggest game of the season – against Northampton in the Heineken Cup – had to be moved to Murrayfield because of the poor surface.) Next, our temporary stand was removed in addition to several hospitality boxes. Both installations had made the amateur club ground look and feel a bit more like something that could host professional rugby. It was bad enough not being able to strengthen our squad adequately given the fact we had only been told we were safe from closure in July; now the supporting structures were being taken away. And this was despite the fact we were ready to move on to the next level after qualifying for the Heineken Cup.

Before the turn of the year we were dealt a further blow. The SRU decided that our two assistant coaches, George Graham and Alan Tait, would be better off working full-time with Frank Hadden and the Scotland squad. It again looked like we might be facing the axe.

Our fears were confirmed on 27 March 2007 when we were summoned to a meeting at Murrayfield to hear the inevitable – the SRU had disbanded the Border Reivers and planned to throw all its resources behind Glasgow. It was the nightmare scenario we had all dreaded. Allan Munro, the SRU chairman, said, 'the professional game in Scotland is in danger of dying'. So, instead of trying to keep one crucial part of it alive, we had our life-support machine switched off.

Although there was a sense of inevitability about the announcement, I still couldn't believe the SRU were making the same mistake again. George Santayana's claim that 'those who cannot learn from history are doomed to repeat it' had never sounded more accurate. After all, hadn't we been here before, in 1998? It was Groundhog Day for Scottish rugby.

Incredibly, the SRU said that they weren't shutting the team down because of their financial situation – they wanted to invest in better facilities, marketing and strengthening of the Glasgow squad, despite the fact that this meant losing one-third of professional rugby in the country and jeopardizing Scotland's second Heineken Cup spot.

The media reaction to the decision was apoplexy. Jim Telfer, who had once taken Scottish rugby near to the top of the world game, blasted the SRU: 'The Borders no longer has any influence because of the Edinburgh–Glasgow mafia that now exists at board level. The whole of Scottish rugby is now driven by the central belt and very few of the people on the board have any experience of being involved in professional rugby. The Borders will become a dust bowl. Nobody is going to see pro rugby in the heartland of the game in Scotland; it will all be in the cities and the past ten years have proved that there isn't huge support for pro rugby in Scotland's cities.'

Edinburgh owner Bob Carruthers revealed in an interview with *Scotland on Sunday* what many in the Borders had thought all along: 'I was told categorically by Gordon McKie back in September, not that the Borders or Glasgow might be closed, but that the Borders would almost certainly be closed. There was no question that Glasgow was under any threat. I was told in confidence but I feel no obligation to honour that confidence in light of what has happened.' With this, my belief in the integrity of the game finally collapsed.

For me, rugby is different to many other sports in that it is built on values like loyalty, unity, honesty and trust. I didn't see much sign of this in the last few weeks of my career. People were talking more about the politics of Scottish rugby than the performances, and the landscape had now become dominated by gossip and suspicion. I believe I have an optimistic outlook on life but I didn't like the growing cynicism I was now feeling. I longed for the sport I once knew.

I read somewhere recently that negative interactions have five times more effect on your frame of mind than positive ones. I think this has been the case in Scottish rugby. The endless arguments, claim and counter-claim and pessimism had fostered cynicism and resistance and had driven many rugby people in the country to apathy. This latest bout of self-destruction was going to turn away many more.

There was a chance of common sense prevailing when a rescue plan was hastily drawn up by businesses and councillors from the Borders. By using existing sponsorship money and having more local autonomy the widely-held view was that crowd numbers would increase, as it would feel much more like a Borders team. Heineken and Magners – the backers of the two tournaments the Scottish sides competed in – gave sponsorship money of close to £3 million a year to the SRU. One–third of that figure, in addition to some local investment, formed the basis of the rescue plan, which incidentally wouldn't have been too far away from the current budget of the Border Reivers. However, the SRU said that the money belonged to them, not to any particular team, and they refused to hand a one-third share to each professional side. The SRU were not going to change their decision.

There were reports of money being offered by investors to the SRU to keep the team in the Borders, move the Borders elsewhere and also move Glasgow to Stirling. So long as the offers were financially viable, I would have thought the SRU had a moral obligation to accept one of them, as the alternative meant the closure of a professional side, and with it the opportunity for over thirty players to get the most out of their talents.

To an outside observer it looked like the SRU were so unwilling to give up control of running a professional team, that they would rather get rid of one altogether than let someone else be in charge. However, no one can be that much of a control freak. I think that the SRU had looked at 'the product' compared to other countries and realized it was not working – and to make it work required investment. They came to the conclusion that they could only afford to provide adequate investment if they removed one team from the equation.

It is undeniable that 'the product' of professional rugby in Scotland hasn't been a success, especially compared to the other leading rugby nations. However, this should not have been the sole rationale for closing down a precious supply-line to the national team. One must take a more holistic approach in considering the benefits of pro rugby.

Scottish professional rugby maybe hasn't made any progress in terms of facilities or crowd numbers over the past ten years, but the playing side has certainly improved. Back in 1996, albeit with a part-time professional side, the Borders lost 85–28 to Pau on their Heineken Cup debut. Ten years later, against the French champions Biarritz, we were leading them on their home ground going into injury time. For all the perceived negativity surrounding the performances of the three Scottish teams, it has been a few years since they occupied the bottom three positions in the Celtic League. I'm not saying for a minute that the Scottish sides have been a resounding success, but they have been competitive. With a better environment, this competitiveness could easily be turned into something tangible. The way Glasgow, under the guidance of Sean Lineen, has improved recently with a settled squad shows what can be achieved.

Just why are three professional teams so important? Well, for starters it gives the opportunity to a further thirty or so Scottish players to train on a daily basis. For many of those selected to play this might be the only chance they have of playing at Magners League or Heineken Cup level. It is also a priceless vehicle for a larger number of up-and-coming young players to develop as professionals. Both Wales and Ireland have shown that four teams work very well and I hope that one day we too can have four sides. It means you can strengthen your squad with quality foreigners – like Leinster have done with Chris Whitaker and Felipe Contempomi and Llanelli with Regan King and Scott MacLeod. With only two sides, signing an overseas player puts at risk having enough Scottish qualified players playing week in, week out.

Of course in the short term, things will be okay – the best players will be playing at big clubs in England and France – but for any late developers it will be very hard to now get a professional contract. Short-termism is never a good policy and it hasn't worked for Scottish rugby over the last ten years. No one involved in the game can dispute the fact that one less professional team will damage Scottish rugby.

It was said that the Borders people didn't want a professional team, but this is nonsense. There were 5,000 people at our matches when we reformed in 2002, and this was after all the pain caused by the initial dissolution of the team in 1998. The fact is that you simply cannot invent a team – it has to be nurtured and supporters must know the money they are spending is not being wasted and that their team has a future.

From the excellent sports marketing book *The Elusive Fan*, the five levels of fan involvement are listed as being: 1. Becomes aware of the team, 2. Checks for results occasionally, 3. Goes to or views events regularly, 4. Follows the team in all distribution channels, and 5. Integrates it as part of his/her life.

The fact that the Borders has a higher proportion of rugby-aware people compared to other parts of the country does not automatically guarantee large crowds, unless there are sustained efforts at attempting to engage potential supporters. I would wager that most rugby people in the Borders were at stage 2, and either better marketing of the team or guarantees over its future would have moved them on through the next three stages. Marketing must be central to any team that is trying to increase its support, as it has to compete with all the alternative ways of spending a Friday evening or a Saturday afternoon.

Sports marketing is a hugely competitive area but for the last three years the Borders did not have a marketing staff at all. Anything that resembled marketing seemed to be the SRU's message to Borders rugby supporters to 'use it or lose it'– hardly a strategy that is likely to feature in many marketing books in the future. Why would people want to invest time and money in a product that looked like being scrapped?

Professional rugby can be shown to be working in the most unlikely of places. An hour or so down the road from the Borders base at Galashiels, in a football-obsessed city, the Newcastle Falcons regularly play to sell-out crowds, despite the fact they have often languished near the bottom of the Guinness Premiership. Professional sport is all about providing an experience for people that is valued and worth paying for – at Newcastle they have clearly got this right. A superb new stadium, match-day entertainment and extensive marketing have been the main reasons why so many new supporters have arrived on the scene.

Those contending that Borders people no longer have the same passion for rugby are well wide of the mark. I saw the disappointment and anger at close quarters, and many people were left distraught by the decision. Given all that the Borders had done for Scottish rugby over the previous 100 years the area deserved an opportunity to establish a team with local autonomy and without the constant threat of being axed. With better marketing – a marketing staff of just one person would even have made a real difference – I believe crowd numbers could have doubled in no time at all.

At the same time, and given that crowds have fallen right across Scotland in both the amateur and professional game, the number of those missing from our matches was still hard to stomach, whatever the reasons. It was particularly frustrating when less than 1,500 were present to watch our home game against French champions Biarritz. The match was live on television, but I would have thought true rugby supporters would still have been present. Those who chose to stay away will soon regret the fact that the likes of Brian O'Driscoll,

James Hook and Paul O'Connell won't be visiting the area anymore.

Perhaps Borderers don't feel a collective sense of belonging as much as they used to or as much as those in Munster do for example. The problems of their own towns and clubs are possibly far more important than the wider picture. Who knows? One thing is for sure, we don't talk up our achievements as a region nearly enough as we should. In Llanelli and Munster they never let you forget the time they beat the All Blacks. I'd be surprised if many people under the age of thirty know about the South's victory against the Grand Slam winning Wallaby team that toured these shores in 1984. The Borders is known the world over for its rugby – I really hope we haven't forgotten our heritage and what we can still achieve in the future.

As a Borderer, not having a professional team is a bitter pill to swallow and I know this will have dire effects for the region. But, as a supporter of Scottish rugby, I would have been less upset if the team had been allocated elsewhere in the country. That is the real travesty – not having a third professional team is plain wrong. Given the fact that outside investors seemed to be at hand, axing the Borders makes a bad decision even worse.

Those that say pro rugby will never work in Scotland are wrong. Although there is compelling evidence that Scotland – one of the most professional nations of the amateur era – has now become the most amateur of the professional era, this can be easily revised. You only have to look across the Irish Sea to see what can be achieved. As good as Scotland were in the period immediately before the game turned professional, Ireland were badly disorganized and never managed to get their impressive school and club rugby set-up translated into international success. Between 1988 and 2000, Scotland were undefeated against their Celtic cousins at Test level. Turn the clock forward to the professional era and you can see the contrasting change in fortunes of the two countries: Ireland have now won seven games in succession against Scotland.

The rapidity of Ireland's success at provincial and international level was breathtaking. In the 1990s, there were far more supporters at club games than those who bothered to watch the provinces. Driven by the likes of Shannon, Garryowen and Cork Constitution, club rugby was very strong, but the provincial route was the only logical way for the game to grow at professional level. Irish rugby accepted this much sooner than the Scots.

Nevertheless, it took a while before the crowds turned up in the numbers we see today at Ravenhill or Thomond Park. Even in 1998 there were less than 200 at some Munster and Leinster matches. This is reminiscent of the woeful crowds who attended home games for Stade Français in the mid 1990s – on a few occasions there were more people on the pitch than had paid to watch. Yet now, because of the imagination and ambition of their president, Max Guazzini, Stade Français have become a marketing phenomenon – on a few occasions last season they played in front of 80,000 at the Stade de France. Irish rugby has also experienced the same transformation.

The IRFU's strategy of investing in provincial rugby and bringing home Irish players paid off in spectacular style. By 2000, Ireland's three leading provinces had a European Cup winner, a runner-up and a semi-finalist between them. The crowd numbers suddenly started to increase exponentially. Winning came first, then the fans – that was the sequence. Today Irish rugby is in fantastic shape, and further building blocks are being laid for the future. With Thomond Park and Donnybrook being redeveloped and huge investments being made in youth rugby, Ireland's model is one that many view as being the ideal template for professional rugby. Fundamentally, they have excelled for the simple reason that investment in growth will pay dividends in the future and that success really does breed success.

In Scotland, there needs to be a change of mindset to accept that professionalism is here to stay and to look at ways of benefiting from it – not just viewing it as an expense on the balance sheet. To do this, the SRU has to be restructured and people who have experience of running, marketing and managing professional sport should be given positions of responsibility and control. Cutting the Borders and the refusal to appoint a Director of Rugby shows that professional rugby still isn't being treated seriously enough. I also believe more can be done for the club game.

The gap between amateur and professional rugby is huge, and increases each year. That's not surprising given that professionals train twice a day compared to twice a week for the amateurs. As such, the amateur game must be treated separately. Before the game went professional, club players had district sides and the Scotland team to aim for. Now these targets are exclusive to the professionals.

The SRU has addressed this a little by introducing one international fixture in the season – against Ireland – but this seems to be a token gesture. There has to be more incentive to our club players. I would like to see the reintroduction of a district championship followed by international matches for club players. This will address two issues. First, it gives the chance for club players to have the pride and challenge of playing at a higher standard. Also, the best club players can come to the attention of pro sides if they are playing at district or amateur level. It is very difficult, although not impossible, to be given a pro contract playing for an amateur club side. This will be an opportunity to see how players perform in more exalted company and should give a boost to the club game.

I know the French wanted a Scottish amateur side to play in an international tournament during the World Cup, and there seems to be a willingness from other countries to have an amateur Six Nations. After all, if there is a tournament for

Scotland Under-20 and the Scotland Women teams, why can't we have one for the amateur players?

Despite the gloom around the professional game, I think now is the best time to put down some foundations for the long-term future of Scottish rugby. I have no doubt in my mind that we can be successful in the future, but to do this we must be absolutely determined to succeed. This will take hard work from everyone involved in Scottish rugby, but our common goal has to be about getting better all the time – a shared spirit of continual improvement. It is a lifelong commitment that requires us all to be ambitious, confident, innovative and passionate.

I remember on my MBA course we studied the amazing postwar recovery of the Japanese economy. From near total devastation, Japan transformed itself to become the second largest economy in the world. All this was achieved without having any comparative advantage, as Japan had a relatively small population with no real natural resources to speak of. Long-term planning, highly efficient operations and an almighty collective effort were the main reasons for the turnaround. Scottish rugby can do the same.

Let's start with some long-term planning … To have any hope of achieving any lasting change, there needs to be a fundamental shift in the culture of Scottish rugby. We have to become much more inclusive and positive, engender a spirit of consensus rather than fear. I am sick and tired of people pointing out what can't be done instead of what can be achieved. I remember hearing a comment from someone in a position of power at Murrayfield about Bryan Redpath, when he was trying to come back to Scotland to start his coaching career. 'What does he know about coaching?' was the dismissive remark. Enough to guide Gloucester to a Premiership final in only his second season in charge – probably more than any Scottish coach has achieved in professional rugby.

It might be job protection, fear or jealousy, but this negativity has been harming our chances of making progress for a number of years. One of our biggest failings seems to me to be an all-consuming lack of optimism. Winston Churchill once said that 'the optimist sees opportunity in every danger; the pessimist danger in every opportunity'. For too long we've heard only about the dangers of professional rugby. I see nothing but opportunities for Scottish rugby.

There are those who say that only money can turn things round for Scottish rugby, but a sporting example from Sweden might hopefully persuade them otherwise. The Swedish athletics association was faced with bankruptcy after hosting the World Championships in Gothenburg in 1995, which were a disaster both financially and in terms of results, as Sweden didn't win a medal. However, this parlous state of affairs did leave a blank canvas for the future. Over the last ten years, Sweden has transformed itself into one of the world's best athletics nations. They have been able to develop and support a substantial number of world-class track and field athletes, many of whom – like Carolina Klüft and Christian Olsson – will be in serious contention for gold medals at next year's Olympics. None of this required a great deal of money.

There was a realization in Sweden that because there was no money they had to stop fighting amongst themselves and start to plan for the future. New interest in athletics led the authorities to begin a process of engagement and simultaneously a programme of building. The government started putting up indoor facilities, and Swedes began using them. There are now around thirty indoor athletics arenas, which is hugely impressive for a country with a population of nine million. Also, allowing experienced athletes to pass their knowledge on to younger talents and trusting clubs and volunteers to fill the facilities was the tipping point to exponential progress. This trust was fundamental to the Swedish success story.

One of the huge advantages Scotland has in being a small country is that we really should have the ability and attitude to co-ordinate and share information to help each other. Arsène Wenger once said that 'some people live off football and others live for football'. We need to get those that live for rugby and genuinely care for the game in Scotland back into the fold. In the last three decades we have produced Grand Slam winners, British Lions and many world-class players – some of whom have either been exasperated by the politics or intentionally sidelined from having any real influence. This knowledge and expertise would be a fantastic help at any level of the game.

The two most fundamental elements of any future SRU policy at growing the game in the country will be, I assume, increasing the overall playing base in Scotland and to expand the number of players who are comfortable performing at the highest level. The key to such a strategy has to be improving training facilities. The Scottish Youth Football Association recently reported that the current standard of facilities in Scotland is 'the biggest barrier to participation at grassroots level'. The situation isn't any better regarding rugby.

While I played at Montpellier we trained on the latest 3rd Generation (3G) artificial turf that the football club had just installed. It left a huge impression on me – in fact I found it better to train on than grass. This type of pitch is completely level, softer to land on than any surface I've trained on and you can use your studs on it just like on a grass pitch.

I've always thought that we are at a disadvantage in a sporting context in Scotland because of our climate and, crucially, our standard of training facilities. I don't feel we currently give young people a good enough choice in deciding whether to get out and play sport or stay inside watching TV or playing video games. I am absolutely convinced that these new artificial pitches would greatly help readdress this, as well as making a drastic improvement to skill levels for all rugby players, especially in the winter months.

It is evident that these 3G pitches (or 'rubber crumb' as they are otherwise known) are fast becoming the accepted normal training surface for football and rugby. Already in England, many schools, colleges and sports clubs have 3G pitches and the RFU have announced that they will install seventy-five of them over the next ten years at a cost of £41 million. Currently, there are only a handful of 3G pitches in Scotland, built by professional football clubs such as Rangers and Hearts, and only one, at Lasswade, for Rugby. 3G is as near to a panacea as I've seen for growing the game and I hope their installation in Scotland soon becomes a reality.

If Scottish rugby is really ready for change, then it is may be time to take a confident, more radical step into the future. Why not move towards playing rugby in the summer? I remember just before I left Scotland to play for the Sharks, I took a session with the Gala Wanderers Under-18 squad. It was a dark, cold winter night and we were restricted to working in the 22-m area because the lighting was poor. The players might have learned something from the session, but nothing compared to what their counterparts in South Africa and France would learn from training in better weather conditions. At schoolboy level in Australia they are passing the ball better than our international team because they have the weather to be outside every day, handling the ball far more than Scottish kids.

I had one day of rain during my five months of playing in Durban and the amount of things you can work on and you can coach properly in better weather means that we are at a real disadvantage being the most northerly country playing rugby union today. Moving to the summer and the long, bright nights of June and July would suddenly give Scotland a veritable advantage. Summer rugby might be the perfect opportunity of breathing new life into a game that many believe is dying on its feet. Rugby league has shown how a game that was previously thought to be in sharp decline has been revitalized since becoming a summer sport.

Three years ago the then SRU chief executive Phil Anderton presented the case for playing in better weather conditions, but the clubs voted to keep the season the way it has always been. At the time I thought this conservatism was typical of Scottish rugby's inability to plan for the future. It reminded me of the story of the 1920s when the SRU secretary at the time, J. Aikman Smith, refused to move with the times and have the players' jerseys numbered. When King George V asked why the Scotland XV bore no identifying numbers on their backs, Aikman Smith, replied: 'This, sir, is a rugby match, not a cattle sale.'

Could it be that football will shake us from our current lack of innovation and foresight? The SFA's new chief executive, the former Rangers player Gordon Smith, has already stated his desire to see Scottish football played in May and June after a winter shutdown of two months. What a difference such a development would make to Scottish rugby.

It is abundantly clear that Scottish rugby will not get itself out of its present situation unless there is some outside help. Sometimes that help, like the franchising of a professional team, hasn't been accepted, and there are still issues of control that need to be sorted out. However, any financial assistance in terms of improving facilities would certainly be welcomed with open arms. Although football dominates the media in the country, rugby is fast becoming the second biggest team sport on the planet. Scotland has consistently punched above its weight in rugby – and at every World Cup so far we have qualified for at least the quarter-finals. This achievement alone means Scottish rugby deserves a more generous settlement from government.

It's not an act of charity – Scottish rugby does not get nearly the same funding as its counterparts in other countries such as Wales or Ireland, or anything like the handouts given to Scottish football. It must be remembered that Hampden Park, the national football stadium, received £45 million of public money followed by a £2 million bail-out from the Scottish Executive. In contrast, the SRU received next to nothing from the government in recognition for building Murrayfield stadium, an arena that has lifted the nation on many occasions. Some would argue that the SRU were desperately unlucky, due to the fact that Murrayfield was already operational before the National Lottery (and the crucial funding it provides) came into existence. The SRU bore the cost of redeveloping a world-class facility and, with 67,500 seats, Murrayfield is still by some distance the largest capacity stadium in Scotland. With the game going professional soon after the stadium was completed in 1994, Scottish rugby has paid a heavy price ever since.

Considering the Irish government are providing £130 million towards the cost of redeveloping Lansdowne Road, it looks like the Scottish Executive have got lucky in the sense that the national rugby stadium in Scotland has already been redeveloped. Surely some sort of retrospective payment is in order? I reckon Scottish rugby's future could be secured for half the amount that was given to the SFA in redeveloping Hampden. Any help would be much appreciated.

Scottish television executives could also play an important role in lending a hand. One reason there is apathy and decreasing playing numbers in Scottish rugby is that there is no television coverage of our game outside the international fixtures. For someone who fondly remembers watching *Rugby Special* without fail on a Sunday afternoon it seems in recent years rugby hasn't even been allowed to compete with football because of an almost total lack of coverage of our domestic and professional game. Ironically, we are the only rugby playing country in Europe where this is the case. I've watched many distinctly average games from the Guinness Premiership this season but Sky TV's coverage allows the game in England to be marketed as a vibrant and exciting sport. It is also no coincidence that with three live matches shown over a weekend in both France and Wales, the game in these countries is in very good health. All those who care for Scottish rugby can only hope that there is a TV executive out there somewhere who shares their love of the game.

Such is the importance of professional rugby to developing young players and aiding the prospects of the national team, I would also urge the SRU to look at anything that might reduce their debt so that they can invest not just in the pro game but also in facilities and club rugby. The most costly item on the SRU's balance sheet last year was not the running of three professional teams but, at £6 million per annum, the running of Murrayfield stadium. This is the biggest burden to growing rugby union in Scotland.

Ten days before the Borders were axed, the SRU were given some excellent news when the Scottish Executive approved a flood prevention scheme for the Water of Leith that doesn't encroach on the back pitches of Murrayfield and so leaves a strip of land adjacent to the stadium free for re-development. It is predicted that this will bring in much-needed money, which will drastically reduce the SRU's debt.

Building luxury apartments and leisure facilities is just the beginning. I think the SRU has to do something visionary with Murrayfield. One sure-fire way of generating funds is selling the naming rights to the stadium. Former Chief Executive Phil Anderton first mooted this idea, but this was one of many proposals that was too radical for the SRU committee and he was later ousted from his post. This conservative, reactionary attitude reminded me of what Mark Twain once said: 'I'm all for progress, it's change I don't like.'

Re-naming Murrayfield should not be viewed as the end to Western civilization but as a stepping stone to restoring the health of Scottish rugby. South African rugby didn't collapse when Kings Park was renamed ABSA Stadium and Loftus Versfeld became Securicor Loftus. The value of being able to build half-a-dozen 3G pitches or guarantee the future of a third (or fourth) professional team would be priceless and well worth the inconvenience of having to change the name to something like RBS Murrayfield or the Vodafone Stadium. You could even have different names for each of the four stands at Murrayfield, as happened at Hampden with the BT Group.

Five years ago the Welsh Rugby Union's debt stood at £75 million – more than three times the current level of debt at the SRU. This figure has now been reduced by over £30 million and rugby is thriving at all levels in Wales. It is not difficult to imagine that this reduction will continue, especially as the WRU are currently sounding out interested companies to purchase the naming rights to the Millennium Stadium at a cost of £5 million a year. The WRU are proving it is possible to have four professional teams and generate profits.

Just as Kevin Costner optimistically put it in the film *Field of Dreams* – 'If you build it, they will come' – I have an optimistic picture of Scottish rugby in the future. It is a million miles away from the many nightmare scenarios that were painted in the aftermath of the Borders closure. Before the 2011 World Cup, I believe that we will have three professional teams in Scotland all playing in front of 5,000-plus crowds and competing at the top end of the Magners League. I also see London Scottish playing in the Guinness Premiership with a team comprised mainly of Scottish-qualified players.

And the pièce de résistance? Well, here's my vision of Murrayfield in five years time: a redeveloped stadium containing the offices of sportscotland and EventScotland as well as a leisure complex situated next to a world-class medical centre. On the back pitches there is a mini-stadium with seating for 7,000 that hosts Edinburgh's matches in the

Magners League. Next door to this is a 3rd Generation training pitch – partly covered by an extending roof, like the one
used at the French rugby centre of excellence at Marcoussi.
Whether all this has been achieved by outside investment, re-
naming the stadium or government assistance, I am optimistic that it is going to happen. After all, we need to have a
dream if we are going to have a dream come true. (And yes, I
realize I am paraphrasing Captain Sensible here!)

Aside from all the politics and disappointments of the last
few seasons from a Scottish perspective, professional rugby
has undoubtedly been a very good thing for the sport. Back in
1998, one of my last games for Northampton was against
Wasps at QPR's Loftus Road. The ground was maybe less than
half full but I remember thinking, 'What a great venue –
wouldn't it be amazing in ten years to be playing rugby at
packed stadiums like this.' Well, that's just exactly what has
happened as a result of rugby becoming fully professional
(except, of course, in Scotland).

The progress the game has made looks likely to continue.
New stadiums are being built for clubs in Ireland, Wales,
England and France and the sport is beginning to establish
itself as a rival to football. In England, attendances have risen
for the ninth season in succession. The average crowd is now
over 11,000 – an excellent return given that a chunk of the
Premiership season takes place without the international
players who are on Test duty. The scenes at the Heineken Cup
final last year would even have made a club like Manchester
United green with envy. Over 60,000 Munster fans filled the
Millennium Stadium to witness the historic victory over Biarritz while thousands more lined the streets of Cork and
Limerick.

A lot of the credit must go not just to the national unions
and the IRB but also the club owners. Although there have
been many conflicts between French and English clubs and
their respective unions over the first decade of professional-

ism, it is undeniable that people like Keith Barwell at Northampton have changed the sport for the better. Many owners have lost vast sums of money, but now the twelve elite English clubs are turning over £100 million a year. If it hadn't been for the drive and financial backing of these pioneers then English rugby might have been in a similar state to Scottish rugby.

Professionalism has also been a good thing for me personally. It made me take my rugby seriously and gave me the tools and environment to adopt a winning attitude. Before the game went professional I saw rugby more as a release and a way to express myself. I was more concerned with experiencing life than doing all I could to become a better rugby player. A keen traveller, I remember once when inter-railing through Europe as a student that I had made up my mind I wanted to live in the Austrian mountains for a year. Professional rugby changed my fanciful notions.

Having toyed with professional rugby at Northampton, I learned from others and was finally taking real responsibility at Brive. It was here that I started to take my preparation much more seriously and I began to study the game I loved. I never had a fixed idea on the limit of my talent, but I realized at Brive that hard work is the only way to get the most out of your talent. I also became much more pragmatic in my approach to the game and systematic in my decision-making. Although I would never have believed it when I first started playing senior rugby, I wanted to become a coach after my playing days were over. It is now an ambition I would like to fulfil in the near future. Professional rugby also gave me the opportunity to develop as a stand-off – far and away my favourite position.

My thanks go to Alan Lyall, the Gala mini-rugby coach who moved me out to stand-off very early in my career. (To think how bad my back would have been now if I'd carried on playing scrum-half throughout my career!) I remember being disappointed at the time as scrum-half in those days seemed to be a much better position. It was closer to the action and there were any number of talented, battling role models to look up to, like Roy Laidlaw, Pierre Berbizier, and Nick Farr-Jones – number 9s were the undisputed kings of the game.

In contrast, in the 1980s and early 1990s, a stand-off wasn't known for anything other than his kicking ability. The only stand-off I liked to watch, or that I could relate to when I was growing up, was Jonathan Davies – and he ended up leaving the game to ply his trade in rugby league. A number 10 tended to play the game deep in the pocket, launching high balls and generally ignoring his outside backs. There would even be a few times when I watched a club match in the middle of a Scottish winter and the only player who left the field without getting his shorts dirty was the stand-off. Tackling was an option then and not the duty it has now become.

I don't think I'm biased in saying that the stand-off has the most decisive role to play in rugby union. It is by far the key decision-making position and, as the role is essentially to give form to a team's movement, it requires the widest range of skills. One of the most satisfying aspects of professional rugby is that stand-offs have been allowed and encouraged to display these skills. Pleasingly, there have been many world-class number 10s who have lit up the game.

There are a number of stand-offs that I love watching perform – Charlie Hodgson, David Humphreys, Ronan O'Gara, Brock James, Felipe Contempomi and Glen Jackson to name but a few. The next generation are just as exciting, as Luke McAllister, James Hook, Shane Geraghty, Toby Flood and Ryan Lamb have even more of an attacking edge to their play. However, even these excellent players are not in the same league as the best number 10s of today. My leading lights would be Jonny Wilkinson, Frédéric Michalak, Dan Carter and Stephen Larkham.

When trying to describe Wilkinson as a player, words that spring to mind are: accuracy, organization, focus, preparation and, above all, excellence. As a stand-off he ticks all the boxes: a decision-maker with tremendous kicking, passing and tackling ability. Other than his world-class goal-kicking, when Wilkinson burst on to the scene in 1999, his defensive capabilities were probably the most talked about facet of his game. His timing, aggression and acceleration in the tackle almost redefined the stand-off role as a leader of the defensive line in addition to that of launching a backline with the ball in hand.

One crucial sector of a number 10's game is that of tactical kicking. Whether it is clearing his lines, turning the opposing pack or kicking for his wingers to win back, Wilkinson is precision personified. What's even harder to believe is that his kicking game is deployed with equal success off either foot. For dodgy left-foot kickers like myself, I can't help thinking what a show-off he is. Wilkinson's accuracy can only be described as breathtaking and underlines the hours upon hours of practice he must have put in over the years to reach such a peerless standard.

Frédéric Michalak was the form stand-off during the 2003 World Cup until France underperformed in their disappointing semi-final against England. Although he has been beset by injury problems since then, his genius is undeniable. Whether for his club side Toulouse or with France, Michalak is a supremely gifted player who looks to attack from anywhere. Although his ability to control a game is sometimes questioned, he has an excellent kicking game and has no visible weaknesses in his repertoire. Just like Stephen Larkham and Dan Carter, Michalak played a lot of rugby in another position – at scrum-half – before moving to stand-off for Toulouse and then the French national team. He seems keen to keep learning as a stand-off and is not afraid to broaden his horizons – it will be interesting to follow his progress next season playing for the Natal Sharks in the Super 14.

After two successful seasons playing with the Crusaders at centre and full-back, Dan Carter took over the stand-off duties from Andrew Mehrtens with amazing results. His performance for the All Blacks in the first Test against the Lions in 2005 must be regarded as one of the best ever in the history of the game. He has shown on many occasions that he is a devastating runner and is a superb goal-kicker. If there is one word to describe Carter it is winner, and his serene style disguises his systematic approach to the game. He knows when and where to break, which can only be the product of hard graft and an intelligent and calculating rugby brain. His fitness base must be amazing, as he never seems to break sweat. Elegance of this calibre puts you in mind of a swan paddling underwater like mad. It must be hard work to make it look that easy.

The final member of the quartet of genuine world-class number 10s is Wallaby stand-off Stephen Larkham. He has the most natural attacking game of any stand-off I have seen and he seems to open up opposing defences with ease. As a first receiver, Larkham always hits the line at pace, which puts pressure on any defensive line. He has a great awareness of where space might open up and will use his bullet-like pass to put a teammate through or ghost over the advantage line himself. His tackling is immense and his kicking has improved substantially in recent seasons. And to think, he only switched to playing stand-off – after previously playing scrum-half and full-back – when he was twenty-two years old. The best news I have heard in Scottish rugby over the past 18 months was Edinburgh's fantastic coup in signing my all-time favourite number 10.

Drawing on the inspiration of these great fly-halves, I prepared for the final match of my career, hoping for one last performance that would do me justice. Our home match against the Ospreys attracted considerable media attention not just because of the fact that it would be the last ever Border Reivers game but because the Ospreys needed a win to be crowned Magners League champions. Whatever happened, it was going to be an emotional night.

It was perhaps fitting that the curtain was brought down on my career on some familiar territory – it was on this turf that I took my first faltering steps as a rugby player, when at seven years old I persuaded my folks to let me join my brother's sevens team. Netherdale was also the setting for my first taste of senior rugby some ten years after that. The symmetry wasn't lost on me and I couldn't help feeling how lucky I had been in the period between making my debut for Gala and coming back to the Borders.

American psychologist Carol Dweck has said that 'the hallmark of successful individuals is that they love learning, they seek challenges, they value effort, and they persist in the face of obstacles'. I couldn't agree more. The quest to seek out new challenges and learn all I could in order to improve as a rugby player meant that I had been living my dream for almost seventeen years.

Despite the wonderful memories I cherished from my assorted rugby experiences, it had been a desperate season for many of my former teams. Scotland's last place in the Six Nations was a setback, but nowhere near as demoralizing as the disappointments suffered by the three club sides I played for the longest: Northampton were relegated to National One, Gala relegated to Premier Three and the Border Reivers axed. Montpellier, Brive and Castres almost suffered the same fate, finishing in the three positions directly above Narbonne and Agen who were both relegated to ProD2. The silver lining seemed to be coming from the Sharks, who became the first ever South African team to host a Super 14 final, and led for most of the match against the Blue Bulls at a packed ABSA stadium. However, their hopes were dashed when winger

Bryan Habana ran in a try with the last play of the game. Derrick Hougaard converted to leave the Bulls with a 20–19 winning scoreline. The trials and tribulations of my former clubs brought home to me the fact that I've had an amazing journey, and that sport has its fair share of disappointments as well as good times.

I've met some great people, played with players I truly admire and had some fantastic life experiences. But the best times have been when I've had the ball in my hands, making decisions and delighting in a game I have always adored. It might sound a bit trivial, but the buzz of running around a rugby field, catching, passing and kicking a funny-shaped ball is going to be hard to replace.

My final game wasn't the vintage performance I was looking for, but there were many times during the match that I felt in control and that I was making telling contributions. Regrettably, there were also occasions when my skills let me down – especially when I wasn't able to complete a tackle on Ospreys number 10 James Hook. His break led to a try and, it seemed at the time that our hopes of pulling off a hugely unexpected victory had been extinguished.

However, we came storming back into the match in the final quarter, urged on by our passionate, loyal group of supporters. At 16–21 going into the last few minutes, we were in the ascendancy. But a bitter-sweet, winning end to the history of the Border Reivers wasn't to be, although we had pushed the champions-elect all the way. James Hook kicked a penalty in injury-time which secured the win and the Magners League title for the Ospreys.

It had been an honour to captain the side and I was proud of the effort the team had put in. The application and perseverance was first class and we had matched one of the best teams in Europe for most of the match. It was a remarkable effort given the circumstances. Steve Bates gave me the honour of a proud send-off by replacing me near the end of

the game. It was a poignant moment as I left the field and I
felt moved by the way both sets of players and the crowd
applauded my exit.

I spent the night with friends, family and my team-mates. It
was good for us all to have a laugh together. I'm glad I was left
with this reminder of the camaraderie and fun I'd always associated with rugby, rather than the politics and negativity of the
preceding few weeks. At three in the morning I was last to
leave the Gala clubhouse, still high from the emotions of the
night and the memory of the many heart-warming messages
I'd received that week from around the world of rugby.

Before getting into a taxi, I looked back at the ground
where I had started my career. As I was about to turn my back
on some wonderful memories – some of the best days of my
life – the thought lingered that I could easily squeeze out
another year or two of rugby at a lower level. But I knew that
this feeling would fade even before the onset of the following
day's hangover. The hunger had gone and I was ready for
new challenges. My new job, with the Scottish Institute
of Sport Foundation, will keep me close to the game that
has given me so much. I can't wait to start the next part of
my life.

Career Statistics

GREGOR TOWNSEND
Full name: Gregor Peter John Townsend
Date of birth: 26 April 1973
Place of birth: Edinburgh, Scotland
Height and weight: 1.83m, 93kg
Position: Fly-half, Centre, Full-back

School: Galashiels Academy
Further Education: University of Edinburgh, Aston University

Club Career

Border Reivers	(2005–2007)	37 appearances
Montpellier	(2004–2005)	30 appearances
Natal Sharks	(2004)	9 appearances
The Borders	(2002–2003)	19 appearances
Castres Olympique	(2000–2002)	51 appearances
Brive	(1998–2000)	48 appearances
Northampton	(1995–1998)	64 appearances
Warringah	(1993 & 1995)	19 appearances
Gala	(1990–1995)	54 appearances

International Career

British Lions	(1997)	6 appearances (2 Test matches)
Scotland	(1993–2003)	82 appearances (17 tries & 164 points)

Scotland XV	(1992–2003)	20 appearances
Scotland 'A'	(1992–1996)	5 appearances
Scotland 'B'	(1991–1992)	2 appearances
South of Scotland	(1992–1993)	4 appearances
Scottish Students	(1991–1992)	9 appearances
Scotland U21	(1992)	2 appearances
Scotland U19	(1991)	1 appearance
Scottish Schools U18	(1990–1991)	11 appearances
Scotland U15	(1988)	1 appearance

Acknowledgments

I began the process of writing this book when I recorded a diary during the 2003 World Cup. Writing it on my own has been a much more cathartic experience than I imagined it would be and hopefully the book is a true reflection of my career and how I approached the game. One of the great benefits is that it has given me reason to reflect on those individuals who had a profound impact on my life and those who have helped me achieve so much. Many of them – players, coaches, journalists and friends – I didn't realize or appreciate at the time. Sincere thanks to all for the support you have shown me over the years. I'd also like to thank all the doctors and physios that have treated me: their good judgment kept me playing well into my thirties.

I would like to thank all those who have assisted with the book. To Tom Whiting and his fantastic team at HarperSport – thanks for your guidance and enthusiasm. Others who have been of great help are Allan Massie and Mike Green for their expertise and constructive criticism. Thank you also to Clive Woodward for permission to reproduce his letter; to Henry Douglas for allowing me to abridge his wonderful 'Kingdom of the Game', and to Chris Cusiter for coming up with the title. A special word to Jamie Crawford from Crawford and Pearlstine whose advice, support and encouragement have been invaluable.

Finally, I must express gratitude to my wife Claire and our young boys, Christian and Luke for all your love and support.

The book has taken me a year longer to write than I had planned and their patience and understanding during those frequent vigils at my computer have provided comfort and strength.

Index